Achieve IELTS

English for International Education

Grammar and Vocabulary

Louis Harrison
Caroline Cushen
Susan Hutchison

mc Marshall Cavendish
Education

First published 2009 by Marshall Cavendish Education
Marshall Cavendish is a trademark of Times Publishing Limited

ISBN: 978-0-462-098975

Marshall Cavendish ELT
32–38 Saffron Hill
London EC1N 8FH
www.mcelt.com/ielts

Prepared for Marshall Cavendish by Starfish Design Editorial and Project Management Ltd.

Editorial Project Manager: Mel Chrisp

Printed and bound by Times Offset (M) Sdn. Bhd. Malaysia

Acknowledgements
We are grateful to the following for permission to adapt or reproduce extracts from the following copyright material:

p.22 The Harris Poll® #63, June 19, 2008, The Environment…Are We Doing All We Can? Harris Interactive Inc. All rights reserved.; p.30 'Favourite food', Somerfield magazine, summer 2007; p.33 'Happy landings', © The Economist Newspaper Limited, London, May 15th 2008; p.34 'What it feels like to be in an avalanche', as told to A.J. Jacobs. By permission of Esquire magazine © The Hearst Corporation. Esquire is a trademark of The Hearst Corporation. All rights reserved.; p.38 (graph) © The Economist Newspaper Limited, London, Jan 22nd 2008; p.40 'Reading styles', taken from 'The brain drain' by Nicolas Carr, published in The Independent on July 18th 2008, Independent News and Media Limited; p.44 'Green shopping in the U.S.', © Greener World Media. This article originally appeared on GreenBiz.com®, and is reprinted with permission. For more news and analysis on environmental business practices, visit http://greenbiz.com; p.45 'Working in the future', taken from 'Work this way' by Liz Stuart, published in The Guardian on September 25th 2004; p.46 'The leap second', taken from 'Tick tock ... tick: Extra second added to 2008' by Jim Wolf published on December 28th 2008 by Reuters.com and 'Parting gift from 2008: An extra second' by Thomas Vinciguerra, published in the International Herald Tribune, on December 29th 2008 © 2008 The New York Times. All rights reserved. Used by permission and protected by the Copyright Laws of the United States; p.51 (graph) © The Economist Newspaper Limited, London, August 14th 2008; p.78 'When food is not pleasure', taken from 'Obese lack pleasure in eating' by Mark Henderson, published in The Australian on October 17th 2008, NI Syndication Ltd; p.80 'Personality and where you sit on a bus', taken from 'How sitting on the top deck is key to what's going on upstairs' by Stephen Adams, published in The Daily Telegraph on January 5th 2008 © Telegraph Media Group Limited 2008; p.84 'Water in desert cities', taken from 'Desert cities are living on borrowed time, UN warns' by John Vidal, published in The Guardian on June 5th 2006. Copyright Guardian News & Media Ltd 2006; p.86 'Latest Swiss army knife technology', edited from 'Swiss army knife that can only be unlocked by fingerprint' by Harry Wallop, published in The Daily Telegraph on January 10th 2009 © Telegraph Media Group Limited 2009; p.97 'High volume', © The Economist Newspaper Limited, London, Jan 30th 2008; p.108 'Social responsibility for big business', © The Economist Newspaper Limited, London, Jan 17th 2008; p.120 'What body shape are you?', taken from 'What body shape are you?' by Craig McQueen, published in the Daily Record on December 3rd 2008; p.129 'Presentation skills', NI Syndication Ltd; p.159 extracts published in The Times on April 8th 2009, NI Syndication Ltd. istock p.159.

Illustrations: William Donohoe

Diagrams: Peters and Zabransky Ltd

Every effort has been made to trace and acknowledge the copyright holders of all material reproduced in this book. The publishers apologise for any omissions and will be pleased to make necessary arrangements when this book is reprinted.

Contents

Comparing

Conditions

Reporting

Defining

Linking words

Vocabulary

Answer key

Do the test to help you find which grammar points you need to practise. Each question is related to grammar units in *Achieve IELTS Grammar and Vocabulary*.

1 **Choose the correct alternatives to complete the passage.**

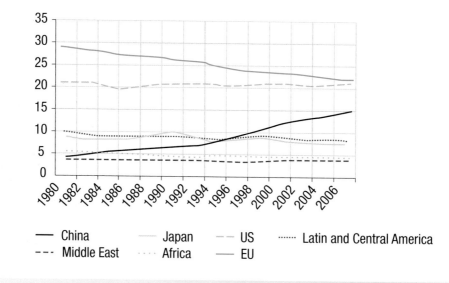

The line graph (1) shows / is showing / has shown the share of world product production. The horizontal axis (2) gives / is giving / has given the time in years, while the vertical axis (3) represents / is representing / has represented the percentage of the share. The graph (4) demonstrates / is demonstrating / has demonstrated some significant trends in the pattern of world production. Overall, China's share of production nowadays (5) rises / is rising / has risen rapidly, while that of the European Union (6) falls / is falling / has fallen. As a result of this swift growth, China's share of world product (7) rises / is rising / has risen from 3.4% in 1980 to 15.4%. Looking at the chart in more detail, we can see that the share of world production for Japan and Latin and Central America (8) drops / is dropping / has dropped since 1980. The US share (9) remains / is remaining / has remained the same over the same period, at around 20% of the total, and the Middle East's and Africa's share (10) stays / is staying / has stayed steady for the past two decades at about 4% each.

2 **Decide which sentences are incorrect and correct them.**

1 Agnes has had terrible headaches for a while now and she's finally gone to see a doctor about it.

2 Recently I've listened to *Highway 61 Revisited* a lot. What have you listened to lately?

3 Farmers have got their produce ready all year round for Thanksgiving celebrations when Americans all over the world sit down for a family meal.

4 Have you been paying attention to your lectures? I hope so, because next week's test is all about them.

5 For the past three years, conservation groups are pushing for a ban on overfishing in the North Sea.

....
....
....
....
....

3 **Complete the passage using the correct form of the verbs in brackets.**

Software testing

Long before a computer program (1)................(ship) to the
customer, software testing (2).................(perform)
by independent testers. Testing can be done on the following levels:
Unit testing (3)................(test) individual pieces
of the software. Each basic component of the software
(4).................(test) to verify that the design (5)...............
(implement) correctly. In the second kind of test, integration testing,
progressively larger groups of tested software units
(6).................(integrate) and tested until the software
(7).................(work) as a system. Then system testing
(8).................(check) the whole system to see that it works.
Before shipping the final version, alpha and beta testing

(9).................(often do). Alpha testing is testing by potential users / customers. Beta testing comes
after alpha testing. Versions of the software, known as beta versions, (10)...................(release) to a
limited audience to make sure the product has few faults or bugs.

4 **Complete the sentences using the correct form of the verbs in brackets.**

1 I'm so angry with Alice. While I................, she................ a party in her room next door.
(study / have)

2 Piotr................ the room when he................ that he didn't have his key. (leave / remembered)

3 In 1969, a Soviet satellite................ the Moon as the American astronauts................ .
(orbit / land)

4 Magali................ even................ the wall; when she................ her car, she
.... the road at all. (not see / crash / not watch)

5 I................ later that my Internet connection wasn't working, but until then I................ for
her email. (realise / wait)

5 **Complete the passage using the correct form of the verbs in brackets.**

It is said that Galileo (1)................(drop) objects of the same material, but of different weights,
from the Tower of Pisa to prove that the time they took to fall did not depend on their weight. This was
contrary to what Aristotle (2)................(teach): that heavy objects fall faster than lighter ones.
Galileo also (3)................(think) that objects keep their speed unless a force — often friction —
slowed them down. But Galileo's discoveries (4)................(not be) entirely original. Nicole Oresme
in the 14th century (5)................ already................(think) about the mathematical law for
acceleration; Ibn al-Haytham (6)................(propose) ideas along the same lines centuries earlier and
Mo Tzu (7)................(discover) it centuries before either of them. However, Galileo was the first
person who (8)................(express) these ideas mathematically and checked them with experiments.

6 Choose the correct alternative.

Joy: What are you doing, Hasan? Are you writing a training programme?

Hasan: That's right – I need to get fit, I (1) 'm doing / will do / 'm going to do the University half-marathon.

Joy: You're joking.

Hasan: No, I'm quite serious, I planned it last month and I (2) 'm seeing / will see / 'm going to see it through. It's for charity.

Joy: So when (3) is it taking / will it take / is it going to take place?

Hasan: It's in three months' time, but entry forms (4) are being / will be / are due to be given in tomorrow and I (5) will not / 'm not missing / 'm not about to miss the deadline.

Joy: You really are serious. Do you know, I think I (6) 'm going to join / 'll join / 'm joining you – I'll help you train.

Hasan: Look, you can if you want, but only if you (7) 're taking / 're going to take / due to take it seriously and not play around.

Joy: I won't play around! I (8) 'm trying / 'm going to try / 'll try my best. Promise.

7 Complete the passage using the correct form of the verbs in the box.

visit	increase	rise	prescribe	work	practise

The rise of the Physician Assistant

The Physician Assistant – health professionals who practise medicine as members of a team with a doctor supervisor – is the third fastest-growing profession in the United States. Approximately 206 million patients (1) .... a Physician Assistant by the end of the year and Physician Assistants (2) .... or recommended approximately 250 million medications during this time. Approximately 55,000 people (3) .... as Physician Assistants at the beginning of next year and the largest number (4) .... in New York and California. By the end of the year the number of Physician Assistant jobs in the US (5) .... by 49%, while total US employment (6) .... by only 15% in the same period.

8 Rewrite the sentences using *should(n't)*, *could(n't)* or *have to*.

1 It's a good idea to wear a warm coat.   You should wear a warm coat.

2 It is necessary to fill in an application form.

3 It's a bad idea to sleep so much.

4 Ann knew how to speak four languages.

5 If I were Marc, I'd apply for a part-time job.

6 It was impossible for Sarah to get home early.

7 Paul wasn't able to believe it when he saw the results of his test.

8 To get a driving licence, you are required to take a written test.

9 **Complete the dialogue using *can('t)*, *may* or *might*.**

Cheng: Excuse me, can you tell me where I (1) .... get an application form for language classes?

Administrator: Yes, just wait a minute while I find them.

Cheng: (2) .... I sit down and wait?

Administrator: Yes, of course – it (3) .... take me a few minutes – I (4) .... remember where I put them now. OK, here we are. We have several options for you – which languages are you interested in?

Cheng: Well, I (5) .... already speak English and Mandarin, of course, so I'm interested in learning French.

Administrator: Let me see ... yes, you (6) .... attend French classes on Wednesday and Friday afternoons.

Cheng: Wednesday afternoon (7) .... be difficult as we (8) .... have an additional lecture then, and I'm sure I (9) .... go on Friday afternoon – we have a tutorial.

Administrator: I wonder, there (10) .... be another possibility here. Yes, here we are – starting next week there will be a class at lunchtime on Monday. Could you make that?

Cheng: That's perfect – thanks.

10 **Correct the mistakes in the passage.**

The bar chart shows the cost of living for eight cities in comparison with New York. In particular, we have the three expensivest cities and three middle-ranked cities and the two cheap cities. The costliest places to live are all in Europe, with Oslo the most priciest city on earth. Paris and London are almost as expensive to live in is each other, with London a little more cheap than Paris. Furtherer down the table are Moscow and Hong Kong, with the same cost of living as each other, but both of these are a lot least expensive than Oslo. Suprisingly, New York is not as costlier to live in as Moscow or Hong Kong. The most least expensive places to live are Mumbai and Caracas. It costs lesser than half as much to live in Caracas as it does to live in Oslo, Paris or London.

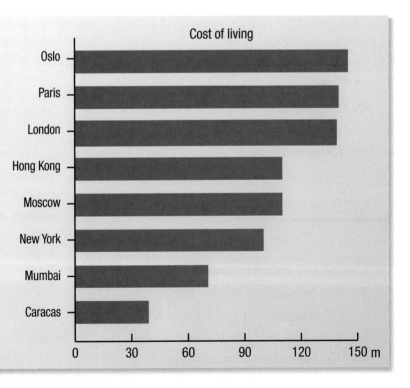

Cost of living

11 **Choose the correct alternative.**

1   **A**: I've got stomachache.   **B**: You've had too much / enough / too many to eat.
2   **A**: His face is red.   **B**: He's been in the sun enough / too many / too much.
3   **A**: I'm exhausted.   **B**: You've been working enough / too many / too much.
4   **A**: I feel tired.   **B**: You haven't had enough / too many / too much vitamins.
5   **A**: Erika's feeling sick.   **B**: She's had enough / too many / too much sweet things.

12 Complete the sentences using the correct form of the verbs in brackets.

1 If Jolanata .... (not leave) now, she .... (miss) her bus.

2 If Helen .... (work) hard, she .... (pass) her exams.

3 In an electrical storm, if you .... (be) outside and away from a building, ...
(take) cover in a vehicle if possible.

4 If you .... (be) not near shelter, ... (avoid) standing under trees or other tall
objects.

5 If Mary .... (not practise) her French, she .... (not improve).

6 The tutor .... (be) angry if you .... (arrive) late again.

7 If I .... (see) Joe tomorrow, I .... (give) him the message.

13 Correct the mistakes in the sentences.

1 If you would meet Peter, you would like him.

....

2 If I have a lot of money, I'd buy a Ferrari.

....

3 If he had time, John will go to the gym more often.

....

4 I wouldn't touch that if I am you.

....

5 Would you still gone to Sydney if you had known it was so expensive?

....

6 Wouldn't you sorry if you failed the exam?

....

7 If I hadn't been so clumsy, I wouldn't break your DVD player.

....

8 What you will do if you missed your train?

....

14 Choose the correct alternative.

1 The Minister of Health denied / refused that there was a crisis.

2 Carmen said me / told me to be quiet.

3 Rory persuaded me / insisted me to stay for dinner.

4 The tutor advised me / suggested me to work this weekend.

5 She explained me / warned me not to leave the light on all night.

6 Tony and Rachel announced / reported that they were going to get married.

15 Rewrite the sentences using the word in brackets.

1   We want to see a film. It starts at seven. (that)
     The film that we want to see starts at seven.

2   Steve's car was stolen. He went to the police. (whose)

     ....

3   A friend met me at the station. He carried my bags. (who)

     ....

4   Rachel cooked the food. It was delicious. (that)

     ....

5   A friend is staying with Peter. He comes from Paris. (who)

     ....

6   I found a man's wallet. He gave me £10. (whose)

     ....

16 Complete the exam tips using the verbs in the box.

work out	pick up	pick out	look up	look for	look back	come across	brush up

Want to (1) .... **on your reading and writing skills for IELTS? Then read on!**
When reading in English, avoid (2) .... every new word or phrase in the dictionary or you will soon feel demotivated. Only check the meaning of something that is really important for understanding the text. When you have finished reading, (3) .... at what you have read, (4) .... a few key words and phrases that interest you and check their meanings in a dictionary. In the same way, when you listen to English, don't panic when you (5) .... some words or expressions that you don't know. Keep listening and you can often (6) .... some clues and get an idea of the overall meaning. When you read or listen to English, it is sometimes possible to (7) .... the meaning of an unknown word before you check it in the dictionary. Decide what part of speech the word is before (8) .... clues from the context or form.

Now check your answers. p166

1 **Read the passage, and put the diagrams in order.**

Japan's changing demography

In Japan, the average population is getting older. People are living longer, and they are not having so many children. The number of people who work is falling, but the number of retired people is growing. This is having an effect on the economy, as fewer people are paying taxes, while the number of people they have to support is increasing. Why is this happening? People are living to a very old age because medical care is improving, and more women are joining the workforce, so they are waiting longer to have a family and the birth rate is slowing.

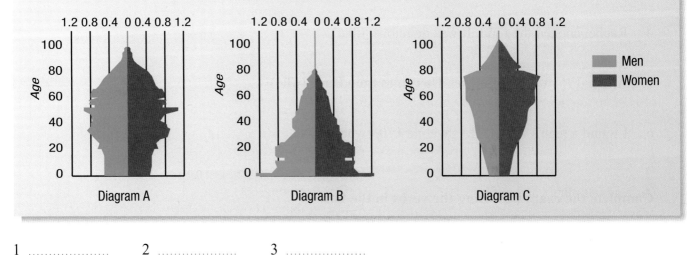

Diagram A   Diagram B   Diagram C

1 .... 2 .... 3 ....

Present continuous

We use the present continuous when we are
- describing a process which is taking place right now or around now (Activities 3 and 5)
- talking about future plans (Activities 4 and 5).

Remember that stative verbs are not normally used in the continuous form (see Unit A8), and that the infinitive is used after modal verbs.

> **Use it for IELTS!**
> You can use the present continuous to describe graphs (especially line graphs) that show trends over recent years.

Form

Affirmative

*People **are living** longer.*
*The number of retired people **is growing**.*

I	am	
You / We / They	are	living longer.
He / She / It	is	

Negative

*They **are not having** so many children.*

I	am not	
You / We / They	are not (aren't)	living longer.
He / She / It	is not (isn't)	

Question

Yes / No questions

To be + subject + present participle
***Are** they **living** longer?*

Wh– questions

Wh– question + *to be* + subject + present participle
*Why **is** this **happening**?*

Spelling rules for present participles

- Verbs ending in *e* – delete *e*, add *ing*
  live – living
- Most verbs ending with a short vowel /e/, /o/, /æ/, /ɪ/, /ʌ/, /ə/
  + consonant – double the consonant, add *ing*
  get – getting
- Verbs ending in *y*, and most other verbs – add *ing*
  hurry – hurrying   wait – waiting

2 Read the passage in Activity 1 again and count the number of present continuous verbs.

3 Complete the passage with the correct form of the verb in brackets, using present continuous where possible.

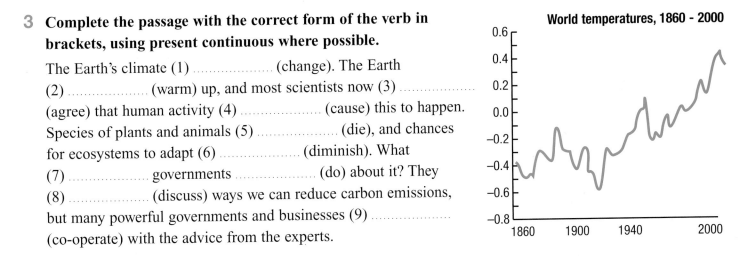

The Earth's climate (1) .... (change). The Earth
(2) .... (warm) up, and most scientists now (3) ....
(agree) that human activity (4) .... (cause) this to happen.
Species of plants and animals (5) .... (die), and chances
for ecosystems to adapt (6) .... (diminish). What
(7) .... governments .... (do) about it? They
(8) .... (discuss) ways we can reduce carbon emissions,
but many powerful governments and businesses (9) ....
(co-operate) with the advice from the experts.

World temperatures, 1860 - 2000

4 Complete the passage with the verbs in the box. Use present continuous where possible.

| increase | hunt | believe | cause | develop | result | poison | disappear | happen | sell | not adapt |

Some people (1) .... that we are in the middle of a mass extinction
of animal life. Why (2) .... this ....? Global warming may
be one reason, but many other factors (3) .... difficulties for wild
animals. In many countries, poachers (4) .... rare animals for
money. They (5) .... the animal parts for traditional medicine. As the
human race (6) ...., natural habitats (7) .... and the
animals (8) .... to the new environment. Chemicals used by farmers
(9) .... the land, and this (10) .... in imbalances between
the species. However, extinction of certain species may also be part of a natural
process, as new species (11) .... to replace those which are lost.

5 🔊 Play Track 1. Listen to Part 1 of an IELTS interview and complete the notes.

Petros (1) .... English and (2) .... as a waiter. He (3) .... to study at
university. After that, he (4) .... his father's business in Athens. Petros (5) .... his
studies, but he (6) .... a problem paying his fees.

🔑 Now check your answers. p167

1 Read the text and the student's response. Complete the labels.

Writing task 1
The chart below shows what working Americans aged 25–65 do during the day. Summarise the information by selecting and reporting the main features.

The pie chart shows how an average American spends their time.

The chart is divided into six sections showing activities per hour over one day. Americans are hard-working – they work 8.2 hours a day. They sleep for 7.6 hours, take part in sports and leisure for another 2.5 hours and do other activities for 2.5 hours. Americans do not take a long time for meals; they eat and drink for 1.5 hours each day.

What do they do for the rest of the day? Care for others.

Time use on an average work day

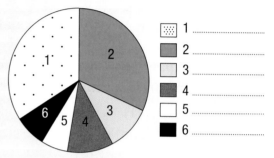

Total = 24 hours

	1 ....
	2 ....
	3 ....
	4 ....
	5 ....
	6 ....

Present simple

We use the present simple to talk about
- something which happens on a regular basis; repeated actions (Activity 3) and feelings
- facts (Activity 4)
- timetables (Activity 5).

Use it for IELTS!
You can use the present simple to write about graphs and tables that show information that is generally true and to write about the main features in a graph or table.

Form

Affirmative

To be

I	am	
You / We / They	are	hard-working.
He / She / It	is	

Spelling

verbs without e + s	drink**s**, show**s**
verbs ending with s, sh, ch + es	finish**es**, teach**es**
verbs ending consonant + y → ies	study – stud**ies**, carry – carr**ies**

Other verbs

I / You / We / They	work	
He / She / It	works	8.2 hours a day.

Negative

I / You / We / They	do not (don't)		
He / She / It	does not (doesn't)	take	a long time for meals.

Question

Yes / No **questions**

***Do* Americans *have* a long time for meals?**

Wh– **questions**

*What **do** they **do** for the rest of the day?*

2 Read the passage in Activity 1 again and underline the present tense verbs.

3 Look at the chart and complete the passage.

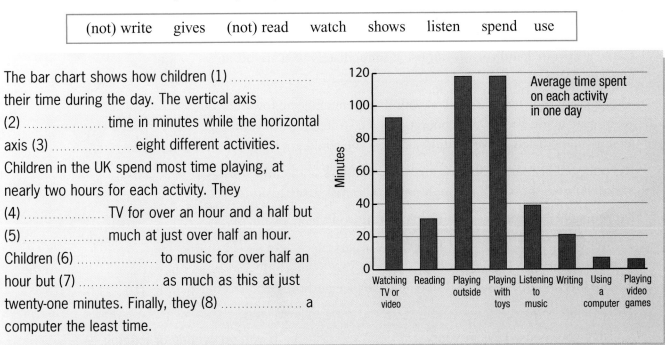

| (not) write | gives | (not) read | watch | shows | listen | spend | use |

The bar chart shows how children (1) .... their time during the day. The vertical axis (2) .... time in minutes while the horizontal axis (3) .... eight different activities. Children in the UK spend most time playing, at nearly two hours for each activity. They (4) .... TV for over an hour and a half but (5) .... much at just over half an hour. Children (6) .... to music for over half an hour but (7) .... as much as this at just twenty-one minutes. Finally, they (8) .... a computer the least time.

Average time spent on each activity in one day

Minutes

Watching TV or video / Reading / Playing outside / Playing with toys / Listening to music / Writing / Using a computer / Playing video games

4 Choose the correct tense to complete the sentences.

The Amazon rainforest

The Amazon rainforest (1) covers / is covering 7,000,000 km² and (2) is crossing / crosses nine nations. Brazil (3) contains / is containing 60% of the rainforest and Peru (4) has / is having 13%. Rainforests (5) are supporting / support over half of our planet's plants and trees. Although the Amazon (6) is representing / represents over half of the planet's remaining rainforests, people (7) are cutting / cut down 16,235 km² of it every year and (8) are growing / grow soy crops on the land.

5 🔊 Play Track 2. Listen and complete the timetable.

Foundation in Civil and Structural (1) ....
Monday – Thursday (2) .... – 12 am (3) ....
Monday / Tuesday pm (4) .... with tutor.
Wednesday / Thursday lab work, Dr Boot (5) .... , Lab Technician also (6) ....

Now check your answers. p167

1 **Read the passage and choose the correct answers.**

Keeping safe

If you often walk home in the dark, get a personal attack alarm. Carry it in your hand so you can use it immediately to scare off an attacker. **(A)**

Always carry your bag close to you with the opening facing towards you. Keep your house keys in your pocket. But if a stranger grabs your bag, let it go immediately. Never put up a fight – you could get hurt. **(B)**

Keep to well-lit roads with pavements. Avoid dark alleys and subways and don't take short-cuts through parks or across waste ground.

Do remember that if you wear an iPod, you won't hear traffic or someone approaching behind you. **(C)**

If you regularly go jogging or cycling, try to vary your route and time. On parklands, keep to the main paths and open spaces, where you can see and be seen by other people. **(D)**

1 Carry your house keys in your
   A   bag.
   B   pocket.
   C   hand.

2 If someone tries to take your bag,
   A   scream for help.
   B   do your best to hang on to it.
   C   give it up immediately.

3 If you go cycling or jogging,
   A   avoid open spaces.
   B   go at the same time each day.
   C   use different routes.

Imperatives

We use imperatives to
- tell people what to do
- advise them
- encourage them
- warn them
- give directions.

Form

Imperatives look the same as infinitives without *to*.

Affirmative

Keep your house keys in your pocket.
We can use *do* to make emphatic imperatives.

Do remember that if you wear an iPod, you won't hear traffic or someone approaching behind you.

Negative

Don't take short-cuts through parks or across waste ground.

Note the position of *always* and *never* before imperatives:
Always carry your bag close to you.
Never put up a fight.

2 Put these sentences into the correct part of the passage in Activity 1: (A), (B), (C) or (D).

1 Always walk facing the traffic so a car cannot pull up behind you unnoticed. ☐
2 Stay clear of wooded areas for this reason. ☐
3 Make sure it is designed to continue sounding if it is dropped or falls to the ground. ☐
4 Remember, your safety is more important than your property. ☐

3 Match the beginning of each sentence on the left with its ending on the right.

1 Never make it easy for a pickpocket so...
2 Keep your bag close to you when in public places and...
3 Tell your bank as soon as your card has been stolen, as...
4 Keep your personal identification number (PIN) separate from your bank card and...
5 Always sign your new bank card as soon as you receive it and...
6 Cash is a favourite target for thieves so...

A someone could use it to make purchases in your name.
B cut up the old one.
C avoid carrying large amounts with you.
D keep the clasp or zip shut.
E carry your wallet in your inside pocket rather than your back pocket.
F never disclose it, not even to bank staff or close friends.

4 Choose the correct alternative.

A thief needs only a minute to steal your possessions so (1) try to / make an effort be careful at all times. (2) Never / Always be on your guard and (3) never / always look away for a second. Wallets carried in back pockets are vulnerable to pickpockets. (4) Put / Don't put them in a front trouser or inside jacket pocket, preferably one which fastens. In public places, (5) make sure / keep your bag is close to you where you can see it and (6) close / open the clasp or zip. If your bank card is stolen, (7) notify / avoid notifying your bank immediately. (8) Have / Don't have the number handy. (9) Make sure / Remember that a delay reporting the loss could lead to a crime being committed in your name. (10) Don't forget / Do make sure that thieves can use cards to make over-the-counter, telephone and online purchases.

5 Complete the passage using the correct form of the verbs in the box.

| ask for | book | give | sit | keep | get in | check | ask |

Staying safe – taxis

If you are going to be out late, try to arrange a lift home with friends or (1) .... a taxi. Always (2) .... the phone number of a reliable taxi firm handy.

At the time of booking (3) .... a description of the car (colour, make, etc.) and (4) .... your name.

When the taxi arrives (5) .... that it is the one you ordered. (If in any doubt, (6) .... the vehicle.)

During the journey always (7) .... behind the driver.

When you get home (8) .... the driver to wait until you are safely inside.

Now check your answers. p167

1 **Read the task and the student's response, and complete the chart.**

> **Writing task 1**
> The chart below shows how numbers of immigrants to Australia have changed over the past ten years. Write a summary of the information given.

The bar chart shows how numbers of people moving to Australia from nine different regions have changed in the past ten years. Overall, there has been a decrease in immigration. Numbers from Europe, southeast and northeast Asia have fallen sharply. Additionally, immigration from India, the Middle East and North America has gone down slightly. Have any regions shown an increase? Numbers from Oceania and Africa have not fallen; in fact, numbers from Africa have more than doubled over the past ten years.

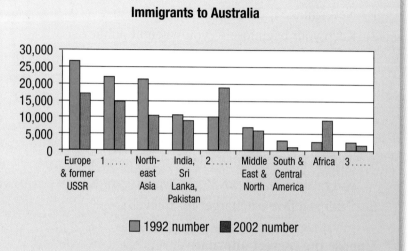

Immigrants to Australia

Europe & former USSR 1 ..... North-east Asia India, Sri Lanka, Pakistan 2 ..... Middle East & North South & Central America Africa 3 .....

☐ 1992 number   ■ 2002 number

Present perfect

The present perfect is always related to present time.
We use the present perfect to talk about
* past events which are still news (Activities 1 and 3)
* actions which are now complete, often with *yet* and *already* (Activities 4, 5 and 6)
* past events with a present result (Activities 7 and 8)
* experiences and news events (Activity 9).

> **Use it for IELTS!**
> You can use the present perfect to write about charts and graphs that show changes which have happened up to now. You can also use it to give examples of recent news stories to support your arguments in Writing task 2, and to talk about your experiences in the Speaking test.

Affirmative

I / You / We / They	have	fallen.
He / She / It	has	

*Overall, there **has been** a decrease in immigration.*

Negative

I / You / We / They	have not (haven't)	fallen.
He / She / It	has not (hasn't)	

*Numbers from Oceania and Africa **have not fallen**.*

Question

Yes / No questions

***Have** any regions **shown** an increase?*

Wh– questions

*Where **have** the immigrants **come from**?*

2 **Read the passage in Activity 1 again and underline the examples of the present perfect.**

3 Complete the sentences using words from the box. Use present perfect where possible.

> more   rise   move   leave   fall   since   fewer   not change

1 Numbers of immigrants from Britain .... considerably .... 2003.

2 The number of people moving to New Zealand from China .... by .... than 1,500.

3 Not so many people from India .... to New Zealand in 2004, compared to 2003.

4 The number of immigrants from South Africa .... very much.

5 .... people from Fiji .... home to live in New Zealand in 2004.

Immigrants to New Zealand

4 🔊 Play Track 3. Listen to the conversation between two IELTS candidates and tick the activities they have done.

	Candidate A (female)	Candidate B (male)
Send application form	☐	☐
Receive confirmation	☐	☐
Find passport	☐	☐
Watch speaking test video	☐	☐
Do practice test	☐	☐
Buy alarm clock	☐	☐

5 🔊 Play Track 3. Listen again, and complete the rule for *yet* and *already*.

1 *Yet* is used with .... and .... sentences.

2 *Already* is used with .... sentences.

6 Complete the conversation between Sally and Bohos, who are preparing to go on holiday. The list shows what they have / have not done.

Book hotel – Sally	✓	Check weather forecast – Bohos	✓
Buy flight tickets – Sally	✓	Do washing – Sally	✗
Apply for visa – Bohos	✓	Call parents – Bohos	✗
Pack suitcase – Sally	✗		

Bohos: (1) .... you .... the hotel (2) .... , Sally?

Sally: Yes, I did it this morning. I (3) .... the flight tickets too, from the airline website.

Bohos: Good. Now, let's look at the list to see what else we have to do. OK – I (4) .... for my visa, but it (5) .... yet. Packing the suitcase is next – that's your job, Sally.

Sally: Well, I (6) .... it (7) .... , because I still (8) .... the washing, and I don't want to pack dirty clothes. You need to check the weather forecast and call your parents.

Bohos: I (9) .... the weather forecast, and it's going to be fine and sunny tomorrow. So there's one more thing I have to do. I (10) .... my parents (11) ....

7 **Complete the passage using the correct form of the words in brackets.**

(1) .... (you / try) making your own bread? If you haven't, you should. It's not difficult. After you (2) .... (measure) the correct amount of flour and warm water, mix them together in a bowl. You now need to add yeast, salt and sugar. When you (3) .... (do) this, work the mixture with your hands, then leave it in a warm place for an hour. When it (4) .... (grow) to double the size, work it with your hands again. It should feel dry to the touch if you (5) .... (follow) the instructions correctly. Put the bread mixture into a tin, and leave it for an hour until it (6) .... (rise) up over the top. Finally, when you (7) .... (heat) the oven, bake the bread for about forty minutes.

8 **Choose the correct tense to complete the sentences.**

1   I took / have taken the IELTS test three times now, and the last time it was / has been much easier for me.
2   When you finished / have finished with the newspaper, can I have it?
3   Yesterday I didn't eat / haven't eaten breakfast, but so far this morning I had / have had three pieces of toast and a banana.
4   This grammar book is no use to me – someone filled in / has filled in all the answers!
5   Good morning, class. Did you do / Have you done your homework? Please give it to me.
6   It rained / has rained nearly every day last month, but this month the weather was / has been very good.
7   There isn't any milk left – the others must drunk / must have drunk it all.
8   A: Can I speak to Gordon, please?
     B: I'm sorry, he's not here. He went / has gone to see a film.
9   I wrote / I've written 2,000 words of my dissertation, but I still have 1,500 to write.
10 The value of the pound sterling dropped / has dropped considerably since last year.

9 **Write the newspaper headlines in full.**

1   Foreign minister returns from Washington
     The foreign minister has returned from Washington.

2   Police catch £30 million bank robber

3   Damaged aircraft lands safely – 200 people survive unhurt

4   Prime Minister caught in love triangle! Offers to resign immediately

🔑 Now check your answers. p167

1 **Read the conversation and choose the correct answer.**

Examiner: How long have you been living in Brisbane, Zhang?

Candidate: I've only been living here for about two months – but I really like it. I've been staying with a host family and they're very good to me.

Examiner: What kinds of things have you been doing?

Candidate: Well, the coast is great here, so I've been surfing quite a lot. Unfortunately I keep falling off because I haven't been practising very much.

1   Zhang has been in Brisbane for
    A one month.   B two months.   C three months.

2   He has been staying
    A at a hotel.   B at a college.   C with a family.

3   He isn't very good at surfing because he
    A hasn't got a good surfboard.   B falls off a lot.   C hasn't been practising.

> **Use it for IELTS!**
> Use the present perfect continuous in the Speaking test to talk about your experiences of working or studying which are continuing up to now.

Present perfect continuous

We use the present perfect continuous to talk about events when
- we refer to longer actions, events or trends (e.g., working, learning, studying) (Activity 1)
- the action or activity leads to a result or is important in the present (Activity 4 and Activity 6)
- we are focusing on the action or activity (Activity 3 and Activity 5)
- the action or activity continues to the present time. (Contrast this with the present perfect, Activity 4.)

We can use the present perfect continuous with words and phrases like *for*, *since*, *recently*, *lately*, or time phrases like *all morning / day / week*.

Form

Affirmative

I / You / We / They	have	been living	here for two months.
He / She / It	has		

*I've only **been living** here for about two months.*
*I've **been staying** with a host family.*

Negative

I / You / We / They	have not (haven't)	been working	very hard.
He / She / It	has not (hasn't)		

*I **haven't been practising** very much.*

Question

Yes / No questions
*Have you **been taking** surfing lessons?*

Wh– questions
*What kinds of things **have you been doing**?*

2 Read the conversation in Activity 1 again and count the number of present perfect continuous verbs.

3 Look at the table and complete the passage with these verbs.

| recycle | pay | buy | use | commute |

What have you been doing to make your lifestyle more environmentally friendly?	total US citizens	age			
		18–31	32–43	44–62	63+
	%	%	%	%	%
recycling	91	89	90	91	94
paying bills online	73	75	77	76	61
buying more locally produced food and / or goods	49	39	44	56	53
bringing my own shopping bags instead of using paper or plastic ones	39	34	47	36	45
commuting to work in a way other than an automobile	16	25	21	15	3

Almost everyone in America has been making changes to their lifestyle because they are concerned about the environment. Recently, 91% of people (1) .... and 73% (2) .... their bills online – the 32–43 age group has been doing this the most. The group which (3) .... the most locally produced food lately is the 44–62 age group, although the 32–43 group (4) .... their own shopping bags the most. Only 16% of people (5) .... to work using a different form of transport than their cars, and the 18–31 group has been doing this the most, at 25%.

4 Match the sentences with their meanings.

1 A My cousin's been staying with me.   i   He's still at my house.
  B My cousin stayed with me for two weeks.   ii He's not at my home now.
2 A I've been repairing my car all morning.   i   The car is working now.
  B I've repaired my car this morning.   ii I haven't finished yet.
3 A Jill's been waiting for you for three hours now. i   She's still waiting for you.
  B Jill waited for you for three hours.   ii She left and went home.
4 A The painters have been decorating the house.   i   You can smell the paint.
  B The painters have decorated the house.   ii They have finished.
5 A Tom's been complaining all day about his phone bill. i   He finally paid it.
  B Tom's complained all day about his phone bill. ii He still hasn't stopped complaining.

5 Complete the text using verbs from the box in the present perfect continuous.

| not work   not eat   not feel   avoid   not go   hurt |

Dear Coach,

I'm sorry but I can't make next week's football match. I (1) .... too well
recently. My feet (2) .... and my knee (3) .... properly
for weeks now. I (4) .... any serious activity – I (5) ....
jogging, for example, for two weeks now and I (6) .... any junk food, either.

Best wishes,

Ehsan

6 Complete the questions.

1 Eva looks really upset. What's the matter? Has .... ? (cry)
2 A: Feridun's just finished his essay.
   B: Really? Has .... all night? (work)
3 Rose looks so suntanned and relaxed. Has .... ? (sunbathe)
4 Lucy – you're covered in mud! What .... ? (do)
5 The flat's really clean now! Who .... ? (tidy up)

Now check your answers. pp167–168

1 Read the passage and choose the correct answer.

The world's favourite drink

Coffee is the second largest export in the world after oil and around two billion cups are consumed every day, making it the world's favourite drink. Where is coffee grown? Two thirds of the world's coffee supply is produced in Central and South America and one third is grown in Brazil. Large amounts of coffee are also grown in Indonesia, Colombia and Vietnam. Worldwide, six million metric tonnes of coffee are produced in countries within 1,600 kilometres of the equator – it isn't produced in colder countries. It takes 4,000 coffee beans to make half a kilo of coffee and 60 to 70 beans are used to make an espresso.

1 .... is the largest export in the world.
   A gold   B coffee   C oil
2 .... of coffee is from Brazil.
   A one fifth   B one quarter C one third
3 .... coffee beans are used to make an espresso coffee.
   A 1,600   B 60–70   C 4,000

Present simple passive

We use the passive when
- we are interested in what is produced and not in the producer
- we do not know who is doing the action
- we do not need to know who is doing the action.

> **Look for...** **IELTS**
> passive sentences in passages about processes and producing things. You will also need to use passives if Writing task 1 asks you to describe a process like producing coffee.

Form

Affirmative	Negative	Question
Object + *to be* + past participle *Two billion cups* **are consumed** *every day.*	Object + *to be* + *not* + past participle *It* **isn't produced** *in colder countries.*	**Yes / No questions** *to be* + object + past participle **Is** *coffee* **grown** *in Brazil?* **Wh– questions** Question word + *to be* + object + past participle *Where* **is** *coffee* **grown?**

2 Read the passage in Activity 1 again and underline the passive verbs.

3 Look at the pictures and complete the passage.

Making coffee

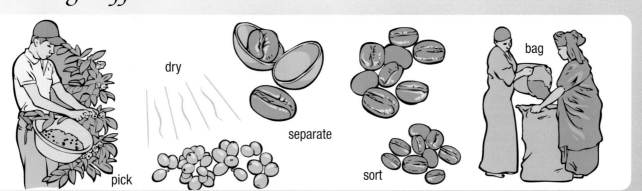

Coffee beans are really the seeds of a fruit. Coffee trees produce coffee cherries, which turn bright red when they are ripe and ready to pick. There are three parts to making coffee: harvesting, sorting and roasting. There is usually one coffee harvest per year. Coffee cherries (1) .... by hand. Then the beans (2) .... and (3) .... from their dry shells. The green coffee beans (4) .... by size and weight. The beans (5) .... and then they are transported around the world in large containers. About seven million tonnes of green coffee are transported worldwide each year.

4 Write the questions.

1   When / coffee beans / pick   ....
2   How / coffee cherries / harvest   ....
3   How / the beans / sort   ....
4   How / the beans / transport   ....

5 Read the passage again and answer the questions in Activity 4.

6 Complete the passage using the verbs in the box. Not all the verbs are in the passive.

| heat   produce   roast   turn down   harvest   turn   occur |

ROASTING COFFEE

After the beans (1) .... and sorted, the green coffee beans (2) .... in ovens. Roasting is where coffee's flavour comes from. The green coffee beans (3) .... to temperatures of about 288°C. The beans first (4) .... a yellow colour and smell a little like popcorn. The beans are heated for another eight minutes until the beans 'pop' and double in size. Then the temperature (5) .... to 204°C and the beans go brown. They are roasted for a further three to five minutes until the second 'pop' (6) .... This means that the beans are ready. The length of the roasting time depends on the type of coffee which (7) ....– shorter for American coffee, longer for espresso.

Now check your answers. p168

1 **Read the task and the student's response, and put the stages of the diagram in order.**

> **Writing task 1**
> The diagram shows how fish are tinned. Write a report describing the process.

| Preserved | Labelled | Soaked | Cleaned | Sealed | Stored | Boxed | Washed |

The diagram shows how fish are tinned after they have been caught. First, they are cleaned. When they have been cleaned, they are washed and soaked. Then they must be preserved with salt because they have not been cooked. After they have been put in tins, the tins are sealed and labels are put on. When the labels have been put on, they are ready to be put in a box and stored in a warehouse. Why have the fish been tinned? Because they will keep longer that way.

1 cleaned .... 2 .... 3 .... 4 ....

5 .... 6 .... 7 .... 8 ....

Present perfect passive

We can use the present perfect passive
- to write about stages in a process which are already complete
- when the person or thing which causes the action is not known
- when the person or thing which causes the action is not important.

> **Use it for IELTS!**
> You can make your description of a process more interesting and natural by using tenses like the present perfect passive in your answer.

Form

Affirmative

I / You / We / They	have	been	found.
He / She / It	has		

*...after they **have been caught***

Negative

I / You / We / They	have (haven't) not	been	found.
He / She / It	has (hasn't) not		

*...they **have not been cooked***

Question

Yes / No questions

Have	I / you / we / they	been	found?
Has	he / she / it		

Wh– questions

*Why **have** the fish **been tinned**?*

2 Read the passage in Activity 1 again and count the number of (a) present passive and (b) present perfect verbs.

3 Complete the passage using the verbs in brackets. Use present perfect passive or present simple passive.

When you post a letter, it (1) .... (collect) and taken to the post office. After it
(2) .... (take) there, it (3) .... (put) through a machine
which cancels the stamps. When the stamps (4) .... (cancel), it is ready to
(5) .... (sort) by district. After this (6) .... (do), the letters
(7) .... (deliver) to the correct house and street by the local postman – but only if the
letter (8) .... (address) correctly by the sender.

4 Correct the incorrect sentences.

1 Alien life have been discovered on the planet Europa.
2 46 species of butterfly have been disappeared because of global warming.
3 Many books have been written on the subject of study skills for students.
4 This book has been written by our Professor of Chemistry in 2001.
5 Has the examination been taken by all the students in the International Department?
6 The classrooms have not cleaned properly this term.
7 30 kilos of potatoes have been eaten in the canteen every day.
8 I cannot finish my dissertation this week because my laptop has been stolen.

....
....
....
....
....

5 Play Track 4. Listen to the fresher's week announcements and decide which of the actions are:

1 happening now, or around now
2 completed
3 repeated

A Cancellation of lecture ☐
B Lectures in Sunleigh lecture theatre ☐
C Register taken ☐
D New students enrol ☐
E New students go to their accommodation ☐
F Lunch in canteen – 12.30 ☐

Now check your answers. p168

1 Read the task and the student's response, and write TRUE, FALSE or NOT GIVEN.

Writing task 1

The diagram below shows how the colour of light from a star changes when it is moving rapidly through the universe. Write a brief explanation of what is happening.

Redshift and the expanding universe

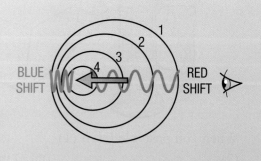

Is the universe expanding? Most scientists believe that it is, but how do they know? The theory can be explained by something called *redshift*. When a star is travelling through the universe, the light waves in front of it are compressed and appear bluer, whereas light from a star which is zooming away is stretched out, and becomes more red. This light isn't travelling slowly: it moves at 1,864 miles per second! Since most light from stars we can see is redshifted, scientists conclude that they are moving away from us – but where are they going? They must be going somewhere, and scientists say that this proves the universe is getting bigger.

1   Redshift can be seen in front of a star.   ....
2   Most scientists believe the universe is increasing in size.   ....
3   Light from stars that are moving away from us is brighter.   ....
4   Light waves are stretched out behind a star.   ....

Stative verbs

Stative verbs are not normally used in continuous structures. Examples of stative verbs in the passage above are *believe, know, appear, become, conclude, see.*

Stative verbs often describe

- mental states

love, hate, understand, want

- senses

seem, look, smell, taste, hear

Many stative verbs can also be used in an active form – compare the two sentences below:

Light waves in front of it are compressed and appear bluer. (a permanent state)

New sunspots are appearing more frequently these days. (a temporary or continuing action)

Transitive and intransitive verbs

- Transitive verbs have an object (something which receives the action):

  *Most <u>light from stars</u> we can **see** is redshifted.* (object)

  *<u>Light from a star</u> is stretched out, and **becomes** more red.* (object)

- Intransitive verbs have no object:

  *This light isn't **travelling** slowly. It **moves** at 1,864 miles per second.*

  Note: Intransitive verbs cannot be used in passive sentences, because there is no object.

- Many verbs can be both transitive and intransitive, depending how they are used:

  *Scientists are looking for the force which **moves** <u>the planets</u>.* (transitive)

  *The planets **move** slowly.* (intransitive)

2 Complete the sentences using the correct form of the verb in brackets.

1 The scientists at NASA .... (have) a meeting tomorrow to discuss their next space launch.

2 The Earth .... (look) very beautiful from space.

3 Can I ring you back later? I .... (look) at the stars and they are really clear tonight.

4 The planet Saturn .... (have) rings around it.

3 Write *C* for correct or *I* for incorrect next to each sentence.

1 I am seeing what you mean. ☐

2 I am seeing a lot of Alan these days. ☐

3 I understand Spanish, but I don't speak it well. ☐

4 This curry is tasting delicious. ☐

5 You are looking very smart today. ☐

6 I'm feeling much better now. ☐

7 This material is feeling very soft. ☐

8 He wants to see you later this week. ☐

4 Correct the incorrect sentences from Activity 3.

....

5 Read the question and the student's response, and choose the correct answers.

> **Writing task 2**
> The extinction of animals is part of a natural process that should not concern us. How far do you agree with this statement?

> When a species of animal dies, the world loses something that can never be replaced. Sometimes, humankind is directly responsible for hunting and killing a species to extinction, as with the example of the dodo. This bird lived on an island called Mauritius. Portuguese sailors visited the island and found the birds, which were easy to catch. The dodo had no fear of humans, so it walked straight up to them. They hunted and ate the birds until there were none left, which changed the ecology of Mauritius forever.

1 The writer
  A agrees with the statement.
  B disagrees with the statement.
  C has no opinion about the statement.

2 When a species of animal dies,
  A another one takes its place.
  B humankind is responsible.
  C it is gone forever.

3 The dodo
  A is an example of an extinct species.
  B could not run fast.
  C was an unintelligent bird.

6 Underline the verbs in the passage in Activity 5, and say whether they are transitive or intransitive.

7 Which of the verbs in sentences 1–4 are intransitive?

1 During the concert, nobody coughed. ....

2 As a child, I wasn't allowed to stay out late. ....

3 I work in Manchester, but I live in Leeds. ....

4 Diamonds are mined in Brazil and South Africa. ....

Now check your answers. p168

1 Read the passage and choose the correct answer.

I like my food. I particularly like duck and eat it regularly, usually with a green salad. I hardly ever eat pasta and I never go near fried potatoes. I've always been a big fan of Asian cooking. I've loved spicy food for as long as I can remember! I normally have fruit for breakfast. It's just become part of my diet over the past few years. I generally mix cereal into that and eat it with milk but occasionally I'll add some yoghurt and honey. I like to relax with a glass of champagne on a Saturday evening. Well, we all need a treat sometimes and it is only once a week! I love barbecues but they generally only work well in warm weather. Climate-wise, Australia is good for barbecues. When the weather gets warm, it's usually one of the first things we do here. People frequently assume that it's all about throwing a prawn on the barbecue at the beach. I don't know if you have ever tried to fry food on a beach but the sand gets everywhere. The reality rarely lives up to the exotic image!

Favourite food

1 The writer tends to avoid
   A drinking alcohol on weekdays.
   B eating breakfast.
   C fried potatoes.
   D Asian food.

3 He regularly eats
   A pasta and salad.
   B cereal and milk.
   C yoghurt and honey.
   D duck.

2 What does he think about barbecues?
   A They take a great deal of time to organise.
   B The quality of the food is good.
   C They should only be held in good weather.
   D The food can be difficult to prepare.

Adverbs of frequency

We use adverbs of frequency to talk about how often something happens. We can use a word or a phrase, such as: *always, usually, generally, normally, regularly, often, frequently, sometimes, occasionally, rarely, hardly ever, never, once a week.*

Adverbs of frequency usually come
• after auxiliary verbs (e.g., *do, have*)
*I don't know if you **have ever** tried to fry food on a beach...*
• after the verb *to be*
*I've **always been** a big fan of Asian food.*
• before other verbs
*People **frequently assume** that it's all about throwing a prawn on the barbecue at the beach.*
*They **generally only work well** in warm weather.*

Note: *Usually, often, sometimes* and *occasionally* can come at the beginning or the end of a clause.
***Occasionally** I'll add some yoghurt and honey.*
*Well, we all need a treat **sometimes**...*
Always and *never* don't come at the beginning or at the end of a clause.
*I've **always** been a big fan of Asian cooking.*
*I **never** add sugar as the honey makes it sweet enough.*
Ever is only used in questions and negative sentences.
*I **hardly ever** eat pasta.*

2 **Read the passage in Activity 1 again and underline the adverbs of frequency.**

3 **Read the passage in Activity 1 again and choose the correct alternative.**

1 He often / hardly ever eats duck and normally / sometimes serves it with a green salad.
2 He frequently / rarely has pasta.
3 Does he ever / never have fried potatoes? No, he doesn't.
4 He doesn't often have / generally has fruit for breakfast.
5 He drinks champagne once a week / occasionally.
6 Australians always / frequently have beach barbecues in warm weather.
7 I have never / always liked spicy food but he does!
8 I occasionally / don't often eat food on the beach because the sand gets everywhere!

4 **Complete the sentences with an appropriate adverb or adverbial phrase of frequency.**

1 My flatmate .... helps with the housework. He's so lazy! I .... end up doing it all myself!
2 I .... go to the supermarket on a Saturday morning but not very .... It's far too busy at weekends.
3 We don't .... go out for meals these days. It's much too expensive!
4 I can .... remember her name. It's so embarrassing!
5 I .... walk to work, although .... , if the weather is bad, I take the bus.
6 I go swimming .... on Friday, but if I had more time I'd go more ....
7 I don't know why they are friends. They .... seem to be arguing about something!

Now check your answers. p168

1 **Read the passage and write TRUE, FALSE or NOT GIVEN.**

> **Writing task 1**
> The figures below give information on the amount of oil used globally in 2008 and the use of oil by sector in the US in 2008. Write a report for a university lecturer describing the information.

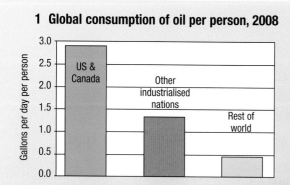

1 Global consumption of oil per person, 2008

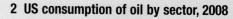

2 US consumption of oil by sector, 2008

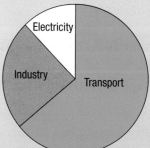

In 2008, the largest users of oil were the US and Canada. They used almost three gallons of oil per day per person, which was double that of other industrial countries and six times that of the rest of the world.

So how did the north American countries use this oil? Figure 2 shows US oil consumption by sector. The biggest demand for oil came from transport; in 2008 this was almost two thirds of the total. The next largest user was the industrial sector, which accounted for 24% of the total. Surprisingly, the US did not consume as much oil to produce electricity as they did for industry.

1 The US and Canada used more than six times more oil than other industrial countries. ....
2 Cars used the most oil in the US. ....
3 Producing electricity consumed the second largest amount of oil. ....

Past simple

We use the past simple to write about completed events. We use it for
* facts, actions or events that happened in the past (Activity 2)
* longer actions, events or trends. (Activity 3)
We often use the past tense with words and phrases like *when*, *in* (+ date), *at* (+ time), *last / the previous* + time period.

> **Use it for IELTS!**
> You can use the past simple for graphs and tables that show information over a number of years, to describe actions in the past or to tell a story.

Form

Affirmative

| I / He / She / It | was | the largest user(s) of oil. |
| You / We / They | were | |

*They **used** almost three gallons of oil.*

Negative

| I / He / She / It / You / We / They | did not (didn't) | consume | as much oil. |

Question

Yes / No questions

Did the rest of the world use up as much oil as the US?

Wh– questions

How did the north American countries use this oil?

2 Read the passage again and underline the regular past tense verbs.

3 Complete the interview with the correct form of the verbs in the box.

| attend | graduate | plan | pass | decide | study | travel |

Examiner: Tell me about your education and how it has changed in your country.

Candidate: Well, I was born in Poland in 1986 and when I was seven years old I (1) .... grammar school for six years until I was 13. Then I went to a gymnasium. I was at high school for three years and after I (2) .... my exams, I took a year out and (3) .... around southeast Asia – I (4) .... to go around Europe but it was cheaper to go to Asia. Then I (5) .... to go to the University of Krakow, where I (6) .... Microbiology and (7) .... in this a few years later. Recently the government decided to...

4 Complete the passage with the correct form of the verbs in brackets.

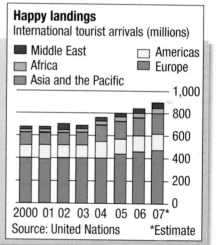

Happy landings
International tourist arrivals (millions)

■ Middle East   □ Americas
▨ Africa   ▨ Europe
▨ Asia and the Pacific

2000 01 02 03 04 05 06 07*
Source: United Nations   *Estimate

International tourism (1) .... (grow) by 6% in 2007, to 900 million tourists. The total (2) .... (go up) by almost 200 million in seven years. The Middle East (3) .... (have) 13% more international tourists, while arrivals in Asia and the Pacific (4) .... (be) up to 185 million. Africa (5) .... (see) an increase to 44 million, but in 2007, growth of international tourism (6) .... (rise) fastest in Asia and the Pacific.

5 Complete the questions with the correct form of the verbs in brackets.

1 **Examiner:** .... you .... a good journey to the test centre? (have)
   Candidate: Yes, it was quite easy – I .... a bus here. (catch)
2 **Examiner:** How far .... you .... this morning? (travel)
   Candidate: Not too far – it .... about fifteen minutes to get here. (take)
3 **Examiner:** .... you .... in Riyadh? (born)
   Candidate: No, I wasn't born in Riyadh. I .... born in Jeddah. (be)
4 **Examiner:** Where .... you .... to university? (go)
   Candidate: I .... from King Saud University. (graduate)
5 **Examiner:** Which subjects .... you .... at King Saud University? (take)
   Candidate: At first I .... Law, but I .... it so I .... to Media and Journalism. (study / not like / change)

Now check your answers. pp168–169

1 🔊 **Play Track 5. Listen to the speaker and complete the sentences with a number for each answer.**

1   The avalanche happened at .... o'clock.

2   He counted from one to .... before taking each handful of snow.

3   He managed to get out of the snow after digging for .... hours.

4   He lay on top of the snow for .... hours before being rescued.

Past continuous

We use the past continuous tense

- to talk about what was already happening at a particular time in the past.

*I **was skiing** in Switzerland.*

- together with the past simple tense. In this case, the past continuous usually refers to the background action or situation and the past simple refers to a shorter action or event that happened in the middle of the longer one.

*I **realised** that I **was lying** in an upside down and backwards position.*

- to talk about temporary actions or situations. When we talk about longer or more permanent situations we usually use past simple.

*I **was living** there at the time.*

> **Use it for IELTS!**
> You can use the past continuous to tell a story or describe an event.

Form

Affirmative

I / It / He / She	was	falling.
You / We / They	were	

Negative

I / It / He / She	was not (wasn't)	falling.
You / We / They	were not (weren't)	

Question

Yes / No questions

Was	I / it / he / she	falling?
Were	you / we / they	

Wh– questions

How	was	I / it / he / she	falling?
When	were	you / we / they	

2   Read the audioscript for Activity 1 on page 184, and underline the past continuous verbs.

3 🔊 **Play Track 5. Listen again and decide which position he was lying in. Circle the correct picture A–D.**

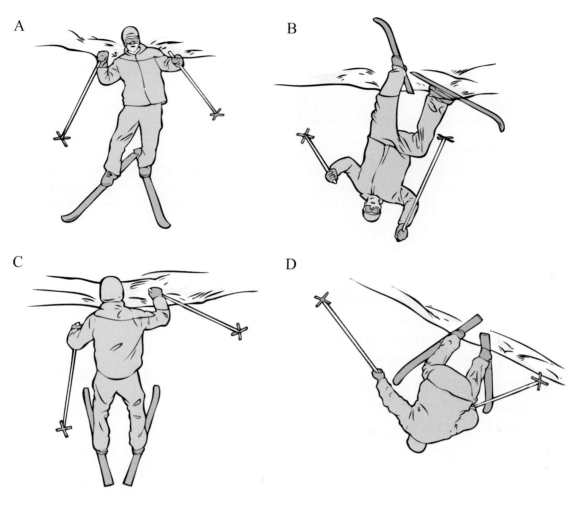

A

B

C

D

4 **Choose the correct alternative.**

1 He skied / was skiing in Switzerland when the avalanche happened / was happening.
2 He remembered / was remembering the day clearly.
3 He wasn't thinking / didn't think he was going to survive.
4 He didn't know / wasn't knowing what to do.
5 He suddenly realised / was realising that his tears ran / were running across his face.
6 He was digging / dug for twenty-two hours before the rescuers arrived / were arriving.

5 **Complete the sentences using the correct form of the verbs in brackets.**

1 .... he (ski) when the avalanche .... (strike)?
2 Where .... he (live) at the time?
3 At first he .... (not understand) what position he .... (lie in).
4 He .... (feel) frightened because it was completely dark.
5 He .... (see) anything while he was trapped under the snow.
6 It .... (take) 14 hours before the rescuers .... (come).
7 .... he (hear) the rescuers as they .... (approach)?

🗝 Now check your answers. p169

1 Read the speaking task and the student's response, and write TRUE, FALSE or NOT GIVEN.

Talk about an event in your childhood that you clearly remember.
You should say:
- where you were at the time
- who you were with
- what happened
and explain why you remember it so well.

The time in my childhood I remember best was when I moved with my parents and my little sister to our new house in the countryside. My father had sold everything to be able to buy it. He had left his job in the city and decided he wanted us to be self-sufficient. He had bought seeds and garden tools so we could grow our own vegetables. It was the biggest adventure I had ever experienced in my life. I hadn't been away from home before, and everything was so different in the country. What had my mother thought of his idea? Well, she supported everything he did, and he was right — it was hard work at first, but we never felt that he had made the wrong decision. We soon became used to our new life in the country.

1 The speaker's father used to work in the countryside.   ....
2 He didn't want to buy their food from a shop.   ....
3 The speaker was very excited about their move.   ....
4 The speaker's mother didn't want to grow vegetables.   ....
5 It was not long before they felt at home in the new house.   ....

Past perfect

We use the past perfect when speaking about things that happened **before** another time in the past.
- When the speaker is talking about the day his family moved to the countryside, he uses past simple:

*I **moved** with my parents and my little sister to our new house in the countryside.*
- When he talks about things that happened before that day, he uses the past perfect:

*My father **had sold** everything to be able to buy it.*

> **Use it for IELTS!**
> You can use the past perfect to tell a story in a more interesting way in the interview. Compare Responses 1 and 2 (Activity 3 and Activity 5).

Form

Affirmative	**Negative**	**Question**
Subject + *had* + past participle	Subject + *had not (hadn't)* + past participle	**Yes / No questions**
He **had bought** seeds and garden tools.	I **hadn't been** away from home before.	*Had* + subject + past participle
		Had he **made** the wrong decision?
		Wh– questions
		Question word + *had* + subject + past participle
		*What **had** my mother **thought** of his idea?*

2 Read the student's response in Activity 1 again and put the events in order.

A They moved house.   ....

B Her father left his job.   ....

C He bought seeds.   ....

3 Read the speaking task and underline the conjugated verbs in Response 1.

> Talk about a party you enjoyed very much. You should say:
> • what the occasion was
> • who attended the party
> • what preparations were made
> and explain why you enjoyed it so much.

Response 1

> I graduated in 2002 with 1st class honours. My friend Anna decided to have a surprise party to celebrate, but she didn't tell me. She invited all my friends, then she booked a large room at the Grand Hotel. She even ordered a stretch limousine to take me there. Imagine my surprise when it turned up at my door! I got dressed up very quickly – but I still didn't know where I was going. When we arrived at the hotel, my friends came out to meet me. We laughed and danced all night long.

4 Write the past simple verbs from Response 1 in the order they appear.

1 graduated   5 ....   9 ....   13 ....

2 .... 6 ....   10 ....

3 .... 7 ....   11 ....

4 .... 8 ....   12 ....

5 Complete Response 2 with past simple or past perfect, using the verbs from Activity 4.

Response 2

> The party I enjoyed most of all was my graduation party. I'll never forget the moment when the stretch limousine (1) .... at my door. My friend Anna (2) .... it. I (3) .... very quickly and got in the car, but I really (4) .... where I was going. Then we (5) .... at the Grand Hotel, and all my friends (6) .... out to meet me. What a surprise! Anna (7) .... all my friends from university. I (8) .... with 1st class honours, so she (9) .... to have a party for me, but she (10) .... me about it. She (11) .... a large room at the hotel, where we (12) .... and (13) .... all night long.

🔊 Play Track 6. Now listen and check your answers.

6 Complete the sentences with the correct form of the words in brackets.

1 We .... for hours because we .... each other for so long. (talk / not see)

2 When the alarm bell ...., I .... that I .... to turn it off. (ring / realise / forgot)

3 Why .... that man yesterday? What ....? (the police / arrest / do)

4 When he .... the meal, he .... it to the children. ●▬▶ **Now check your answers. p169**
   (prepare / serve)

1 **Look at the graph and complete the passage. Use these dates and figures.**

| 2008 | 2005 | 2000 | 12% | 8% | 4% | 10% |

> **Writing task 1**
> The chart below shows the exports and carbon dioxide emissions for two countries between 1990 and 2008. Summarise the information by selecting and reporting the main features and make comparisons where relevant.

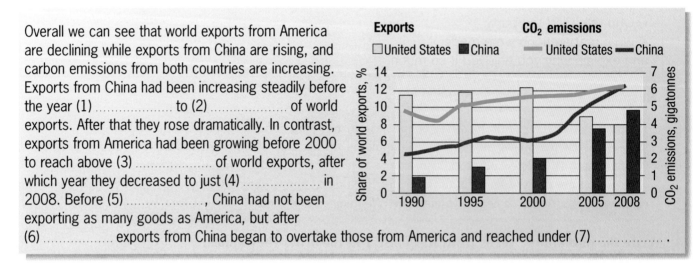

Overall we can see that world exports from America are declining while exports from China are rising, and carbon emissions from both countries are increasing. Exports from China had been increasing steadily before the year (1) .... to (2) .... of world exports. After that they rose dramatically. In contrast, exports from America had been growing before 2000 to reach above (3) .... of world exports, after which year they decreased to just (4) .... in 2008. Before (5) ...., China had not been exporting as many goods as America, but after (6) .... exports from China began to overtake those from America and reached under (7) ....

Past perfect continuous

When we refer to an action or event that happened before the time we have already referred to, we can use the past perfect or the past perfect continuous. We use the past perfect continuous

- to write about longer actions and events
- with words and phrases like *previously, before this, prior to this*
- with *for* and *since* to show the period of time.

Form

Affirmative

| I / He / She / It / You / We / They | had | been | waiting. |

*Exports from China **had been increasing** steadily.*

Negative

| I / He / She / It / You / We / They | had not (hadn't) | been | waiting. |

*China **had not been exporting** as many goods as America.*

Question

Yes / No questions

***Had** China **been exporting** as much as the US before 1995?*

Wh– questions

*What kind of goods **had** America **been producing** before 2000?*

2 **Read the passage in Activity 1 again and say what**

1 had been increasing steadily. ....
2 had been growing before 2000. ....
3 China had not been exporting. ....

3 Complete the conversation using the verbs in the box. Use the past perfect continuous where possible.

think	find	work	do	change

Examiner: What did you do before you came to Australia?

Candidate: Before I came here I (1) .... in IT. I worked for Computech for five years, then I (2) .... jobs and became an IT trainer.

Examiner: Why did you decide to move into education?

Candidate: Well, while I was working for Computech, I (3) .... about changing career for a few years. I (4) .... the job a bit boring – the job was about fixing computer problems and I (5) .... this for five years. It was time to move on really.

4 Complete the sentences using the past perfect continuous.

1 John was hurt in the car crash.
(not wearing / seatbelt)   *He hadn't been wearing a seatbelt.* ....

2 The company lost its share of the market.
(not investing / new products)   ....

3 Jane didn't do well in her exams.
(not working / hard enough)   ....

4 Ayse didn't know what to do.
(not listening / instructions)   ....

5 Kevin couldn't talk about the TV series.
(not / watching it)   ....

5 Look at the chart in Activity 1 again and complete the passage using the verbs from the box.

increase (×2)	fluctuate	decrease	rise (×2)	produce

The amount of carbon dioxide (CO_2) from both countries (1) .... Before 2000, emissions from China (2) .... – between 1990 and 1998 they (3) .... steadily, and between 1998 and 2000 they (4) .... , in contrast to the US, where emissions (5) .... steadily since 1993. However, after 2000, emissions from China (6) .... very quickly. But (7) .... China really .... as much CO_2 as America? In reality, CO_2 emissions per person are much lower in China than in America.

Now check your answers. p169

1 **Read the passage and choose TWO correct letters A–E.**

Reading styles

Reading a book or an article used to be so easy for me. I would get fully involved in the narrative. In fact, I used to love reading long texts but I don't now. After reading two or three pages my concentration starts to drift. I never used to think like this. I didn't use to have a problem with deep reading, but recently I've been spending a lot of time online, surfing the Internet. Research that in the past would require days searching through books can now be done in minutes. But when I'm reading online, I'm 'power browsing' instead of deep reading in the way I used to.

A recent study of online habits suggests that new ways of reading are emerging. Researchers found that users would hop from one source to another and that they wouldn't necessarily go on to read texts that they had saved. The style of reading promoted by the Internet may be weakening our capacity to think; to interpret text and to make the mental connections that form when we read books and other printed material.

A   People have less time to read nowadays compared to the past.
B   More research into online reading habits is needed.
C   People read in different ways when they are online.
D   People are reading fewer books than they did in the past.
E   People tend to concentrate better when they read books.

Used to

We use *used to*

- to talk about things that we habitually did in the past but no longer do. It expresses a past situation which contrasts with the present.
  *I **used to** love reading long texts but I don't now.*
- to refer to past states.
  *Reading **used to** be easy for me.*

Form

Affirmative	Negative	Question
used to + infinitive	*did not* + *use to* + infinitive	**Yes / No** questions
*Reading a book or lengthy article **used to** be so easy for me.*	*I **didn't use to** have a problem with deep reading.*	***Did** you **use to** read a lot of books when you were a child?*
	Or, less commonly,	
	used not to + infinitive	
	*I **used not to** have a problem with deep reading.*	
	Mid-position adverbs can go before or in the middle of *used to*. The position before *used to* is more common.	
	*I never **used to** think like this.*	
	*I **used** never **to** think like this.*	

Would

Would can also be used to describe habitual actions in the past.
*I **would** get fully involved in the narrative or argument.*
*I **used to** get fully involved in the narrative or argument.*

However, *would*

- is more common in written language and often occurs in reminiscences.

*Research that in the past **would** require days searching through books can now be done in minutes.*

- is also used to express the idea of 'future in the past' (to talk about a past action which has not yet happened at the time we are talking about).

*After I read one thing, I **would** hop from one source to another.*

2 **Read the passage in Activity 1 again and underline the examples of *used to* and *would*.**

3 **Complete the grammar rules using A, B or C.**

A *used to*   B *would*   C *used to* and *would*

1 .... can be used to talk about past habits.
2 .... can express past states.
3 .... refers only to repeated actions.
4 .... emphasises the contrast between past and present.
5 .... has no present form.
6 .... may be more commonly used in written form.
7 .... may express the idea of future in the past.

4 **Write *C* for correct or *I* for incorrect next to each sentence.**

1 I would read much more as a child than I do now. □
2 Did you use to enjoy reading adventure stories? □
3 When he was a student he would spend hours in the library. □
4 She has always been a keen reader. Even as a child she would put down a book until she
   had finished it. □
5 It would take ages for him to find all the information he needed but now it takes only a few seconds! □
6 Do you think people read less nowadays than they use to? □

5 **Correct the incorrect sentences from Activity 4.**

....

....

....

....

6 **Complete the sentences using the correct form of *would* or *used to* and a verb from the box.**

make   buy   study   be (x2)   take

1 I .... second-hand books but now I do. They are much cheaper than new ones!
2 When he was a child he .... the same route to school and back.
3 Andreas has lost a lot of weight! He .... overweight.
4 My grandmother was a wonderful cook. She .... delicious cakes every weekend.
5 You look familiar. .... at Manchester University together?
6 There .... so much traffic in the city centre. It's so congested these days!

Now check your answers. pp169–170

1 Read the task and the student's response and label the diagram.

> **Writing task 1**
> The diagram below shows an experiment in which iron was extracted from flakes of breakfast cereal. Write a report explaining the stages of the experiment for a university tutor.

The diagram shows the stages of an experiment for removing iron from flakes of breakfast cereal. Firstly, a beaker was filled with water and some cornflakes were put on top. After that, a magnet was put in the water and the cereal moved towards it, showing that there was iron in it. At the next stage, some cereal was crushed into a powder with a mortar and pestle. The powder was spread on a piece of paper, and the paper was moved over a magnet. Specks of iron in the powder were attracted to the magnet, which could then be removed from the cereal.

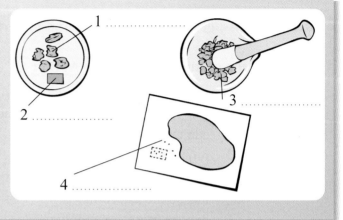

Past simple passive

We use the past simple passive
- to describe a process which took place in the past
- when we are more interested in the stages of the process than in who was doing the actions.

Form

Affirmative	Negative	Question
Object + *was / were* + past participle	Object + *was / were not (n't)* + past participle	**Yes / No questions**
*A beaker **was filled** with water.*	*The experiment **was not (wasn't)** conducted in a laboratory.*	*Was / Were* + object + past participle
*Some cornflakes **were put** on top.*		***Was** the experiment **conducted** in a laboratory?*
*The powder **was spread** on a piece of paper.*		
		Wh– questions
		Question word + *was / were* + object + past participle
		*Where **was** the experiment **conducted**?*

2 Read the passage in Activity 1 again and underline the past simple passive verbs.

3 Complete the passage using the verbs from the box. Use past simple or past simple passive.

> **Writing task 1**
> The diagrams below show a simple experiment in which salt was extracted from a sand and salt mixture. Write a report of the stages of the experiments for a university tutor.

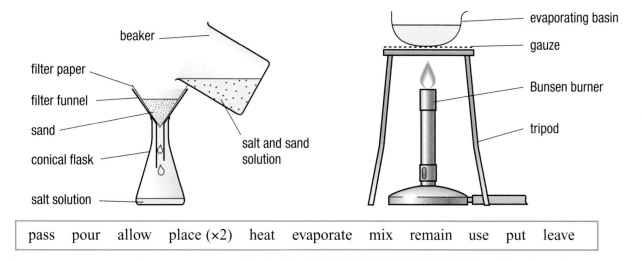

| pass | pour | allow | place (×2) | heat | evaporate | mix | remain | use | put | leave |

In the first part of this experiment, filter paper (1) .... to separate sand from a mixture of sand and salt. First, a few grams of salt and sand (2) .... with water in a beaker, then a filter funnel with filter paper inside it (3) .... on top of a conical flask. When the salt and sand solution (4) .... through the funnel, the sand (5) .... on top of the filter paper, but the salt solution (6) .... through. After that, the salt solution (7) .... into an evaporating basin, which (8) .... over a Bunsen burner on a tripod. When the solution (9) ...., the water (10) .... into the air and (11) .... the salt in the basin. Finally, the salt (12) .... to dry.

4 Rewrite the sentences in the passive. Do not include the agent if it is not necessary.

1 The students took care when they mixed the chemicals.
   Care ....

2 The teacher showed the class how to use a Bunsen burner.
   The class ....

3 All the boys chose science as their favourite subject.
   Science ....

4 You have to describe an experiment in the Chemistry exam.
   An experiment ....

5 🔊 Play Track 7. Listen and complete the report. Use past simple or past simple passive.

In this experiment, glue (1) .... from milk.
First, a cupful of milk (2) .... with some
vinegar in a beaker. Then the mixture (3) ....
and (4) .... until it (5) .... into curds
and whey. The whey (6) .... into a flask,
leaving the curds in the funnel. After that, the curds
(7) .... with a paper towel, and some water
(8) .... The curds and water (9) ....
again. The glue (10) .... by sticking pictures
in notebooks.

filter paper
filter funnel
conical flask
curds and whey
curds
whey

🔑 **Now check your answers. p170**

1 Read the passage and complete the sentences using NO MORE THAN THREE words or a number for each answer.

Green shopping in the US

A survey of 6,036 people in the US showed that people aged 55 and older purchased the most green products for the home, contrary to beliefs that environmentally conscious buying is largely done by young people. Another survey of 30,000 people found that respondents gave 'a sense of responsibility' as the leading motive and 'to give back to society' and 'make the world a better place' as the other reasons for buying eco-friendly goods. Researchers think what will happen is that eventually green (environmentally friendly) products will not be a small market. It will become an expectation among all consumers that all products will be environmentally friendly. The main question isn't 'Will the green market become mainstream?' but 'When will the green market become mainstream?'

1 The passage says that people think that environmentally friendly products are most often bought by ....

2 The main reason for buying environmentally friendly goods is a ....

3 Eventually, consumers will .... all products to be eco-friendly.

Will

We use *will* to make:

- predictions about the future (Activity 3)
- for promises, quick decisions and offers (Activity 6)

We can use *will* with words and phrases that refer to the future like *next* (*week / month / year*), *later, tonight, this* (*afternoon / evening / year / Summer / Winter*), *in 10 years' time*.

We can use *will* with *still* and *as ever* to emphasise that we do not expect any changes or that the changes will not have any effect. (Activity 3)

Will or *shall*?

We use *shall*:

- to show that we are determined to do something

The economic conditions of the next two years will be very bad, but I know that we **shall** *come through the hard times.*

- to make (formal) suggestions

I'd like to see that film too. **Shall** *we go together?*
We only use *shall* with *I* or *we*.

> **Look for...** **IELTS**
> *will* in listening or reading passages about future trends or scientific developments.

Form

Affirmative

Subject	will	verb

All products **will be** *environmentally friendly.*

Negative

Subject	will not (won't)	verb

Environmentally friendly products **won't be** *a small market.*

Question

Yes / No questions
***Will** the green market* **become** *mainstream?*

Wh– questions
When **will** *the green market* **become** *mainstream?*

2 Read the passage in Activity 1 again and find six examples of *will*.

3 Complete the passage with *will* and a verb from the box.

| be (× 3) work not use do not work have need not be |

Working in the future

Predicting the future of work is not a science. Most employment in Britain in 20 years' time (1) .... still .... the same as it is now: the majority of us (2) .... still .... for other people doing a job that is recognisable today. So what (3) .... different? Although we (4) .... the same jobs, we (5) .... in the same way – there will be more flexibility of working hours and where we work. Everything that can be done from home, (6) .... Companies will be smaller and more specialised; offices will be for 'face time' only, when meeting other people is essential. That (7) .... wider benefits, too. Half the greenhouse gas emissions in Europe are the result of office work – people's journeys to their workplace, heating and air conditioning. While homeworkers (8) .... still .... to keep warm, we (9) .... as much energy. But (10) .... we .... happy in our jobs? Sadly, in spite of all the corporate attempts to please us, and the chance to work from home a couple of days a week, it seems likely we (11) .... happier than we are now.

4 Match the questions with the answers.

1 What time will the sun set this evening?
2 What's your schedule for this week?
3 What time does the tutorial start?
4 Where will the first experiment be held?
5 Who will be the next head of state?

a Well, tomorrow I'll be in London...
b That will be Prince William.
c It begins at 3 pm, after the lecture.
d It won't get dark until around 7.30 pm.
e It will take place in laboratory 3.

5 Complete the replies using the correct form of the verbs in brackets.

1 Oh no, we've run out of milk again.
   Don't worry, ... (go) to the shop.
2 Did Sally bring her holiday photos to show us?
   No, she's forgotten – .... (bring) them next week.
3 And what can I get you for your main course today?
   .... (have) pizza, please.
4 Ali, you're late again. Why can't you be on time for once?
   I'm sorry, ... (happen) again.
5 I can't put this bag onto the luggage rack; it's much too heavy.
   Let me take it. .... (lift) it up for you.

6 Decide whether the replies to 1–5 in Activity 5 are offers, promises or quick decisions.

🔑 **Now check your answers. p170**

1 **Read the passage. Choose TWO correct letters A–F.**

Clocks around the world are about to change. The world's official timekeepers are going to add a single second or leap second to atomic clocks on Wednesday, the last day of the year. This will be the 24th leap second since 1972, when the practice began. It is going to be the first leap second since 2005.

The leap second

The move will help match clocks to the Earth's slowing spin on its axis. Because of tidal friction and other natural phenomena, that rotation is slowing down by about two-thousandths of a second a day.

The extra second is due to be added in co-ordination with the world's atomic clocks on New Year's Eve at 23 hours 59 minutes and 59 seconds Co-ordinated Universal Time or UTC. This is the timescale kept by the precise atomic clocks around the world.

In today's digital world, the smooth operation of everything from cash machines to the Internet depends on the exactly timed transmission of electronic data. Leap seconds can crash mobile phones and computer networks. However, the passing of the leap second on December 31st won't make much of a difference to most people. We're not going to notice it.

The leap second

A was first added to atomic clocks in 2005.
B may be removed from atomic clocks in future.
C was introduced in 1972.

D usually causes machinery to break down.
E can affect the transmission of electronic data.
F may vary from the Earth's rotational time.

Going to

We use *going to* to talk about
- our plans and intentions
- future actions which are already decided

*The world's official timekeepers are **going to** add a single second or leap second to atomic clocks on the last day of the year.*

- to talk about things which we can see now are certain to happen.

*We're **not going to** notice it.*

Form

Affirmative

I	am going to	
It / He / She	is going to	notice.
You / We / They	are going to	

*The world's official timekeepers **are going to** add a single second or leap second to atomic clocks on the last day of the year.*

Negative

I	am		
It / He / She	is	not going to	notice.
You / We / They	are		

*We **are not going to** notice it.*

Note:

*It / He / She **isn't going to** notice.*
*You / We / They **aren't going to** notice.*

Question

Yes / No **questions**
*Are you **going to** notice it?*

Wh– **questions**
*When **are** you **going to** notice it?*

Be about to / be due to

We use *be about to* and *be due to* to talk about planned future events that we expect to happen very soon.
About to is often used with *just*.
Clocks around the world **are about to** *change.*
The extra second **is due to** *be added in co-ordination with the world's atomic clocks.*

Form

Affirmative		
I	am about to due to	
It / He / She	is about to due to	go.
You / We / They	are about to due to	

Negative		
I	am not about to / due to	
It / He / She	is not about to / due to	go.
You / We / They	are not about to / due to	

Question

***Yes / No* questions**
*Is the data **about to** change?*
*Are the clocks **due to** change?*

***Wh–* questions**
*When **are** the clocks **due to** change?*
*Why **are** the clocks **about to** change?*

2 Read the passage in Activity 1 again and find examples of *going to, due to* and *about to.*

3 Choose the correct alternative.

1 The world's atomic clocks are about to be changed / due to be changed on December 31st.
2 Are you going to do / about to do anything special on New Year's Eve?
3 I don't think we are going to notice / about to notice an extra second!
4 Wait! It is 23 hours 59 minutes and 57 seconds so the clocks are just about to change / due to change!
5 I hope my mobile phone isn't due to crash / isn't going to crash on New Year's Day!
6 Do you think there is about to be / going to be a leap second next year too?

4 Write *C* for correct or *I* for incorrect next to each sentence.

1 Be quiet! The concert is just about to start! ☐
2 Are you due to go to the shops later? Can you get some bread? ☐
3 I haven't got time to discuss it now. The train is about to leave in five minutes. ☐
4 The plan is that we are all going to meet up on Friday night. Do you want to come too? ☐
5 When are you about to take your driving test? ☐
6 Quick! Pass me a tissue. I'm just due to sneeze! ☐
7 When is the meeting about to finish? I thought it was scheduled to be over by 2 pm! ☐

5 Correct the incorrect sentences from Activity 4.

....
....
....
....
....

Now check your answers. p170

1 **Read the dialogue and complete the summary using NO MORE THAN THREE words from the dialogue for each answer.**

Examiner: Let's talk about what you do, Carlos. Do you work or are you a student?

Candidate: Well, at the moment I'm a student, but I'll be starting work next month in a restaurant.

Examiner: And what will you be doing there?

Candidate: I'll be waiting on tables, and working behind the bar with the owner. He'll be serving the customers and I'll be mixing the drinks. I've worked as a barman before, but not as a waiter.

Examiner: Will you be earning a good salary?

Candidate: I won't be earning very much per hour, but I hope I'll be making a lot more from tips, if the customers like me. I'll be trying my best to make sure they do.

Examiner: Good. Now let's move on to talk about names...

Carlos is currently (1) .... , but soon he is starting work (2) .... His duties are going to be (3) .... and (4) .... behind the bar. He has some experience (5) .... , but he has never worked (6) .... before. Although he will not be paid very much, he hopes to make more money (7) ....

Future continuous

We use the future continuous to talk about
- future plans (Activity 1)

I'll be waiting on tables, and working behind the bar.
He'll be serving the customers, and I'll be mixing the drinks.
- actions which will be taking place at a certain time or over a certain period in the future (Activity 2)

I'll be starting work next month in a restaurant.
- a person's future plans. (Activity 3)

I hope I'll be making a lot more from tips.
I'll be trying my best.

Form

Affirmative

I / You / We / They He / She / It	will be	mixing the drinks.

Negative

I / He / She / It You / We / They	will not (won't) be	earning very much per hour.

Question

Yes / No questions

Will	I / you / he / she / it / they / we	be earning a good salary?

Wh– questions

What	will	I / you / he / she / it / they / we	be doing there?

2 **Read the task for part 2 of the Speaking test and complete the dialogue using the verbs from the box in future continuous form.**

Talk about something you enjoy doing in your spare time.
You should say:
• where you do it
• who you do it with
• how you started doing it
and explain why you enjoy it so much.

develop   do   fly   take part   play   move   break   not play

Examiner: So, you've told me you enjoy playing volleyball. Do you think people (1) .... still .... volleyball in the next century?

Candidate: Oh, yes. I'm sure they (2) .... as much sport as now. But maybe they (3) .... the same kinds of sports. Perhaps they (4) .... over the field instead of running! And more disabled people (5) .... in the Olympics. The Paralympics is growing every year. Of course, technology (6) .... very fast, so sports equipment (7) .... too, and athletes (8) .... more world records every year. I think sport will always be part of our lives.

Examiner: Thank you very much. That is the end of the speaking test.

3 🔊 **Play Track 8. Listen and match the answers with the questions.**

Question 1   Answer ....
Question 2   Answer ....
Question 3   Answer ....
Question 4   Answer ....
Question 5   Answer ....
Question 6   Answer ....

A   No. You can use it, if you want to go out.
B   Yes, do you need stamps or anything?
C   I'm going to drive there. Would you like a lift?
D   No, my presentation ends before lunch.
E   Sorry, I didn't realise it was so late. I'll ask them to leave.
F   I'll be out in a couple of minutes.

🔑 Now check your answers. p171

1 Read the task and the student's response, and write TRUE, FALSE or NOT GIVEN.

> **Writing task 2**
> Change is an inevitable process in human societies. However, some people prefer to keep their traditional customs whereas other people like the latest trends. To what extent do you agree or disagree with this opinion?

In conclusion, when we look back at today 20 years from now, we may wonder why people were so worried about their traditions and customs. By that time many things will have changed: the way we work will have altered, the population will have increased by 3 billion people, multinational companies will have products in every shop and our news will have become more international and easier to get. But how will cultural traditions have changed? In my opinion many things will not have altered: the way we behave with other people, for example, and traditions — they won't have lost their local importance.

1   People worry too much about their culture and traditions.   ....
2   American brands will be available everywhere.   ....
3   Traditional activities will have been forgotten by local people.   ....

Future perfect

We use the future perfect when we think about a time in the future and describe the actions and events that we imagine will take place before this time.
We use the future perfect to
* make guesses and predictions (Activity 5)
* talk about quantity and amounts before a future date. (Activities 3 and 4)
*By 2030, the world population **will have increased** by 3 billion people.*

We can also use *am / is / are going to have* + past participle with the same meaning.

We often use the future perfect continuous with words and phrases like
* *by / before* + future time point (*by 2020, before the end of today, by next week, by the time*)
* *when* + present tense (*when we look back, when she arrives*), *tomorrow, (two days) later*.

Form

Affirmative

I / He / She / It / You / We / They	will	have changed.

*Many things **will have changed**.*

Negative

I / He / She / It / You / We / They	will not (won't)	have changed.

*Traditions **won't have lost** their local importance.*

Question

Yes / No questions

Will you **have passed** your driving test by the time you're 21?

Wh– questions

How **will** traditional cultures **have changed** in 20 years?

2 Read the passage in Activity 1 again and say how many things will have changed in 20 years' time.

3 Connect the two events using *by (the time)*, *before* or *when*.

1st event	**2nd event**
1 I will be in Australia for one year.	I will see you next Summer.

I will have been in Australia for one year before I see you next Summer.

2 She will complete her Masters.	Tahiye will be 28 years old.
3 Hsiao Wen will lose five kilos.	Summer will arrive.
4 A lot of things will happen.	We will meet again.
5 They will repair your computer.	You will return to the shop.
6 We will be in business for two years.	We will start making a profit.

4 Write questions for 1–6 from Activity 3.

1 Where will you have been for one year?

2 When .... ?

3 How many kilos .... ?

4 What .... ?

5 When .... ?

6 How long .... ?

5 Look at the chart and complete the passage with the correct form of the verbs in brackets.

In 2042, America's minorities (1) .... (become) the new majority, eight years earlier than previously thought. Non-Hispanic whites now represent nearly two thirds of America's population but this figure has been falling. By 2042, the Hispanic population (2) .... (grow) steadily to 30% of the total and by 2050, it (3) .... (reach) 36% of the total. The black minority (4) .... (not increase) but the Asian population (5) .... (increase) to 9% of the total population by 2042.

By 2050, America overall (6) .... (become) more like present-day Texas and California, which are already majority-minority states.

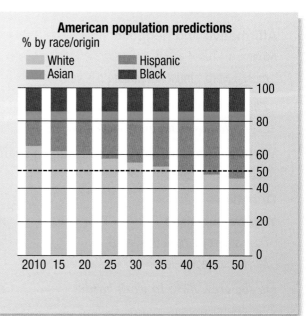

American population predictions
% by race/origin

White   Hispanic
Asian   Black

Now check your answers. p171

1 Read the passage and match the headings i–vi with the paragraphs A–C. You will not need to use all of the headings.

> i Health and hygiene   ii Resting   iii Keeping fit   iv Repairing the space station
> v Working   vi The effects of zero gravity

Life in space

250 miles above the Earth is a small group of people learning to live and work in space. What do they have to do in the International Space Station?

(A) .... Zero gravity and a sunrise every 90 minutes can disrupt an astronaut's health. The crew must combat motion sickness every day and mustn't get homesick. Also, they must be prepared for any medical emergencies. But astronauts don't have to worry about germs – the only germs aboard the International Space Station are the ones they take with them. Astronauts are required to exercise two hours per day, to avoid bone and muscle deterioration.

(B) .... Sleeping can be a problem when you are weightless. Astronauts must remember to tie themselves down when they sleep. When the commander allows everyone to sleep, the astronauts may sleep anywhere in the station, as long as they attach their sleeping bags to something.

(C) .... Crews have to spend six to nine months on the space station and they have to put in a lot of work. The average workday for an astronaut in space is sixteen hours; after this they are allowed to wash and rest – they don't have to do duties. If something breaks down, the astronauts must repair it at a moment's notice. Communications must be fixed and power has to be restored.

Obligation

We use *must* and *have to* for rules.

- We use *must* when we want to do something or feel that we need to do something.

*Astronauts **must** remember to tie themselves down when they sleep.*

- *Have to* is used when **another person or organisation** wants us to do something.

*Crews **have to** spend six to nine months on the space station.*

> **Look for...** **IELTS**
> modals and other verbs of obligation in passages explaining rules or describing the regulations of an organisation.

Form

Affirmative and negative

Must

must + verb	*must not (mustn't)* + verb

*The crew **must** combat motion sickness every day and **mustn't** get homesick.*

Have to

have / has to + verb	*do / does not (don't / doesn't) have to* + verb

*They **have to** put in a lot of overtime.*
*Astronauts **don't have to** worry about germs.*

We use *mustn't* to say that something is against the rules, but we use *don't have to* to say that we do not need to do something.

Question

Yes / No questions

Do + subject + *have to* + verb?
Must + subject + verb?

*Do the crew **have to** work hard?*

Wh– questions

What do + subject + *have to* + verb?
What must + subject + verb?

*What do they **have to** do in the International Space Station?*

Note: To talk about obligation in the past we use *had to.* There is no past form of *must*.

We use *can* and *may* to give permission to do something. We can also use *allowed to*.

*The astronauts **may** sleep anywhere.*
*After this they are **allowed to** wash and rest.*

We can also use the passive forms *is to* and *be required to*.

*Power **is to** be restored.*
*Astronauts **are required to** exercise two hours per day.*

2   **Read the passage again and write *R* for rules and *P* for things the crew need permission for.**

1   be prepared for medical emergencies ☐   4   sleep anywhere ☐

2   exercise every day ☐   5   repair the space station ☐

3   rest after a sixteen-hour workday ☐

3   **Complete the sentences with *must(n't)* or *(don't) have to*. For one answer you can use both.**

1   NASA needs the crew to keep healthy in space, so they .... exercise everyday.

2   Any air loss from the space station .... be found and repaired immediately.

3   On the International Space Station you .... worry about getting a virus – it's a sterile environment.

4   I haven't called Jen for three weeks now – I .... remember to call tonight.

5   Aziz really .... fail the test again; it's his last chance.

4   🔊 **Play Track 9. Listen to the talk about IELTS exam regulations and complete the notes.**

IELTS test day
Before the test, you must (1) .... who you are, take your (2) .... with you.
Leave (3) .... outside the room and don't take (4) .... with you.
During the test, you can't use (5) .... and you must (6) .... your phone.
Don't talk to other (7) .... and don't ask the supervisor about the (8) ....
At the end of the test, (9) .... your answers, don't take away (10) .... the test paper.

5   🔊 **Play Track 9. Listen again and complete the sentences from the talk.**

1   You .... to prove who you are.

2   Remember, you .... leave your bags and coats outside the test room.

3   People have asked me if they .... use a dictionary in the test.

4   Dictionaries ....

5   You .... remember to switch off your mobile phone.

6   You .... take it into the exam room.

7   You .... talk to any other candidates.

8   He or she .... let you in.

9   During the test you .... ask about any of the questions.

10   Remember you .... transfer your answers to the answer sheet.

11   You .... remove any part of the test.

12   After the test you .... wait for around two weeks for the results.

🔑 Now check your answers. p171

1   Read the task and the student's response, and answer the questions.

> **Writing task 1**
> The diagram shows two possible locations for a new leisure centre. Write a report for a university lecturer, describing the information shown.

The map shows two locations where a new leisure centre could be built in the town of Ullston. Location 1 is in farmland near the river Chand, and Location 2 is between the school and the town centre. Location 1 **may** be more attractive, as it is surrounded by fields. Land is **probably** cheaper there, too, so the leisure centre **could** be bigger, and **might** even have an outdoor sports area. On the other hand, Location 2 is **certainly** more convenient for the townspeople, as it is close to the town centre. Children **could** use it after school, and it **might** attract people from Waston, too. However, the land price in town will **definitely not** be as cheap as in Location 1, which **must** be an important consideration for the leisure centre company, as they **might not** be able to provide as many facilities. Making the choice between the two locations **can't** be easy for them.

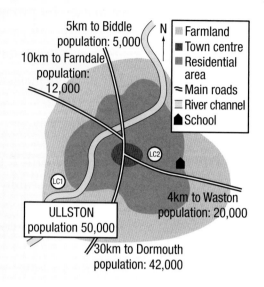

1   What are the two main advantages of Location 1?

....

2   What are the three main advantages of Location 2?

....

3   What is the main disadvantage of Location 2?

....

Possibility

- Modal verbs *may*, *might*, *could* + infinitive (without *to*) are used when the possibility of something happening is around 50%.
  *Location 1 **may** be more attractive.*
  *It **might** attract people from Waston, too.*
  *...where a new leisure centre **could** be built...*
- *May* and *might* followed by *not* can be used when something negative is possible.
  *They **might not** be able to provide as many facilities.*
- The adverb *probably* (*not*) is used when the possibility is more (or less) than 50%.
  *Land is **probably** cheaper there, too.*

Certainty

- *Must* + infinitive (without *to*) means that something is surely true. (Activities 3 and 5)
  *...which **must** be an important consideration for the leisure centre company.*
- *Can't* or *cannot* + infinitive (without *to*) means that something is surely not true. It is the opposite of *must be.*
  *Making the choice between the two locations **can't** be easy for them.*
- *Certainly* (*not*), *definitely* (*not*) can also be used to talk about things we are sure about. (Activities 4 and 5)
  *...Location 2 is **certainly** more convenient for the townspeople.*
  *...the land price in town will **definitely not** be as cheap as Location 1.*

Note: you cannot use two modal verbs together.

2 Read the passage again and count how many phrases are used to express possibility and certainty.

3 Complete the sentences using *must be* or *can't be*.

1 Achieving a 9.0 at IELTS .... easy.
2 Are you asking me to do your homework for you? You .... joking!
3 There's a light on in his office – he .... working late.
4 There aren't any cars outside the house, so it .... the one where they're having the party.
5 Susan's on holiday in Spain, so that .... her.
6 He's wearing a white coat and carrying a clipboard; he .... a doctor.
7 There are three expensive cars in the drive, so they .... making a lot of money.
8 This phone bill .... right. It's over £100 and I've only made a few calls!
9 I've got a sore throat and a headache. I .... catching a cold.
10 That .... the right answer. It doesn't fit the question.

4 Complete the sentences with a word or phrase from the box.

> probably not   definitely   may be   probably go   might not   might have   might
> could make   might wait

1 Selling home-made soup at the college fair .... a lot of money for charity.
2 I've almost decided – I'll .... to Greece for my next holiday.
3 Laptops are getting cheaper all the time, so I .... until next year before I buy one.
4 Revising before taking an examination is .... a good idea.
5 I haven't made up my mind. I .... go to the party, but then again I ....
6 Eating raw chillies is .... a sensible thing to do, unless you are used to them.
7 I'm not sure if any food will be provided, so I .... something to eat before I go.
8 There .... something wrong with her car – perhaps that's why she's late.

5 Read the task and complete the conclusion using words from the box. More than one answer may be possible.

> **Writing task 2**
> In the future, libraries will not have any part to play in learning. All study will be computerised, and books and newspapers will die out. To what extent do you agree or disagree?

> may not be   might   may   certainly not   must be   probably   certainly   definitely

In conclusion, I strongly disagree with the statement. Libraries (1) .... change in the services they provide, but they will (2) .... disappear altogether. Students (3) .... use computers more and more, but there (4) .... a place for books in education. Online newspapers will (5) .... become more popular, too, but paper ones will (6) .... continue to be printed. To sum up, libraries (7) .... the same in the future, but there will (8) .... always be a role for them to play.

Now check your answers. p171

1 Read the passage and complete the sentences 1–3 with the correct endings A–F.

Ambidexterity

Ambidexterity is the ability to use both hands or both feet with equal ease. However, ambidextrous people still tend to have a 'dominant' hand. Ambidexterity is encouraged in activities requiring skill in both hands or both feet, such as juggling and swimming. In pool and snooker, a player can reach further across a table if they are able to play with either hand. In skateboarding, a person is considered to be exceptionally talented if they are able to skate with either foot forward, hence the term 'switch skating'. In surfing, those who can ride in either stance are said to be surfing 'switch foot'. In soccer, being skilled at kicking with both feet provides more options for passing and scoring. Therefore, players who can use their weaker foot with proficiency are more valuable in a team than those who can't.

To be able to use either hand equally well, practice is the key. Wherever you normally use one hand, try to use the other instead. Consciously switch when you are about to do everyday actions such as pouring a glass of water. When you next put on your clothes you could put your other hand or foot into the garment first. You may have difficulty in doing these things at first or be unable to do them at all, but with regular practice you'll gradually become good at using your less dominant hand.

1	Your dominant hand	A	is a technique used in some sporting activities.
2	Switch foot	B	may become more comfortable to use by regular training.
3	The ability to switch hands	C	may be less advantageous when doing some sports.
		D	may determine whether someone is ambidextrous.
		E	may enable you use both of them equally well.
		F	is likely to be more flexible and stronger.

Ability

Can, could, be able to

Affirmative

We use *can* and *could* to talk about 'general' ability. This means the ability to do something any time you want to. (Activity 3)

Go on! You can do it!

When you next put on your clothes you could put your other hand or foot into the garment first.

Negative

The contracted negative forms are *can't* and *couldn't*.

Players who **can** *use their weaker foot with proficiency are more valuable in a team than those who* **can't**.

It is also possible to use the form **be able to** to talk about present ability, but this is less common.

In pool and snooker, a player can reach further across a table if they **are able to** *play with either hand.*

To talk about future ability, we normally use *will be able to*.

With regular practice **you'll be able to** *use your less dominant hand more easily.*

We can use *could* as a conditional, meaning *would be able to*.

Other phrases

We also use these other expressions to talk about ability (Activities 4, 5 and 6)

* to be *good / bad / clever at* something

So, if you want to **be good at** *using both hands equally well, practice is the key.*

* to *have difficulty with* something
* to *have difficulty in doing* something

*You may **have difficulty in doing** these things at first.*
- to *be adept at, skilled at, skilful at* something
- to have *skill at* something.

*It takes years to develop real **skill at** juggling.*

2 Read the passage in Activity 1 again and underline the expressions used to talk about ability.

3 Complete the sentences using the correct forms of *can, could* or *will be able to*.

1 I .... come round and see you tonight if that suits you.
2 I'm practising really hard, so I think .... juggle quite well in a few weeks.
3 You .... be a better surfer if you were ambidextrous.
4 She .... play tennis really well and she's only ten years old.
5 I .... hear Katya playing the guitar next door. She's very good!
6 If I .... use both feet equally well, I'd be a much better skater.

4 Choose the correct alternative.

1 I'm not that good at / bad at pool. I can get a perfect shot and still mess it up!
2 By being ambidextrous you are able to / skilled at do tasks with either hand.
3 He's only six years old but already he is skilled / has no difficulty at reading and writing.
4 He plays the piano so beautifully I think he could / can well become a professional musician one day.
5 She's broken her leg, so she won't be able to / can't walk for a few weeks.
6 Are you any good at / skilled at juggling?

5 (🔊) Play Track 10. Listen to the conversation and choose TWO letters A–E.

Which TWO sports is Ahmed good at?

A tennis   D badminton
B swimming   E basketball
C football

6 Complete the passage using NO MORE THAN FOUR words for each answer.

Examiner: So, Ahmed, do you do any sports?
Candidate: Yes, I'm (1) .... and I've won a couple of tournaments. But I'm (2) .... getting up in the morning to do two hours of training, though! That's the hardest part for me. I'm (3) .... football either – I've (4) .... coordination. However, I injured my knee during a game last weekend so (5) .... for a few weeks. I like playing tennis but I'm (6) .... I (7) .... enough and have difficulty keeping my eye on the ball. It's the same with basketball. In fact, I think it would be true to say that I'm (8) .... all. I'm (9) .... badminton too – I've never won a game yet!

Now check your answers. pp171–172

1 **Read the task and the student's response, and write TRUE, FALSE or NOT GIVEN.**

Writing task 2
Ought governments to pay for childcare, or should it be the responsibility of the family?

In my opinion, the government ought to provide free childcare for everyone who needs it. Families shouldn't have to spend their money on nurseries so they can go to work. Working people pay a lot of tax in this country, so why not use it to fund nurseries and encourage more people to go to work? Governments should stop complaining about unemployment and start helping people to stay in their jobs after they have children. How about training young people to look after children as part of their education, and what about giving them volunteer work in nurseries during the school holidays? Then they could use this work experience to help them find jobs when they leave school.

In the writer's opinion

1   people should not have so many children.   ....
2   government-funded nurseries would encourage people to work.   ....
3   tax-payers should pay for their own childcare.   ....
4   looking after children should be taught in schools.   ....
5   doing volunteer work helps you to find a job.   ....

Advice

We can use the following structures to say what we think is the right thing to do:
- *should* (*not*) + infinitive (without *to*)
- *ought to* + infinitive.

> **Use it for IELTS!**
> Use these words and phrases when the question asks you to give your opinion.

Form

Affirmative

*Governments **should stop** complaining about unemployment.*

*In my opinion, the government **ought to provide** free childcare.*

Question

Should + subject + infinitive (without *to*)
***Should** it **be** the responsibility of the family?*

Ought + subject + *to* + infinitive
***Ought** governments **to pay** for childcare?*

Other structures (Activity 3)

- *Why not* + infinitive (without *to*)?
  ***Why not use** it to fund nurseries and encourage more people to go to work?*
- *Why don't (you, they)...? Why doesn't (he, she)...?*
  ***Why don't they** use it to fund nurseries?*

Negative

Should not + infinitive (without *to*) (Activity 4)
*Families **shouldn't have to** spend their money on nurseries.*

Ought not to + infinitive (rarely used)
*They **oughtn't to have** left their child at home alone.*

Note: *could* + infinitive can also be used for giving advice, but only in positive statements:
*They **could use** this work experience to help them find jobs.*

- *Stop* + *ing* and *start* + *ing*
  *Governments should **stop complaining** about unemployment and **start helping** people to stay i‌ their jobs after they have children.*
- *What / How about* + *ing*?
  ***How about training** young people..., and **what about giving** them volunteer work?*

2 Read the passage in Activity 1 again, and count how many pieces of advice there are.

3 Rewrite the advice using the words in brackets.

1 You should go to the library if you want a quiet place to study. (how about)

....

2 If you're feeling sleepy, why not have a cup of coffee? (should)

....

3 They shouldn't build more roads, they should improve public transport. (stop, start)

....

4 You could try acupuncture if you want to stop smoking. (what about)

....

5 If you have a problem with your accommodation, how about going to a local estate agent? (why not)

....

6 If you want to lose weight, stop eating so many biscuits and start doing more exercise! (shouldn't, should)

....

7 What about taking the bus to London? It's cheaper than the train. (ought to)

....

4 Write *You should* or *You shouldn't* to complete the study skills advice for degree students.

1 .... rely on your tutor for help.
2 .... work by yourself.
3 .... look up unknown words in the dictionary.
4 .... guess the meaning.
5 .... know the different types of words.
6 .... try to read faster.
7 .... read with a friend.
8 .... ask questions to test comprehension.
9 .... look back at the text.
10 .... test how much you remember.

5 Play Track 11. Listen and complete the summary.

Now you have reached the second year of your degree, it's time to (1) .... on your tutor and (2) .... independently. You (3) ....a dictionary to look up all the words you don't know; you (4) .... the context to guess the meaning. Students (5) .... recognising the type of word. The other thing you (6) .... is to improve your reading speed. First of all, (7) .... with a friend? When you have finished reading, (8) ....each other questions to test how well you have understood? But when you do this, (9) .... look back at the text again. Instead, you (10) .... how much you remember.

Now check your answers. p172

1 **Read the passage and write TRUE, FALSE or NOT GIVEN.**

VELCRO

The hook-loop fastener (or Velcro) was invented in 1941 by George de Mestral. On a hunting trip he noticed small seeds on his dog's fur. When he looked at these seeds under the microscope he could see they were made of hundreds of hooks that caught on anything with a loop, such as animal fur, clothes or hair. He saw the possibility of attaching materials together in a way that could replace the zip – but could he figure out how to duplicate the tiny hooks and loops? At first people didn't take his idea seriously and de Mestral couldn't make the process work with natural materials. Eventually, he managed to find a material that formed tiny hooks and loops – nylon. He was finally able to use nylon for large-scale production in 1951.

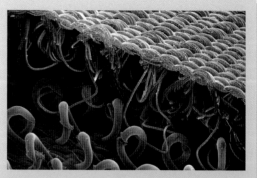

1   De Mestral found that the seeds were made of small loops.   ....
2   He had no difficulty in making the hooks and loops artificially.   ....
3   De Mestral's invention became a successful way of fastening things together.   ....

Could / was able to / managed to

Only two modal verbs have past tenses:
* *can – could*
* *will – would* (see Unit A14 for *would*).

We use *could* to talk about:
* general ability
* our senses (sight, smell, hearing, touch and taste)
* understanding (beliefs, remembering, deciding).

When we want to talk about what happened in a specific situation, we use *was able to, managed to* or, formally, *succeeded in.* Compare:

*Maria **could** do complicated mathematical problems from an early age.*

*She had a Maths test last Thursday and **was able to** pass it very easily.* (Not *She **could** pass it,* because we are referring to a particular situation – her Maths test.)

Form

Affirmative

*He **could** see they were made of hundreds of hooks.*

*He **was** finally **able to** use nylon for large-scale production in 1951.*

*He finally **managed to** use nylon for large-scale production in 1951.*

Negative

For negative sentences in the past we can use *couldn't* or *wasn't able to / didn't manage to.*

*De Mestral **couldn't** make the process work.*

*When de Mestral went to Lyon, he **wasn't able to** / **didn't manage to** convince people that his idea would work.*

Question

Yes / No questions

Could he figure out how to duplicate the tiny hooks and loops?
Was Maria able to finish the Maths test last Thursday?
Did Maria manage to finish the Maths test last Thursday?

Wh– questions

How could de Mestral make hooks and loops in nylon?
How was Maria able to finish the Maths test last Thursday?
How did Maria manage to finish the Maths test last Thursday?

2 **Read the passage in Activity 1 again and underline the ways to talk about ability.**

3 **Write *C* for correct and *I* for incorrect next to each sentence.**

1 My brother is very good at chess. At a recent competition he could get the third prize. ☐
2 When I was younger, I managed to run ten miles each week. ☐
3 As soon as you started the experiment, I could see it wasn't going to work. ☐
4 I was very lucky when I went to the concert because I could book a seat at the front. ☐
5 My best holiday was when we drove around Italy for a week. Although the car broke
down twice, we could repair it each time. ☐

4 **Correct the incorrect sentences from Activity 3.**

....
....
....
....

5 **Complete the sentences with positive or negative forms of *could / were able to / managed to.***

At the end of our research we (1) .... reach some interesting conclusions. First of all, we
(2) .... see that many students were not happy with their accommodation. Last year, only one in
ten students (3) .... rent reasonable accommodation, and three in ten students (4) ....
find a place they were satisfied with. However, when they went to their landlord at the start of term, they
(5) .... negotiate a better rent.

6 **Complete the questions using the words in brackets.**

1 You completed the writing test in 40 minutes! .... finish the test so quickly?
(how / able to)
2 After your accident, ... do sports again? (how long / it / before / able to)
3 I need that paper immediately. .... find the document I asked you for?
(were / able to)
4 François looks very puzzled. .... that lecture about operational management?
(could not / understand)
5 You're back already! .... the train? (not manage / catch)

Now check your answers. p172

1 Read the task and the student's response. Write *S* if the meaning is the same, or *D* if it is different.

Academic writing, task 1

The charts below show average monthly rainfall and temperatures in three cities: New York, Tokyo and Sydney. Write a report for a university lecturer describing the information below.

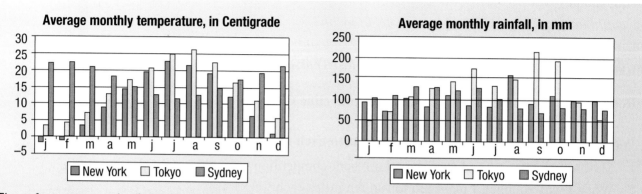

The information in the first chart compares average temperatures in New York, Tokyo and Sydney. We can see that January and February are the hottest months in Sydney, but the coldest in New York and Tokyo. In Tokyo, Winter temperatures are warmer than in New York, but the warmest Winters are in Sydney. Sydney also has the least variation in temperature of the three cities, while New York is the most extreme. Tokyo is around 6° hotter than New York in the middle of Summer, making it the hottest city of all.

The second chart shows the average amount of rain the cities get each month. Patterns of rainfall vary more widely than temperatures. September in Tokyo is the rainiest month on the chart, with more than 200 mm on average. However, it is slightly less rainy than New York in August. Sydney is much drier than Tokyo in September, and a little drier than New York. Rainfall in Tokyo is the most variable, with a minimum in January of 50 mm, showing a difference of around 150 mm between January and September.

1 When Sydney is hot, the other cities are cold. .... *S*
2 Temperatures in Sydney change more than in Tokyo and New York. ....
3 Average monthly rainfall is easier to predict than temperatures. ....
4 New York is drier than Tokyo in September, but wetter in August. ....
5 In September, there is not much difference in rainfall between New York and Sydney. ....

Comparatives and superlatives

Comparative forms

We use comparatives when comparing two or more things.

*In Tokyo, Winter temperatures are **warmer than** in New York...*

*However, it is slightly **less rainy than** New York in August.*

*Patterns of rainfall vary **more widely than** temperatures.*

Superlative forms

We use superlatives when comparing a group, to say which has the greatest degree of something.

*January and February are **the hottest** months in Sydney...*

*Sydney also has **the least variation** in temperature ...while New York is **the most extreme**.*

Adjective spelling rules

- Adjectives with one syllable take –er or –est.

cold	colder	coldest

- Adjectives ending with short vowel /æ/, /e/, /ɪ/, /ɒ/, /ʌ/ + consonant, double the consonant.

hot	hotter	hottest

- Adjectives ending in –y normally change to –i before –er, –est.

dry	drier	driest

- Adjectives with three or more syllables take more and most.

variable	more variable	most variable

- Some common adjectives are irregular.

bad	worse	worst
far	farther / further	farthest / furthest
good	better	best

- Two-syllable adjectives can take either –er, –est or more, most.

common	commoner / more common	commonest / most common

- Quantifiers such as *a little* and *much* can be used to show large or small differences.
  *Sydney is **much drier** than Tokyo in September, and **a little drier** than New York.*

2 **Read the passage again and count the number of (a) comparative and (b) superlative forms.**

3 **Complete the passage using the correct comparative form of the words in brackets.**

The chart shows how much people have to pay for things they buy every day in three cities: New York, Tokyo and Sydney. A ride on the bus or subway is (1) .... (cheap) in Sydney than in New York, but Tokyo is (2) .... (expensive) of all three. Buying a newspaper in Sydney, however, is (3) .... (much / costly) than in Tokyo, which is (4) .... (inexpensive) of the three cities. The cost of a cup of coffee is (5) .... (high) in New York, at over £2. In Tokyo or Sydney you can buy one (6) .... (cheaply), at around £1.50 per cup. For a hamburger meal, New York is (7) .... (dear), and Sydney is (8) .... (expensive). Overall it seems that prices in Sydney are (9) .... (low) than in New York, unless you buy newspapers. If you want to save money, it's a (10) .... (good) place to live.

4 **Write C for correct or I for incorrect next to each sentence.**

1 The climate in Eastern Europe is much more colder than in Western Europe. ☐
2 The Taj Mahal is far more widely known than the Egyptian pyramids. ☐
3 It is much more costlier to live in the US than in Africa. ☐
4 The graphs show which commuters travel the further to work. ☐

🔑 **Now check your answers. p172**

1 Read the passage and write TRUE, FALSE or NOT GIVEN.

Lie Detectors

Polygraphs (or lie detectors) measure changes in the body that often occur when people tell lies, such as breathing rhythms and body temperature. They can even monitor the response of the eye during questioning. If the iris contracts too suddenly, this may indicate that a person is lying. The questions used fit into three categories. The first are a set of control questions such as 'Have you ever borrowed anything and not returned it?' These are questions which almost everyone should answer 'yes' to, but which may be too uncomfortable for some people to give honest answers to. These are followed by irrelevant questions such as 'Do you think you drink too much coffee?' 'Do you take enough exercise?' They can help distract the respondent from the relevant questions that follow. These are specific questions such as 'Did you drive too fast last night and exceed the speed limit?' that should determine whether you are telling the truth or not. The problem is that polygraphs only really work with those who become stressed when they lie. Those able to remain calm enough can easily beat the test. Recent scientific research also suggests that the tests themselves may not be reliable enough. One study has found their level of accuracy to be as low as 65%.

1   Polygraphs are more commonly known as lie detectors.   ....
2   There are three different types of question used during polygraph tests.   ....
3   People taking the test are asked every question twice.   ....
4   Specific questions are followed by irrelevant questions.   ....
5   The majority of questions asked during a polygraph test are irrelevant.   ....
6   There is general agreement among scientists that polygraphs are unreliable.   ....

Too many / much

We use *too* to say that something or someone has an excessive amount of a quality. We use it before an adjective without a noun or an adverb.
*Did you drive **too** fast?*
We use *too many* or *too much* before a noun.
*Do you think you drink **too much** coffee?*

Enough

We use *enough* to say something is sufficient. It comes after an adjective or adverb. It comes before a noun.

*Do you take **enough** exercise?*

*Those able to remain calm **enough** can easily beat the test.*

As... as

We use *as* + adjective / adverb + *as* to say that something or someone is like something or someone else, or that one situation is like another.

*One study found their level of accuracy to be **as** low **as** 65%.*

2 Read the passage again and underline examples of *too, enough* and *as... as*.

3 Read the grammar rules again and classify them as referring to **A** *too*, **B** *enough* or **C** *as... as*.

1 means more than you want or more than is good for you ☐
2 comes before an adjective ☐
3 means as much as you need or is good for you ☐
4 is placed after an adjective or adverb ☐
5 describes the similarity between things or people ☐

4 Rewrite the sentences using *too* or *enough*.

1 He is strong. He can carry the machine.

....

2 You are very young. You can't take the test.

....

3 She was nervous. She couldn't answer the questions.

....

4 You weren't calm. You didn't pass the test.

....

5 She is very honest. She doesn't tell lies.

....

6 I'm not very clever. I can't understand how the machine works.

....

5 Complete the sentences using an appropriate phrase with *too, enough,* or *as... as*.

1 The film wasn't .... funny .... I thought it would be. I didn't laugh once!

2 I can't drink this tea. There's .... sugar in it.

3 We couldn't get a good view of the stage. There were .... people in front of us.

4 I won't go back to that restaurant. There was .... choice for vegetarians.

5 I can't see to read in this room. There's .... light.

Now check your answers. pp172–173

1 **Choose the most suitable headings from the box below for sections A–C.**

INTERNATIONAL OFFICE – HERE TO HELP

A   Where do you go if you want some advice? Our role is to support and advise you during your studies. If you want help with your visa and you don't know where to go, or if you are having problems with your accommodation, we can try to help you.

B   If you want to see us, office hours are between 9.30 am and 4.30 pm Monday to Thursday. When you want to call us, telephone 0800 835222 – it's free. If we are not here, you can always leave a message. When we pick up messages we call the person back right away.

C   Alternatively, if you want to book an appointment with an adviser online, send an email to us, then we can arrange a time to see you. Of course, if you don't need help, don't call us!

i Opening times and contacting us   ii International Office trips   iii International Office duties
iv Contacting us electronically   v People in the International Office

A   ....
B   ....
C   ....

Look for...   **IELTS**
real conditionals in passages about experiments and research or when people are giving advice, alternatives or warnings.

Zero conditionals

We use real conditionals to talk about results based on real events and situations. Real conditionals are divided into zero and first conditionals. When we know the same result always happens after an event or situation, we use a zero conditional.

*If you **want** to see us, office hours **are** between 9.30 am and 4.30 pm, Monday to Thursday.*

Form

Conditional sentences have two parts:
* the *if–* clause
* the result clause. (Activity 1)

We can put the *if–* clause first, or we can put the result clause first. We do not need a comma when the result clause comes first.

*Office hours **are** between 9.30 am and 4.30 pm, Monday to Thursday **if** you **want** to see us.*

We can use present continuous and past tenses with real conditional sentences, as well as modal verbs like *can* and passive forms. (Activities 3, 4 and 6)

*If you **are having** problems with your accommodation, we **can try** to help you.*
*Janos **stopped** studying if he **felt** tired and **took** a break instead.*

With zero conditionals, *if* can be replaced by *when* to make the result of the condition more certain.
***When** you want to call us, **telephone** 0800 835222.*
We use *then* to focus on the result of the condition.
*If the International Office **is** closed for lunch, **then** leave a note at main reception.*

Because real conditionals refer to something that is generally true, we can use adverbs of frequency (Unit A9) like *always* and *never* with them.

*If we are not here, you can **always** leave a message.*

Negative

We can make the *if–* clause or the result clause or both clauses negative, but this changes the meaning of the sentence. (Activity 6)

*If you **don't need** help, don't call us!*

*If you **don't know** how to use the University computer system, we **teach** you how to do it.*

Question

Yes / No questions

***Do** students **go** to their tutors **if** they need advice?*

Wh– questions

***Where do** you **go if** you **want** some advice?*

2 **Read the passage in Activity 1 again and underline the zero conditional sentences.**

3 **Match the beginnings with the ends of the quotations.**

1 If the facts don't fit the theory,
2 If you have only one smile in you,
3 If a friend is in trouble,
4 If you don't like something change it. If you can't change it, change your attitude.
5 If you're not part of the solution,

A don't annoy him by asking if there is anything you can do. Think up something appropriate and do it. (Edgar Watson Howe)
B you're part of the problem. (Sydney J. Harris)
C Don't complain. (Maya Angelou)
D change the facts. (Einstein)
E give it to the people you love. (Maya Angelou)

4 **Read the passage and choose the correct answer.**

Hurricanes are enormous heat engines that generate huge amounts of energy. When a thunderstorm (1) forms / is forming / formed over the Atlantic, it (2) gains / is gaining / gained in size and power. The Atlantic ocean acts as a giant solar collector, and when the seas are over 27 degrees Celsius, low pressure (3) is created / creates / created, making warm air rise. If the warm air (4) is rising / rises / rose, a cycle is created and more warm air comes up from the sea into the atmosphere. At the same time, dry air from the upper atmosphere is sucked into the low-pressure centre. If upper level winds and surface winds (5) are blowing / blow / blew in opposite directions, then the storm starts to spin. When this happens, a circular pattern of clouds known as a tropical depression forms. If the wind (6) is reaching / reaches / reached 119 kilometres per hour, a hurricane is born.

5 **Look at the diagram and complete the passage using the correct form of the verbs in the box.**

take   separate   want   stick   find   cut (×2)

If you (1) .... to make a Moebius strip, (2) .... a strip of paper about 250 mm long by 25 mm wide and twist it once. When you (3) .... the ends of the paper together, you (4) .... that the strip has strange properties. If the band (5) .... in half (along the length of the paper), the strip forms one long strip. If the band (6) .... a third of the way across and cut around once again, then the strip (7) .... into two strips – one twice as long as the other.

How to make a Moebius strip

Cut a strip of paper about 250 mm long x 25 mm wide and twist it once. Stick the ends together to form a band.

How to double the length of a Moebius strip

Cut the strip all the way round. Instead of separating into two, it surprisingly forms one long strip.

If the strip is cut round twice, it will separate into two, one twice as long as the other.

6 **Match the meanings.**

1 If you need help, call me.
2 If you don't need help, call me.
3 If you need help, don't call me.
4 If you don't need help, don't call me.

A There's no reason to call me if you don't want me to help you.
B I'll only speak to you if you don't want anything.
C Talk to someone else if you need help.
D Talk to me when you want some help.

7 **Complete the sentences using the correct form of the words in brackets.**

1 If you .... the sand and salt mixture through a filter, it .... the sand from the salt. (pour / separate)

2 I need to finish this essay. Don't .... me when I .... to do my homework. (disturb / try)

3 I'm sorry, visitors are not allowed at the moment. If Kristina .... better later, you .... her. (feel / see)

4 If you .... the answer immediately, ... read the question again carefully. (not find / not worry)

5 When we're making porcelain, the temperature must be over 1,200°C. If the clay .... , the temperature .... (not harden / not high enough)

Now check your answers. p173

1   **Read the passage and complete sentences 1–3 with the correct endings A–E.**

> **Writing task 2**
> Some people argue that it is too late to do anything about global warming, while others say it should be taken more seriously. What is your opinion on this?

Many scientists agree that if carbon dioxide emissions continue to grow at current rates, then the level of this gas in the atmosphere will double during this century. However, even if there is a slight increase in the global temperature, this will lead to climate change, affecting the temperature of the Earth, the frequency and strength of storms, and the length of seasons. If this happens, increasing temperatures will raise sea levels, causing flooding along coastlines worldwide. Furthermore, when the environment changes, many endangered species are not going to survive. If climate change is happening, we must work together against its worst effects.

1   There will be twice the amount of carbon dioxide
2   If there is even a small rise in world temperature
3   Many animals already in danger

A   sea levels go up.
B   the duration of the seasons will change.
C   in the next 100 years.
D   will not have enough to eat.
E   will not be able to survive.

First conditionals

We use real conditionals for possible results based on real situations. Conditional sentences have two parts
- the *if–* clause
- the result clause.

We can put the *if–* clause first or we can put the result clause first. We do not need a comma when the result clause comes first.

*If this **happens**, increasing temperatures **will raise** sea levels.*
*Increasing temperatures **will raise** sea levels **if** this **happens**.*

> **Look for...**   **IELTS**
> real conditionals in passages about experiments and research or when people are giving advice, alternatives or warnings.

Form

Affirmative

We can use tenses such as present continuous or present perfect in the *if–* clause and *will*, *going to* or modal verbs in the result clause.

*If climate change **is happening**, we **must** work together against its worst effects.*

If +	present tense present continuous present perfect	subject +	will be going to must should could	+ verb

Negative

Like zero conditionals (Unit A27), we can make either or both parts of the sentence negative.

When the environment **changes**, many endangered species **are not going to** survive.

If + verb	subject + *will* (*not*) + verb

With first conditionals, *if* can be replaced by *when* to say we believe the result of the condition is more certain to happen. We can use *if..., then...* to focus on the result.

If the level of carbon dioxide **continues** to grow, **then** the level of carbon dioxide in the atmosphere **will double** during this century.

We use *even if* to show that something may happen whatever we do.

Even if there is a slight increase in the global temperature, this **will lead** to climate and weather changes.

Question

Yes / No questions

If the Earth's temperature increases, **will** we be able to stop animals becoming extinct?

Wh– questions

Who will be affected most **if** global warming **is happening**?

2 **Read the passage in Activity 1 again and count the number of first conditional sentences.**

3 **Read the passage and correct the mistakes. There are four mistakes.**

Theories X and Y

In 1960 Douglas McGregor formed two theories about employee motivation: Theory X and Theory Y. Theory X says that people dislike work – and if people will dislike work, their manager needs to control them. On the other hand, Theory Y says that work is natural and if the job is satisfying, when the result will be a good worker. Under Theory Y, if managers will explain problems to their employees, they see better results than when they simply are telling their employees to do something.

. . . .

. . . .

. . . .

. . . .

4 **Match each sentence from the condition box with one from the result box and use them to write longer sentences.**

condition	result
1 You think the equipment for your laboratory experiment is too old.	You think his eyesight may get damaged.
2 Your computer is old and crashes often.	You could lose your work.
3 Agata doesn't use her dictionary very much.	American products will be cheaper to buy.
4 Your friend is playing computer games all night.	The experiment may not work.
5 The value of the dollar may fall.	Her vocabulary is not improving.

1 ....

2 ....

3 ....

4 ....

5 ....

5 **Complete the sentences with the correct form of the verbs in brackets.**

1 If you .... already .... dinner, we .... straight to the cinema. (have / go)

2 Don't worry about finding a bed for me. I .... with Helen if Mike .... you. (stay / visit)

3 You .... a lot of money to the library if you .... that book soon. (pay / not return)

4 If you .... back late at night again, I .... you out of the flat. (come / lock)

5 If you still .... the project, I .... you at the weekend. (not finish / help)

6 If you .... to Budapest, you .... the Fisherman's Bastion. (go / visit)

7 Alex .... your car if he .... it already. (fix / do)

8 If you .... to live off-campus, you .... to make arrangements well in advance. (plan / need)

6 **Complete the questions.**

1 .... Shabana, ... her the lecture was very useful? (you see / you tell)

2 How was the interview? What .... you the job? (you do / they offer)

3 .... sorry, ... him? (Joe says / you forgive)

4 .... the date to give in our report, ... the course? (we miss / we fail)

5 What .... more than 150 words for task 1? (happen / I write)

Now check your answers. p173

1 Read the passage and complete the summary.

> **Writing task 2**
> Many of the problems in the world today are caused by overpopulation. Governments should limit the number of children people have. How far do you agree or disagree with this statement?

I agree with the first part of the statement, but not with the second. It is true that there are too many people in the world today, but if people were better educated, I believe this could solve the problem. It is often poorer people who have a lot of children. They might not do this if they understood the problems it causes. If they had proper education in schools, they would know how to control their lives. If the women used birth control and didn't have so many children, they would be able to go back to work, and then they would have more money. However, if the government punished people for having children, people who are already poor would become even poorer. If that happened, who would suffer? The children would, of course. If only governments would spend more money on education, we could avoid the problem altogether.

The writer believes that the solution to (1) .... is to give people a better (2) .... Many large families belong to (3) .... parents, who don't understand the (4) .... which can result. Women could use (5) .... to limit the size of their families, meaning they could return to (6) .... to earn (7) .... Government regulation would only result in more suffering for the (8) ....

Unreal conditionals – second conditional

We use unreal or second conditional forms when we talk about a situation which is imagined. The verbs are in the past tense, but we imagine the situation is in the present. (Activities 3 and 5)

Form

Affirmative

If + past simple + *would / could / might* + infinitive
*If they **had** proper education in schools, they **would know** how to control their lives.*
Or:
*They **would know** how to control their lives **if** they **had** better education in schools.*
Note: When the subject of the *if*– clause is *I*, the verb *to be* is often *were*, not *was*.
*If I **were** the president of the USA, I **would live** in the White House.*

Negative

Either clause can be made negative, or both clauses.
*They **might not** do this if they **understood** the problems it causes.*
*If the women **didn't have** so many children they **would be able** to go back to work.*
Note: we cannot say *would can*.

Question

Yes / No questions
***Would** the children suffer, **if** that happened?*

Wh– questions
***If** that happened, who **would suffer**?*

I wish / If only

We use *I wish* and *If only* to talk about things we would like to be true, but are not. They are both used in the same way. (Activity 4)
I wish / If only + *would / could* + infinitive

I wish / If only governments **would spend** more money on education.
Other verbs are used in the past tense:
I wish / If only they **had** better education.

2 Read the passage again and underline the examples of the second conditional.

3 **Complete the sentences using the correct form of the verbs in brackets.**

1 If governments .... (spend) less money on developing weapons and more on health and education, the world .... (be) a better place.

2 In an ideal world, everybody .... (have) enough to eat.

3 If I .... (rule) the country, I .... (build) houses for homeless people.

4 There .... (be) a lot more happiness if there .... (be) no more wars.

5 Which people .... you .... (help) if you .... (win) £1,000,000?

6 I .... (not touch) that red button if I .... (be) you – it looks dangerous.

7 If teachers and nurses .... (earn) a higher salary, they .... (have) more respect.

8 If leaders of some countries .... (value) people more and money less, fewer people .... (starve).

4 **Study the examples and complete the sentences with *I wish* or *If only*.**

If I had more money, I'd buy a car.
*I **wish** I **had** more money. **If only I could buy** a car.*

If I didn't have eight cats, I'd go on holiday.
*I **wish** I **could go** on holiday. **If only I didn't have** eight cats.*

1 I want to go to England, but I can't get a visa.
I wish ....
If only ....

2 I'd like to study psychology, but I have to work.
If only ....
I wish ....

3 I'd love a big piece of chocolate cake, but I'm on a diet.
I wish ....
If only ....

4 This lecture is so difficult. I can't understand what he's saying.
If only ....
I wish ....

5  **Play Track 12. Listen to the lecture about overpopulation, and complete the sentences.**

1 If we had fewer people, there .... and food for everyone.

2 If .... the average north American, we would need six planets the size of Earth.

3 Statistics show that the average Chinese woman ...., if there was no law against it.

4 If they all had the lifestyle of a citizen of the USA, how much .... for the rest of us?

Now check your answers. p173

1 Read the passage and write TRUE, FALSE or NOT GIVEN.

The Women's Rights Movement in America

The Women's Rights Movement in America began on July 13th, 1848 when Elizabeth Cady Stanton was invited to tea with four women friends. During tea they talked about the limitations placed on them under America's new democracy. The American Revolution had established a new democracy – with the help of America's women – but, although women had taken equal risks during the Revolution, they had not gained equal rights. The Women's Rights Movement worked to create a better world, and they succeeded. If they had ended their meeting without further action, America would have been very different. Women might not have won the vote in 1920 if Elizabeth Cady Stanton and her friends had not met. If they hadn't campaigned for financial independence, women may not have had control over their own money. Would the 1972 Equal Rights Amendment have been passed if it had not been for the Movement? We cannot imagine today's American women without a vote, equal rights and financial security – their rights would be very different today if the Women's Rights Movement had not been formed.

1   During tea they talked about how unfair American society was.

....

2   Women won the vote in America because of the American Revolution.

....

3   The 1972 Equal Rights Amendment was passed because of the Women's Rights Movement.

....

Unreal conditionals – third and mixed conditionals

We use third conditionals when we are talking about:
- the past and what might have happened in a certain situation
- regrets, or what we could have done better. (Activity 3)

*If they **had ended** their meeting without further action, America **would have been** very different.*

We can use *should have, could have, might have* instead of *would have*.
We can use the past perfect continuous (Unit A13) in the *if*– clause instead of the past perfect (Unit A12) when we want to focus on the length of time of the action.

*If Elizabeth Cady Stanton and her friends **had not met**, women **might not have won**...*
With mixed conditionals the clauses refer to different times; for example, the *if*– clause may refer to the present and the result clause may refer to the past. (Activity 4)
*Their rights **would be** very different today if the Women's Rights Movement **had not been formed**.*

Question

Yes / No **questions**
Would the 1972 Equal Rights Amendment *have been passed if* it *had not been* for the Movement?

Wh– **questions**
How different *would* women's lives *have been if* the Women's Movement *had failed?*

2 Read the passage again and underline the examples of the third conditional.

3 🔊 Play Track 13. Listen and complete the form.

Final project feedback form
Project subject: new archaeological sites in (1) ....
About project:
– group good at (2) ...., but would have done (3) .... activities
– group good at (4) .... – but one group member didn't (5) ....
– would have been better if the team (6) .... earlier.
Question: would the team have worked well without the pressure (7) ....?
If the student had to do the project again she would have (8) .... and started sooner.

4 Look at the pictures and complete the sentences.

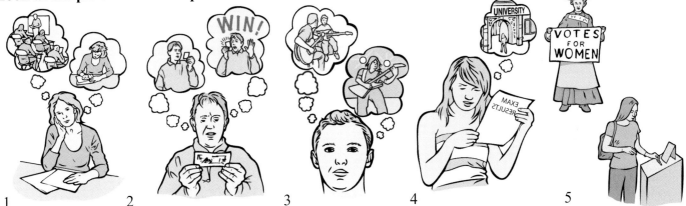

1   2   3   4   5

1 If I had arrived at the start, I would have understood the lecture. .... (arrive / understand)
2 .... (buy / win)
3 .... (learn / be)
4 .... (pass / go)
5 .... (not fight / not be able)

5 Choose the correct alternative.

1 If John hadn't missed the bus, we wouldn't still have waited / be waiting for him.
2 If email hadn't been invented, we would have written / write letters more often.
3 Arzu wouldn't be working for her present employer if she had got / gets a better offer.
4 You wouldn't have such a bad headache if you had taken / took a painkiller.
5 If I had enough money, I'd go / went to America to do a Masters degree.

🔑 **Now check your answers. pp173–174**

1 **Read the task and the student's response, and label the charts.**

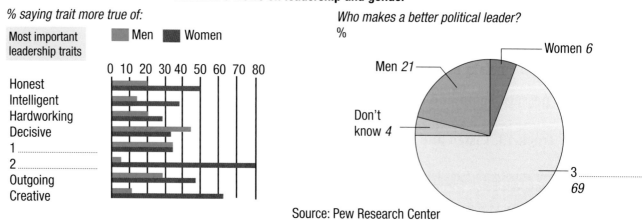

America's views on leadership and gender

% saying trait more true of:

Most important leadership traits

■ Men ■ Women

0 10 20 30 40 50 60 70 80

Honest
Intelligent
Hardworking
Decisive
1 ....
2 ....
Outgoing
Creative

Who makes a better political leader?
%

Men 21 —
Women 6
Don't know 4
3 ....
69

Source: Pew Research Center

> **Writing task 1**
> The first chart shows the results of a survey on leadership and gender. The second chart shows the results of a survey asking who makes the best leader. Write a report describing the information.

The results of a survey in America by the Pew Research Center regarding the most important leadership qualities in men and women showed significant differences. For men, over 40% said that decisiveness was the most important quality. For women, Americans told Pew Research Center that compassion was the most important thing. Surprisingly, they said compassion was not important at all for men. Americans believed the next most important quality for men was ambition, but in contrast, they told the Pew Research Center that the next most important characteristic for women leaders was to be creative. Interestingly, when they were asked whether it was important for a woman to be ambitious, people put this characteristic in sixth position for women, but second for men. When they were asked who would make the best leader – whether a man or a woman was the best – 69% of people said that men and women were equal.

Reported speech

We use reported speech when we write or talk about what other people say. (Activity 3)

We often use *say* or *tell* to introduce what the person said.
With *tell* we use the structure *tell* + person + what they said.
*Over 40% **said** that decisiveness was the most important quality.*
*For women, Americans **told** the Pew Research Center that compassion was the most important thing.*

We can use other verbs such as *believe*, *think* or *state*.
With reported speech we need to change the verb tense of the original sentence.
*'Decisiveness **is** the most important quality.'→ 40% said that decisiveness **was** the most important quality.*

> **Look for...** **IELTS**
> reported speech in passages which give opinions or the results of surveys.

Form

Direct speech	Reported speech	Tense change
Compassion **is** the most important thing.	*They said compassion **is** / **was** the most important thing.*	present → present *or* present → past
Eisa **is working.**	*Jemal said Eisa **was working.***	present continuous → past continuous
They **didn't like** the film.	*They said that they **hadn't liked** the film.*	past → present perfect
I **have done** my homework.	*Phung said that she **had done** her homework.*	present perfect → past perfect
Wei**'s been waiting** for hours.	*Wei told me that he **had been waiting** for hours.*	present perfect continuous → past perfect continuous
You **can't** sit next to the door.	*The lecturer told the student that she **couldn't** sit next to the door.*	present modal verb → past modal verb
I **must** finish this essay.	*Nawaf said that he **had to** finish his essay.*	*must → had to*
I**'ll** help you with your presentation.	*Rana told Sultan she **would** help him.*	*will → would*
no change: past continuous, past perfect, past perfect continuous		

Other changes		
Person I think ambition is important in a leader.	***She** said she thought ambition was important.*	*I → he / she* *we → they*
Place I wish Jon was **here** with us.	*Jules said she wished Jon had been **there** with us.*	*here → there*
Time It's raining here **now.**	*Ebru said it was raining there **then.***	*now → then / at that time* *my → his / her* *today → that day / on Monday* *yesterday → the day before / the previous day* *tomorrow → the next day / the following day* *last week → the week before / the previous week*
Demonstrative **These** are my books.	*He said **those** were his books.*	*this → that* *these → those*

Question

Yes / No questions

In reported speech we use *ask / want to know + if / whether.*

***Is** it important for a woman to be ambitious? → They were **asked whether** it **was** important for a woman to be ambitious.*

Note: the sentence structure after *ask* or *want to know* is the same as the affirmative form.

2 Read the passage in Activity 1 again and underline the sentences with *say* or *tell* – write these again in direct speech.

....

....

....

....

....

3 Read the sentences and complete the report.

When food is not pleasure

Researchers have found that obese people may be overweight not because they love food, but because eating is not rewarding for them. A US study said some people (1) .... to eat more food than normal to activate their brain's reward chemicals and satisfy their appetites. Researcher Dr Eric Stice said the research (2) .... fewer dopamine (the chemical important to the sense of reward) receivers, so they overate to compensate for this decrease in reward. He believes that people with fewer dopamine receivers (3) .... food to experience the same pleasure as other people. He went on to say that (4) .... less pleasure when eating, and therefore ate more to compensate. Dr Stice told the journal *Science* that (5) .... in the design of new treatments for appetite control.

4 Look at the charts and complete the passage with reported questions using the words in brackets.

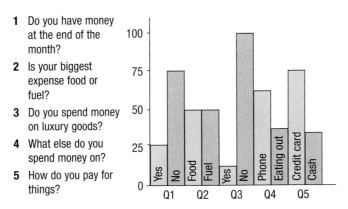

1 Do you have money at the end of the month?

2 Is your biggest expense food or fuel?

3 Do you spend money on luxury goods?

4 What else do you spend money on?

5 How do you pay for things?

Where the money goes!

In a survey of students' spending patterns, researchers asked (1) .... (if / have / money) at the end of the month — only 25% said they did. When students were asked (2) .... (if / spend / more money) on food or fuel, 50% said they spent more money on fuel, and another 50% said on food. The survey asked (3) .... (if / spend / money) on luxury goods, but only 10% told researchers they bought luxury items. When they were asked (4) .... (what / spend / money on), 60% said they spent money on mobile phones and a further 40% said they spent money on eating out. Finally, researchers wanted to know (5) .... (how / pay) for things, and most students said they used credit cards.

5 Play Track 14. Listen and complete the sentences with NO MORE THAN THREE words.

Lili: Were you ill today? You (1) .... a good lecture about accounting this morning.

Andreas: No, I'm not ill. I (2) .... a lot about accounting lately, and I'm not really interested in it. I (3) .... to take the option in it.

Lili: Dr Kesevan covered more than just accounting. He (4) .... about the marketing mix too – the 4Ps: Product, Price, Place and Promotion.

Andreas: Oh, really. I (5) .... about that.

Lili: Well, it was only a short introduction; he (6) .... talk about it in more detail next week, so you (7) .... make sure you're there.

Andreas: Don't worry – I (8) .... there for sure.

6 Write the conversation again using reported speech.

Lili asked Andreas if he had been ill. She said that he had missed a good lecture about accounting that morning.

....

....

....

....

....

....

Now check your answers. p174

1 Read the passage and label the picture. Choose NO MORE THAN THREE words from the passage for each answer.

PERSONALITY AND WHERE YOU SIT ON A BUS

It has been suggested in a recent study that there are definite patterns in people's behaviour depending on where they sit on a double-decker bus. Researchers from Salford University discovered that forward-thinking people sat at the front of the bus and noticed that the independent-minded chose the middle. It was also noted that those with a rebellious character usually opted for the rear. The findings revealed seven distinct groups of passengers.

Passengers at the front on the top deck are said to be forward thinkers, while those at the back are believed to be rebellious types who tend to guard their own personal space. Passengers sitting in the middle are thought to be independent thinkers because they read a newspaper or listen to music during their journey.

It is claimed that people who sit on the bottom deck at the front are outgoing and sociable, while those in the middle are strong communicators. Passengers who head for the rear of the downstairs deck are said to be risk takers.

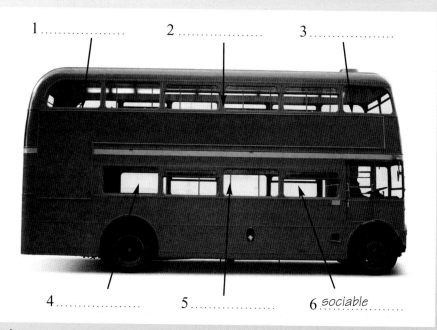

1 .... 2 .... 3 ....

4 .... 5 .... 6 *sociable*

The researchers defined one final group as chameleons and explained that these are travellers who do not care where they sit because they feel that they can fit in anywhere.

Reporting verbs

We use reporting verbs when we write or talk about what other people say or think. We may report the views of a group of people (such as a group of researchers).

With the verbs *believe, claim, explain, think, suggest, note* and *discover,* we use

> Verb + *that* + what they said or thought.

When we use reporting verbs, we need to change the original sentence (see Unit A31 for a table of verb changes).

These reporting verbs can be used in the passive, introduced by *it:*
* *believe, claim, suggest, note, report* and *think.*

It was also noted that *those with a rebellious character usually opted for the rear.*
It is claimed that *people who sit on the bottom deck at the front are outgoing and sociable.*
*Passengers at the front on the top deck **are said to be** forward thinkers, while those at the back **are believed to be** rebellious types who tend to guard their own personal space.*

Some reporting verbs describe a function rather than report words. Examples are *admit, suggest* and *agree.*

2 Read the passage in Activity 1 again and underline the reporting verbs.

3 Classify the parts of the bus with the passengers' comments. Write the correct letter A, B or C.

A front	B middle	C back

1 'OK, I suppose it is true to say that I don't always obey the rules.' ☐
2 'You see, it's like this. I always think ahead and don't only focus on the present.' ☐
3 'I really do mean it! I can take responsibility for myself.' ☐
4 'Yes, I feel the same way. I also like to keep my distance from other passengers.' ☐
5 'That's quite correct. I prefer being around other people.' ☐
6 'I think I find it quite easy to express my ideas clearly.' ☐
7 'You may not believe me but I always want to try something new even when there's a chance I won't succeed.' ☐

4 Match the statements in Activity 3 with the correct reporting verbs A–G.

1 ....   5 ....   A explain   E admit
2 ....   6 ....   B claim   F reckon
3 ....   7 ....   C confirm   G insist
4 ....   D agree

5 Rewrite the highlighted statements in Activity 3 using an appropriate reporting verb.

1 He admitted that he didn't always obey the rules. ....
2 ....
3 ....
4 ....
5 ....
6 ....
7 ....

6 ⊙ Play Track 15. Listen to the recording and complete the sentences below. Write NO MORE THAN TWO WORDS AND / OR A NUMBER for each answer.

1 .... items go missing on buses, trains and taxis in London every year.
2 Items which passengers frequently leave are mobile phones, ... and ....
3 Approximately .... of items are reclaimed by their owners.
4 Lost items are retained by the lost property office for a period of ....
5 One unusual item of lost property was a briefcase which contained ....

7 Complete the summary using the verbs in brackets.

(1) .... (think) that Transport for London deals with more than 130,000 items of lost property each year on its buses, trains and taxis. (2) .... (understand) that last year alone over 10,000 mobile phones (3) .... (hand in). A spokesman for the lost property office (4) .... (explain) that items were auctioned off if they (5) .... (remain) unclaimed after a period of three months. The office has dealt with some very unusual items over the years. (6) .... (believe) that someone once (7) .... (find) a briefcase containing £10,000!

⟶ Now check your answers. p174

1 **How much do you know about the IELTS test? Try to answer the questions.**

IELTS QUIZ

1 Do you know the name of one of the three organisations which administer the IELTS test? ....
2 What is the correct word for the examiner who asks the questions in the IELTS speaking test? ....
3 What do we call the place where the test is taken? ....
4 What is the day of the week when the test is usually taken? ....
5 What is the reason why most people take the IELTS test? ....
6 Can a doctor whose IELTS score is 6.5 work for the National Health Service in Great Britain? ....
7 Name a type of question which might be in the listening test. ....
8 What is the word for a person who sits in the room while people are taking an examination? ....
9 Can you name the part of the IELTS test that takes about 35 minutes? ....
10 What is the maximum length of time that you should spend on Writing task 1? ....

🔊 **Play Track 16. Listen and check your answers.**

Defining relative clauses

A defining relative clause gives you essential information about the subject of the sentence. In the questions in Activity 1, it is not possible to leave out the relative clause and still be able to answer the question. For example, for question 1, *Do you know the name of one of the three organisations?* does not make sense. We need to know more about the organisations before we can answer.

Relative pronouns

Depending on the type of subject, there are various relative pronouns we can use.

Person + who
*What is the correct word for **the examiner who** asks the questions in the IELTS speaking test?*

Person + whose
*Can **a doctor whose** IELTS score is 6.5 work for the National Health Service in Great Britain?*

Thing + which / that (that is less formal)
*Name **a type of question which** might be in the listening test. Can you name **the part of the IELTS test that** takes about 35 minutes?*

Time + when
*What is **the day of the week when** the test is usually taken?*

Place + where
*What do we call **the place where** the test is taken?*

Reason + why
*What is **the reason why** most people take the IELTS test?*

Leaving out the relative pronoun

When the pronouns *which / that* or *who(m)* refer to the *object* of the sentence, they can be left out.
What is the maximum length of time (which / that) you should spend on Writing task 1?
            object   subject

2 Read the quiz again and underline the people or things that are being defined.

3 Combine the clauses into sentences using *who, whose, which / that, when, where* or *why*.

1	Those are the people	A	Her dog bit the Vice Chancellor.
2	I'd like to buy a book	B	I will be teaching this afternoon.
3	He isn't the same man	C	He was in the canteen yesterday.
4	That reminds me of the day	D	She set fire to the school.
5	Do you know the reason	E	I saw real snow for the first time.
6	That lady over there is the one	F	Their test papers have been lost.
7	The police are looking for the girl	G	The sky is blue.
8	There are some subjects	H	It will help me to pass the test.
9	Is this the room	I	All the clocks go back in Europe.
10	The end of Autumn is the time	J	They are harder to learn than others.

1 ....   6 ....

2 ....   7 ....

3 ....   8 ....

4 ....   9 ....

5 ....   10 ....

4 Find seven sentences in the reading passage which do not need a relative pronoun. Rewrite them without the pronoun.

Charles Darwin (1809–1882)

Charles Darwin was the man who first put forward the theory of evolution. This is the theory which suggests animals and plants can change over time to become more successful. The book which he wrote was *On the Origin of Species*.

Darwin studied medicine, but it was a subject which he hated. He thought Religious Studies was a topic that he might be more interested in. Consequently, he went to study Theology at Cambridge. There he met a man who was a botanist, Reverend John Henslow. He encouraged Darwin to go on the sea voyage which would provide him with the evidence for his theories. South America was the place where he gathered most of his information.

When he returned to England, he wrote about his theory. These were papers which he did not publish until 1859. This was the same year that he published his book. Many scientists who read the book were shocked. Most people believed God had created the universe.

Darwin believed in God but he could not ignore the evidence which he had found. He married a woman whom he loved very deeply, Emma Wedgewood. In later life, Darwin suffered a painful illness which hardly left him for a day. He died in 1882, after a life which has changed the way we see the world.

1 ....   5 ....

2 ....   6 ....

3 ....   7 ....

4 ....

Now check your answers. p175

1 **Read the passage and complete the summary with NO MORE THAN THREE words.**

Water in desert cities

Desert cities in the US and the Middle East, which include Phoenix and Riyadh, may be living on borrowed time as water supplies become undrinkable, says a UN report. Riyadh, which is the capital city of Saudi Arabia, is situated in the centre of the Arabian Peninsula, and has a population of over four million people, many of whom are foreigners (about 35%). Although the city is located in a very arid area, where temperatures can reach 45°C in Summer, it still receives some rainfall. Today, Riyadh has developed into a dynamic city, in which government, education and commerce are important elements. But, for people who live in the world's desert regions, life may become increasingly unbearable as already high temperatures rise and water is used up or turns salty.

Cities in the desert may be in danger as water supplies cannot be (1) .... Riyadh is centrally (2) .... in Saudi Arabia and has a population of four million, some of whom come from (3) .... Although it is in a dry area, it gets some (4) ...., but increasingly, its people and others living in desert cities will find life difficult (5) .... as temperatures rise.

Non-defining relative clauses

We use non-defining relative clauses
- to give additional information or more detail about something
- to avoid repeating information.

*Riyadh, **which is the capital city of Saudi Arabia**, is situated in the centre of the Arabian Peninsula.*

We put commas around the extra information in the sentence – if the additional information is at the end of the sentence, we put a comma after the main clause only.

We do not use *that* in non-defining relative clauses and we always include the relative pronoun. (Activities 3 and 4)

> **Look for...** **IELTS**
> non-defining relative clauses in descriptions about graphs, people and places. Using them can make your writing more detailed and interesting.

To add extra information about all or part of something, or for people, we use

all / part / both	
most / many / some	of which / whom
neither / none	

or to talk about a period of time, we use

at / by / during	which time / point
at / by	which point

We use *in which* and *on which* in formal writing to be more exact about places and times and to avoid ending the sentence with a preposition, which sounds informal. (Activity 6)

*Riyadh has developed into a dynamic city, **in which** government, education and commerce are important elements.*

When we want to give more detail we can use *which means / shows (that)*...

2 **Read the passage in Activity 1 again and underline the extra information.**

3 Complete the passage using relative pronouns and punctuate where necessary.

Making glass

Huge containers (1) .... hold the raw materials for glassmaking. The base material is silica (2) .... is normally found as sand but may contain other materials (3) .... can produce greatly different results. The materials are delivered by rail to the factory (4) .... the mixture is melted at 1,425–1,600°C in pots (5) .... are called refractory pots. Refractory pots hold up to 1,400 kg of glass. Loading, melting and working go on continuously from (6) .... the fires are first lit until they are extinguished at the end of a period called 'a campaign'. A campaign may last as long as ten years.

4 Look at the graphs and complete the sentences.

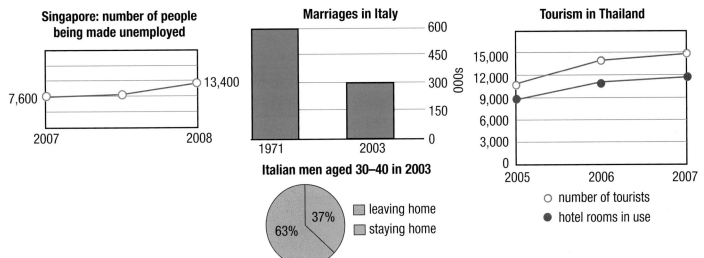

1 If we look at the first graph, ... in Singapore, we can see that there has been a significant increase in people out of work. (show / number of people being made unemployed)

2 We can see that in 2003, 37% of men in Italy lived at home, ... of marriage to under 300,000. (may account for / falling rate)

3 There was a very sharp rise in tourism in Thailand from 2005 to 2007, ... a similar rise in the number of hotel rooms in use. (mean / be)

5 Join the sentences with a relative clause.

1 The speed of economic growth is influenced by many factors. We can control some of these.
2 The rugby society has many members. Three members of the society play for Bradford Bulls.
3 The Prime Minister has visited Japan many times. The most recent time was in May.
4 The Prime Minister had dinner with the Prime Minister of Japan. He made a speech during dinner.

6 Rewrite the sentences in a more formal way.

1 I live in Izmir, which is the city my parents still live in.
   I live in Izmir, the city ....

2 Gyorgi hurt her head in the accident, which she can't remember much about.
   Gyorgi hurt her head in the accident, ...

3 Banks work to improve customer confidence, which they rely on for their business.
   Banks work to improve customer confidence, ...

Now check your answers. p175

1   Read the passage and complete the diagram labels. Choose NO MORE THAN THREE words from the passage for each answer.

I magine having fingerprint recognition, bluetooth and a laser in your Swiss army knife! The company which has made pocket knives for more than a century and still supplies the Swiss army has

LATEST SWISS ARMY KNIFE TECHNOLOGY

managed to produce a model which provides you with all the tools you would ever want or wish to use. It even allows you to deliver boardroom presentations! It enables you to store documents, too, because the removable flash drive has a memory capacity of 32 gigabytes. If you decide to give a presentation, you can point the laser at projected images. The bluetooth technology means that you can even choose to use the tool as a remote computer mouse! You don't even need to touch your computer! The memory stick is security protected by your fingerprint. This biometric fingertip sensor stops anyone hacking into the information, even if you happen to lose the knife. The technology also lets you put all your passwords for Internet banking and shopping websites onto it. It doesn't expect you to remember them – it automatically does it for you.

1   Removable flash drive with a 32-gigabyte .... to store documents.

2   Flash drive will only work if you place your finger on a ....

3   Bluetooth-powered remote control which can act as a ....

4   The laser enables you to point at ....

Verb + gerund / infinitive

Verbs normally followed by the infinitive with *to*:

afford, choose, decide, expect, forget, happen, remember, want, manage, need

- *The company which has made pocket knives for more than a century and still supplies the Swiss army has **managed to** produce a model which offers you all the tools you could possibly want to use.*
- *If you **decide to** give a presentation, you can point the laser at projected images.*
- *You don't even **need to** touch your computer!*
- *The bluetooth technology means that you can even **choose to** use the tool as a remote computer mouse!*

Verbs normally followed by *ing*:

appreciate, avoid, enjoy, involve, practise, suggest, spend time, imagine, finish

- ***Imagine having** fingerprint recognition, bluetooth and a laser in your Swiss army knife!*

Verbs that can be used in the form: verb + object + *to*:

allow, expect, need, want, wish, order, leave, ask
- *It even **allows you to** deliver boardroom presentations.*
- *It doesn't **expect you to remember** them. It automatically does it for you.*

Verbs normally followed by the infinitive without *to*:

make, let
- *The technology **lets you put** all your passwords for Internet banking and shopping websites on to it.*

2 Read the passage from Activity 1 again. Put the verbs from the passage into one of the following groups.

A verbs followed by infinitive with *to*
B verbs followed by *–ing*
C verbs followed by an object and *to*
D verbs followed by infinitive without *to*
E verbs followed by an object and *–ing*

A ....
B ....
C ....
D ....
E ....

3 Choose the correct alternative.

1 It allows / lets you to store all your Internet passwords.
2 The Bluetooth technology lets / offers you go back and forward in a presentation.
3 I can't find my Swiss army knife! If you happen see / to see it, let me know!
4 How did the company manage to develop / developing a knife that can only be unlocked by a fingerprint?
5 Imagine owning / to own a knife like that!
6 I can afford to buy my own knife! I don't expect / expect you to pay for it!

4 Complete the sentences using the correct form of the verb in brackets.

1 I didn't want .... (work), so I spent the day relaxing in the garden.
2 Did you remember .... (book) the seats?
3 Leave the dishes. I don't expect you .... (do) them for me!
4 You don't need .... (ask) my permission every time you want .... (leave) the room!
5 He offered .... (lend) me the money but I didn't take it.
6 You are required .... (complete) three assignments this term.
7 Do you happen .... (know) where the nearest bank is?
8 Could you imagine .... (win) a million pounds on the lottery?

Now check your answers. p175

1 Read the passage. Write TRUE, FALSE or NOT GIVEN.

Britain's favourite food

Britain's most popular 'fast food' has got to be fish and chips. The dish is simplicity itself: fish (usually cod, haddock or plaice) is dipped in batter made from flour, eggs and water, and then deep-fried in hot fat. Chips are made from thick batons of potato and then deep-fried.

Fish and chips are served wrapped in paper and traditionalists prefer to eat them straight out of the paper because they say they taste better that way. Many people like to eat them with bread and butter and a cup of tea or a bottle of beer.

The best known British dish eaten at home has been roast beef, traditionally eaten on a Sunday, when people have more time to prepare food. It is served with roast potatoes, vegetables and gravy – a sauce made from meat juice and stock, thickened with flour. The dish used to be so popular that in French the word 'rosbif' refers to the British!

Most recently, the British diet has been enriched by the wide variety of ethnic dishes available in our shops and restaurants, from Indian curry to Italian spaghetti. Indeed, curry, a spicy dish with meat such as chicken, fish or vegetables served with rice, is now Britain's most popular meal.

1   Fish and chip shops date from the early nineteenth century.   ....
2   Batter is a mixture of water, flour and egg.   ....
3   People generally agree that fish and chips taste better when they are wrapped in paper.   ....
4   Gravy is a sauce which is made from meat.   ....
5   Chicken is the most common meat used in curries.   ....

Countable and uncountable nouns

Countable nouns

Countable nouns have two forms:
- the singular form, which is used to talk about one person or thing
- the plural form, which is used to talk about more than one person or thing.

Some countable nouns have the same form for both singular and plural forms. Many of these nouns refer to animals or fish.

Before countable nouns we can use *a / an, few / fewer, a few, many, not many, several.*

Uncountable nouns

These nouns have only one form. They refer to general things such as qualities, substances and topics, rather than to individual events or items.

Uncountable nouns are not used with
- numbers
- articles (*the / a / an*).

There are some words which are uncountable in English but which refer to things that are considered countable in other languages. Here is a list of the most common uncountable nouns of this type: *advice, baggage, furniture, hair, homework, information, knowledge, luggage, money, news, progress, research, spaghetti, traffic.*

Before uncountable nouns we can use *some, any, (quite) a lot of, lots of, plenty of, a lack of, much.*

Nouns which can be countable or uncountable

The following groups of nouns can be both countable and uncountable:
- nouns we think of as single things or substances

*Can you buy **a chicken** from the supermarket? Let's have **chicken** for dinner.*
- normally uncountable nouns which are used to refer to particular varieties

*Would you like some more **bread**? They sell **a** delicious rye **bread** in that shop.*
- words for drinks such as *coffee, tea* and *beer*.

Uncountable nouns can be modified by countable nouns:
- *a glass of, a cup of, a bottle of, a plate of,* etc.

*I prefer **tea** to **coffee**. Many people have **a cup of tea** or **a bottle of beer** with their fish and chips.*
- *time, space, room*

*We had **a really good time** at the restaurant.*

Some and *a lot of* can be used with both countable and uncountable nouns.

2 Classify these nouns from Activity 1 as:

C countable	U uncountable	B both

food	☐	flour	☐	vegetable	☐	water	☐	cup of tea	☐
simplicity	☐	paper	☐	sauce	☐	spaghetti	☐	curry	☐
fat	☐	gravy	☐	country	☐	potato	☐	batter	☐
century	☐	egg	☐	haddock	☐	beer	☐	chicken	☐
fish	☐	dish	☐	rice	☐	meal	☐	diet	☐

3 Choose the correct alternative.

1 I wish she would take my advices / advice and eat healthier food.
2 Research show / shows that curry is the most popular dish in Britain.
3 My first job / work was in a fish and chip shop.
4 It's no surprise that she became a head chef. She's got 15 years' experience / experiences in the kitchen.
5 How much flour / eggs do you need to make the batter?
6 Do you want some sauces / salt on your chips?
7 There's no meat juices / stock left. I need to make some / several more.
8 I don't like cooking so I never spend a lot / much of time in the kitchen.
9 The sauce is too thick. Why don't you add a little / much water?

4 Underline the errors in the passage. There are 10.

The wide range of British regional food are reflected in the names of our favourite dish. Several region are famous for their local produces. Cheeses is produced in many area and Cheddar is one of the most popular variety. Many dishes are named after place, such as Bath buns – a very sweet cake containing much sugar, some dried fruit and a little spices.

Now check your answers. p175

1 Read the task and the student's response, and find examples of *a / an*, *the* and *no article* for each of the rules below. You may use some of the examples more than once.

Speaking test, part 2 – long turn
Talk about an older person you know whom you admire.
You should say:
- how you came to know them
- what you know about their life
- what they enjoy doing
and say why you admire them so much.

Candidate: I'm going to talk about my grandfather. After he left school in 1922, he joined the army. He was a soldier in the Second World War in India. His regiment was stationed near the River Ganges, in Rishikesh under the Himalayas. They lived on rice and vegetables. The rice was dirty and the vegetables were usually rotten. He was very brave and won a medal for saving an officer from drowning. The officer is still alive now, and my grandfather still has the medal. These days he lives in a retirement home. He has a lot of friends there and once a week they go by bus to the White Swan Hotel for lunch and a few drinks. He may be old now, but he is one of the happiest men under the Sun.

Articles

---

a is used:
1 before consonant sounds
   Example – ....
2 before *few* and *lot of*
   Examples – ....

an is used:
3 before vowel sounds
   Example – ....

a or an is used:
4 with jobs
   Examples – ....
5 the first time we mention something
   Examples – ....
   ....
6 after *once*, *twice*, etc. to say how often
   something happens
   Example – ....

---

the is used:
7 when we know which thing it is
   Examples – ....
   ....
   ....
8 when there is only one of a thing
   Examples – ....
9 for names of rivers and mountain ranges
   Examples – ....
10 for names of hotels
   Example – ....
11 before a superlative, e.g., *most*, *luckiest*
   Example – ....

No article is used:

12 for names of towns and countries

Examples – ....

13 for uncountable nouns and plurals, when we talk about things in general

Examples – ....

14 before the names of meals

Example – ....

15 for institutions, e.g., *university, hospital*, when talking about their use

Example – ....

16 to say how we travel

Example – ....

2 **Complete the chart. Put ✓ if you think it is possible to make a sentence using the combination for each square, and ✗ if it isn't. (You may not use determiners such as *my, his, these, those*, etc.)**

Example:

In square 1, you need to make a correct sentence using *the* with the uncountable noun *water*:

The water in the pool is too cold to swim in today.

The + *water* is possible, when the speakers understand which water you mean, so you can put a tick in the box.

	the	*a / an*	**no article**
Uncountable noun *(e.g., water)*			
Plural noun *(e.g., tables)*			
Singular countable noun *(e.g., chair)*			

3 **Write TRUE or FALSE for this rule:**

A singular countable noun **MUST** have an article.   ....

4 **Read the task and the student's response, and correct the errors. There are 17 errors.**

Writing task 2
It is impossible for children to succeed at school unless they have help from their parents.
How far do you agree or disagree?

I agree with statement. When I first started the school, I could already read and write a bit because my mother had taught me. She always used to read me bedtime story, and I got to know shapes of the different letters. Some of the other children in a class couldn't even count up to ten.

Only problem was, I was very bored at first. Everything teacher taught us, I already knew. Book we had was too easy for me, but girl who sat next to me couldn't read it. I asked a teacher if I could read book from library, but she said I had to use same one as the other children in our class.

To sum up, I think all the parents should help their children learn to read and write before they start a school. They should also teach alphabet and numbers up to ten. Unless they do this, their children will learn more slowly and they will never be top of class.

1	7	13 ....
2	8	14 ....
3	9	15 ....
4	10	16 ....
5	11	17 ....
6	12	

5 **Write *C* for correct or *I* for incorrect next to each sentence.**

1   Moon is very bright tonight. ☐
2   I usually have a breakfast at 7.30 am. ☐
3   Can you shut the door, please? I'm cold. ☐
4   Large numbers of the Japanese tourists travel abroad every year. ☐
5   China produces lot of the rice. ☐
6   Anton had to go to hospital for an operation on his arm. ☐
7   I usually like chocolate, but bar I had yesterday was horrible. ☐
8   Once week I go to Manchester by the train. ☐
9   She's a engineer, I'm student and he's an teacher. ☐
10 There are 15 people in the IELTS preparation class. ☐

6 **Correct the incorrect sentences from Activity 5.**

....
....
....
....
....
....
....

7 **Write *the, a / an* or – (no article).**

1   We saw .... light in .... sky which looked like .... spaceship.
2   Will you have .... dinner with me tonight at .... Hilton?
3   .... Thames is one of .... most famous rivers in ....world.
4   .... advice from friends can be hard to take, but .... advice Sharif gave me was a great help.
5   I had .... sandwich, ... banana and .... apple for lunch.
6   Look! There's .... football in .... garden.
7   I need to buy .... new mobile phone – I've lost .... one Michelle gave me.
8   After leaving .... school, many young people now take .... year off before they start .... university.
9   I don't like .... snakes, but I'm not afraid of .... spiders.
10 My uncle was born in .... Manchester, but now all my cousins live in .... Spain.

Now check your answers. p176

1 **Read the passage and write TRUE, FALSE or NOT GIVEN.**

BIG BEN

Big Ben is the name of the bell in the famous clock at the Houses of Parliament in London. The bell was named after Sir Benjamin Hall, who commissioned the bell as part of the rebuilding of the Palace of Westminster following a fire there in 1834. The original bell was cast in 1856 but during a sounding test in December of that year it cracked and had to be broken up shortly after. A new bell was installed two years later – in 1858. This second bell has been a tourist landmark and symbol of London ever since.

The clock is wound up by hand on Mondays, Wednesdays and Fridays. The process takes over an hour because it is not possible to wind while it is chiming. And when it is going a bit fast or a bit slow (which is nearly always the case) a mechanic places or removes a penny from the pendulum; adding one speeds up the clock by two-fifths of a second a day. The keeper of the clock checks the clock by ringing up the speaking clock. He does this from a phone in the clock room at five minutes to the hour precisely, before going to the belfry to check that the hammer on Big Ben strikes on the hour. Over the years the clock has been stopped by snow in Winter and mechanical failure but is still going strong. And it looks likely that it will continue to ring out across London during the twenty-first century too.

1   Sir Benjamin Hall's nickname was Big Ben.   ....
2   The bell made in 1856 was later replaced.   ....
3   The clock is wound up three times during the week. ....
4   Repairs to the clock are usually carried out in Winter. ....

Prepositions of time

In

We use the preposition *in* when we want to talk about what happened in a month, season, year or century.
*The original bell was cast **in 1856.***
***In December** of that year it cracked and had to be broken up.*
*Over the years the clock has been stopped by snow **in Winter.***

At

We use the preposition *at* to refer to clock times.
*He does this from a phone in the clock room **at five minutes to the hour** precisely.*

On

We use the preposition *on* when we want to mention the day something happens.
*The clock is wound up by hand three times a week – **on Mondays, Wednesdays and Fridays.***

Other prepositions

If we want to be less precise about when something happened, we can use approximate expressions and prepositions, such as *over, nearly, by, before, shortly after, following.*
We often use these words
• when the exact time of an event is not known
• when events happen gradually, continuously or several times.

*The process takes **over** an hour because it is not possible to wind while it is chiming.*
*And when it is going a bit fast or a bit slow (which is **nearly** always the case) a mechanic places or removes a penny from the pendulum; adding one speeds up the clock **by** two-fifths of a second a day.*
Note: *Nearly can only be used after the verb to be.*

*He does this from a phone in the clock room at five minutes to the hour precisely, **before** going to the belfry to check that the hammer on Big Ben strikes on the hour.*
*It had to be broken up **shortly after**.*
*...as part of the rebuilding of the Palace of Westminster **following** a fire.*

We can use *during* instead of *in* with periods of the day or week, months, seasons, years, decades and centuries.
*It looks likely that it will ring out across London **during the twenty-first century** too.*

2 Read the passage in Activity 1 again and underline the expressions and prepositions of time.

3 Classify the prepositions and expressions in Activity 2 as referring to:

A Specific time		**B** Non-specific time	
1	☐	1	☐
2	☐	2	☐
3	☐	3	☐
4	☐	4	☐
5	☐	5	☐
6	☐	6	☐
7	☐	7	☐
8	☐		
9	☐		

4 Choose the correct alternative.

1 Big Ben was cast in / at the nineteenth century.
2 The bell is never wound up in / at weekends.
3 The bell sometimes stops working during / following Winter.
4 A sounding experiment was carried out on the first bell before / in December 1856.
5 The bell is still working well after / nearly 150 years.
6 Do you think the bell will still be working by / before the end of the twenty-first century?

5 Complete the sentences using an appropriate time preposition or expression.

1 The Summer term ends .... June 30th.
2 The train leaves .... 3.30.
3 What did you do .... the weekend?
4 My flat tends to be very cold .... Winter. I need to buy a new heater.
5 I'll phone you .... the morning.
6 She's written many books .... her long career.
7 They've been great friends .... the years.

Now check your answers. p176

1 **Read the student's response and choose which task card they spoke about.**

1. Describe a long journey you went on.

2. Describe a tourist destination you would recommend to a visitor to your country.

3. Describe a memorable experience.

We were staying in a hotel in Kintamani on Bali, when we decided to go to Komodo National Park – where the Komodo dragons live. We caught the ferry across to Komodo – it was a long trip and there weren't many people on the boat, under 20, I guess. When we arrived at the island, our guide met us. He was nervous and hurried us along the path through the forest. We were annoyed by this, but a dragon had gone up to him and attacked him earlier that day and he didn't want to repeat the experience. As we walked towards the place where the dragons were, we saw they had caught a water buffalo – and more dragons were coming from all corners of the island to feed. They can smell death from miles away, and we had walked straight into their feeding ground – it was an amazing experience but quite frightening at the same time.

Prepositions

We use prepositions to show the relationship between

- a noun and another noun
- a noun and a verb
- a noun and an adjective.

The three basic relationships that prepositions of location and movement show are

- vertical relationships (something on, above or below something)
- horizontal relationships (something next to or along something)
- facing relationships (something opposite another thing).

Vertical relationships

on (top of), above, over, up / below, under(neath), down
Note: we use *over* or *under* for prices, ages, speeds, distances and quantities to mean *more than* or *fewer than*. (Activity 7)
*There weren't many people on the boat; **under** 20, I guess.*

Horizontal relationships

against, at, beside, between, by, in, near, next to, on the left / right (of)
Note: we use

- *at* with a point in space
  *…we arrived **at** the island…*
- *on* with a line or surface
- *in* for something surrounded by something
  *…**in** Kintamani on Bali.*

Because prepositions describe relationships between things, the preposition we use depends upon how the speaker sees the relationship. Compare

*The guide met us **at** the national park office. (inside or outside)*

*The guide met us **in** the national park office. (inside)*

Facing relationships

across, before, behind, facing, in front of, opposite, over

Note: with *across* and *over* we must say what is between the things. Compare

*Let's meet in the café **opposite** the theatre.*

*Let's meet in the café **across** the road from the theatre.*

Movement in one direction

around, along, away from, into, onto, out of, towards, up (to)

*A dragon had gone **up to** him and attacked him.*

*As we walked **towards** the place where the dragons were...*

Note: we use *up to* when we want to say something was very close (touching) another thing, but we use *towards* to say that something approached another thing, but was not close to it.

Passing movement

across, over, past, through, up, down

*...**through** the forest*

> **Listen for...** **IELTS**
> prepositions of location and movement in listening tasks where you need to follow directions or label a map or diagram.

2 Read the passage in Activity 1 again and count the prepositions of location and movement.

3 🔊 Play Track 17. Listen and label the rooms on the map. Choose your answers from the box and write them next to 1–5.

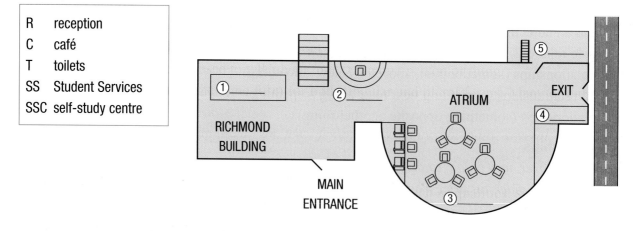

```
R    reception
C    café
T    toilets
SS   Student Services
SSC  self-study centre
```

4 🔊 Play Track 17. Listen again and complete the sentences with prepositions of location.

Yes, it's in C101, just (1) .... this building here. ...just there, and (2) .... you, you'll see the main stairs into the main part of the building. ...you'll see the main stairs in front of you, and Student Services (3) ....And (4) .... is the main reception ...You'll see students (5) .... the computer cluster station ...with the café (6) .... you, you'll see a door.

5 🔊 **Play Track 18. Listen and label the map.**

Write the correct letter next to 1–5.

1   Senior common room   ....
2   Kitchens   ....
3   Foundation Studies office   ....
4   Sharwood room   ....
5   Dining room   ....

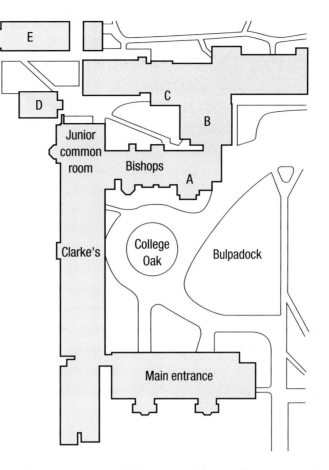

6 🔊 **Play Track 18. Listen again and complete the sentences with prepositions of movement.**

Go straight on (1) .... the College Oak... go (2) .... Bishops... Go right
(3) .... the path... Go (4) .... the stairs, (5) .... the senior common
room building and straight (6) .... the other side... Go (7) .... Sharwood Court.

7 **Look at the chart and complete the passage with these words.**

| up to   over   above   under   at |

High volume

In 2004 sales of digital music came in (1) .... just
2% of the total revenues in the music industry. This increased
to (2) .... $1 billion in 2005 and rose again in 2006
to (3) .... $2 billion. By 2007, sales of digital music
had risen (4) .... 15% of total industry revenues to
just (5) .... $3 billion.

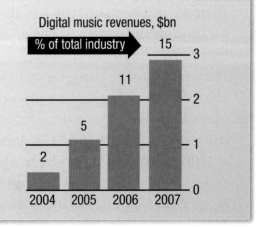

Digital music revenues, $bn
% of total industry

Now check your answers. pp176–177

1 Read the passage and write TRUE, FALSE or NOT GIVEN.

CONTAINER CITY

Although the number of people in London looking for homes has increased, house building hasn't kept up with demand and now there simply aren't enough homes to go round. But Eric Reynolds has come up with a solution. Container City is the name of his modular housing system. Old shipping containers are set up as the external structure of homes and offices, meaning 80% of the finished apartments are made up of recyclable materials. Container City was originally aimed at providing artists with affordable living and studio space in the capital. The container homes go straight back to the principles of ready-made homes and cater for the needs of single professional people. They have also been tried out as classrooms, youth centres, retail space and nurseries. But don't let the way they look from the outside put you off. What initially looks like a giant experiment is modern and fashionable, with interiors that are unrecognisable as shipping containers. Inside, Container City apartments are stylish homes that won't let the buyer down. Will they catch on, though? In the end it could come down to price: a one-bedroom apartment will set you back £50,000.

1   Container City is the name of a model house.   ....
2   Container City satisfies the demands of young professional people.   ....
3   The inside of the house looks like the inside of a shipping container.   ....

Multi-word verbs

There are three types of multi-word verbs
- **Types 1(a)** and **1(b)** verb + adverb
- **Type 2** verb + preposition
- **Type 3** verb + adverb + preposition.

There are two kinds of **Type 1** multi-word verbs
- **1(a) Intransitive** (verbs that do not take an object)
Intransitive multi-word verbs cannot be separated.
*There simply aren't enough homes to **go round.***
The meaning of intransitive multi-word verbs can be different from the separate parts of the verb. (Activities 2 and 3)
*Will they **catch on**, though? Catch on* means *become popular*, not to catch something.
- **1(b) Transitive** (verbs with an object) (See Unit 9 for transitive and intransitive verbs.)
Transitive multi-word verbs can be separated by their object. (Activities 5, 6 and 7)
*Inside Container City are stylish apartments that won't let **the buyer** down.*
Note: pronouns usually go between the verb and adverb.
*A one-bedroom apartment will set **you** back £50,000.*
Not: *A one-bedroom apartment will set back **you** £50,000.*

Type 2 and **3** multi-word verbs end with a preposition and are transitive, but they cannot be separated. We put the object after the preposition. (Activity 7)

*Eric Reynolds has **come up with** a solution.*

Not: *Eric Reynolds has **come** a solution **up with**.*

For **Type 2** multi-word verbs (verb + preposition) we can sometimes guess the meaning of these verbs from the preposition. (Activity 3)

*The number of people in London **looking for** homes has increased. (look for = search)*

However, for **Type 3** verbs (verb + adverb + preposition) it can sometimes be difficult to understand the meaning from the parts of the verb.

Some **Type 2** multi-word verbs are mainly used in the passive.

*Container City was originally **aimed at** providing artists with affordable living.*

There are sometimes other, more formal verbs with similar meanings to multi-word verbs. (Activity 2)

*But Eric Reynolds has **come up with** a solution.*

*Eric Reynolds has **designed / discovered / invented** a solution.*

> **Listen for... IELTS**
> multi-word verbs and words with a similar meaning in summarising and *TRUE / FALSE / NOT GIVEN* questions. You may find a word with the same meaning expressed in a multi-word verb that helps you with the answer.

2 Read the passage in Activity 1 again and find the multi-word verbs that mean:

1   cost   ....
2   disappoint   ....
3   constructed   ....
4   satisfy   ....
5   return   ....
6   match   ....

3 Read the sentences and match the meanings with the multi-word verbs.

> A be somewhere as a result of something bad   B destroy something   C explain (× 2)
> D make sense   E conclude   F understand   G learn new things   H establish   I use   J complete

1   The glass is sorted and then **broken up** before it is melted down again.   ☐
2   When astrophysicists try to **account for** all the matter in the universe, things just don't **add up**.   ☐
    What we can see accounts for only about 4% of everything.   ☐
3   If we can **figure out** how we remember words, we'll have a much better idea how we learn languages.   ☐
4   Many people buy digital music online rather than on CDs, as it **takes up** no space.   ☐
5   Although many organisations try to help street children, children **end up** on the street due to a combination of several factors and not single issues.   ☐
6   Philip has many good ideas – his main problem is **getting** them **across** to other people.   ☐

7 To **sum up**, there has been a lot of research into the disease, but we are still a long way from a cure.

8 Radiation scientist Louis Slotin died during an experiment and didn't **see** his work **through**.

9 The World Heritage Sites programme was **set up** to preserve the world's cultural and natural heritage.

10 Researchers have found that criminals watch documentaries about crimes to **pick up** ideas for their next crime.

4 **Choose the multi-word verb in brackets with the same meaning as the word before it.**

Smart Living

How does a Japanese tea house combine with advanced materials technology? In the microhouse. Researchers and designers based in London and Munich **admired** (1 looked up to / looked down on / looked around) the scale and order of the tea house and **considered** (2 thought through / thought about / thought up) these when designing the microhouse. In 2001, Professor Richard Horden requested (3 asked for / asked in / asked over) his students to design a 2.6m cube house to answer the demand for short-stay living for students and business people, as well as sports and leisure use. The microhouse was **tested** (4 tried on / tried out / tried for) at the Technical University Munich and in 2005 a student village of microhouses was **produced** (5 brought forward / brought up / brought out).

5 **Read the sentences and write *S* if the multi-word verbs are separable and *I* if they are inseparable.**

1 Tony and John can't agree on a plan at all. They are meeting today to <u>iron out</u> their differences.

2 The talk was very interesting but there was so much information, I couldn't <u>take in</u> all of it.

3 Don't laugh at Bora. Just because your essay is better, you shouldn't <u>look down on</u> him.

4 Katerina is so lazy – she just wants to <u>veg out</u> and sit in front of the TV all day.

5 For my next point, I'm going to talk about eco-homes and how they save energy – but I'm <u>getting ahead of</u> myself now. Let me <u>deal with</u> this point first.

6 **Write *C* for correct or *I* for incorrect next to each sentence.**

1 Can we go to a bar tomorrow night instead? I'm tired now and I just don't feel up to going out tonight.

2 Mike's feeling very nervous – he's got six exams this week and he can't face up them to.

3 A: Demet – You're still at university!

   B: I know – I wanted to travel abroad, but my plans just fell through.

4 Here are the handouts for the next lecture – can you pass them out please? ☐

5 Look, go and hand in your essay now, don't put off it until the last minute as usual. ☐

6 Even though Stephen Hawking didn't work very hard at university, he stood still out as an exceptional student. ☐

7 Correct the incorrect sentences from Activity 6.

1 ....

2 ....

3 ....

8 Complete the sentences using the multi-word verbs from the box and pronouns.

hold up   throw out   fill out   watch out for   get along with   work out

1 Miklos told his wife about his new girlfriend last night, so she ....

2 Henrietta is a real star, she's going to do very well – ....

3 Fermat's Last Theorem was such a difficult mathematical problem, no one could .... for two hundred years.

4 I still haven't had your application form for a visa extension letter – have you .... ?

5 When he won the bike race, he took his medal and .... for everyone to see.

6 I like Elisia very much – she's a lovely person – I .... very well.

9 Match the prepositions with the multi-word verbs.

out   up   off   on

1 I'd like to tie .... this tutorial now – Kathleen, could you summarise what you think are the main points, please?

2 Don't be afraid to say what you want Yang – speak ....

3 And when we've finished our walk we can stop .... at a pub nearby for a drink.

4 That Xinzhu, she's so greedy – every time I go to the fridge to get something, she's used .... all the food!

5 Aircraft give .... lots of carbon dioxide. They are responsible for 3% of the USA's carbon emissions.

6 Susie knows all about operations management – she read up .... it last week.

7 Hey, stop hitting me – cut it .... now!

8 I wonder when we'll get our test results – they been sitting .... them for weeks now.

Now check your answers. p177

1 **Read the passage and choose the correct answer.**

Life without numbers

The Piraha, an Amazonian tribe of hunter-gatherers, have fascinated linguists and ethnologists for years, mainly because they appear to have no words at all for numbers in their language. In fact, there are only three words that roughly describe quantity and so it is not actually possible to distinguish between, for example, one big fish and several small fish. Furthermore, the language is one of the most phonologically simple known. (1) ....

Not only do the Piraha live in a world without numbers, they also inhabit a world without colour. (2) ....Moreover, they cannot write or draw and they seem to communicate solely by humming and whistling. (3) .... This means that few can remember the names of all four grandparents. Food is readily available to them, yet they frequently starve themselves. They change their names frequently, too, because they believe spirits regularly take them over and intrinsically change who they are.

Dan Everitt, who has studied the tribe for three decades, argues that what prevents the Piraha from counting is not their language but their unique way of life. As hunter-gatherers they clearly have little need for counting in their everyday lives. (4) .... This means that they have no concept of the abstract (hence no words for number, colour or memory) and no past tense. (5) ....

1 The language	2 The Piraha people
A has very complex phonological patterns.	A communicate by whistling.
B has no written form.	B survive by trading.
C has a wide range of vocabulary.	C have good numeracy skills.

Addition and concession

We add information using linking words for addition and give contrasting or opposite ideas with linking words for concession.

Addition	Concession	Contradiction
Furthermore, *the language is also one of the most phonologically simple known.*	***In contrast*** *to other cultures, they put huge emphasis on immediate physical experience.*	***In fact***, *there are only three words that roughly describe quantity.*
Not only *do the Piraha live in a world without numbers,* ***they also*** *inhabit a world without colour.*	*Food is readily available to them,* ***yet*** *they frequently starve themselves.*	***As a matter of fact***, *there are only ten phonemes.*
Moreover, *they... seem to communicate solely by humming and whistling.*	*What prevents the Piraha from counting is not their language* ***but*** *their unique way of life.*	*It is not* ***actually*** *possible to distinguish between, for example, one big fish and several small fish.*
What is more, *they have no collective memory going back more than two generations.*		***Indeed***, *as far as the Piraha tribe is concerned, everything exists in the present.*
They change their names frequently, ***too***.		

2 **Put sentences A–E below into the correct part of the passage 1–5.**

A   In contrast to other cultures, they put huge emphasis on immediate physical experience.

B   As a matter of fact, it has only ten phonemes.

C   Indeed, as far as the Piraha tribe is concerned, everything exists in the present.

D   What is more, they have no collective memory going back more than two generations.

E   They actually have no distinct words to describe them.

1   ....

2   ....

3   ....

4   ....

5   ....

3 **Choose the correct alternative.**

1   The language has a number of unusual features. As a matter of fact, / What is more, it is so strange that it fascinates linguists and ethnologists.

2   The Piraha can't count and / yet communicate through humming and whistling.

3   There is no past tense in the Piraha language. Moreover, / Actually, there is no means of saying, for example, 'I ate'.

4   Life for the Piraha is about the present. Indeed, / Furthermore, they have no desire whatsoever to remember where they came from.

5   In contrast / In addition to other societies, the Piraha are hunter-gatherers who seldom trade.

6   Not only are the Piraha unable to write, they too / also cannot draw.

4 **Complete the summary using words and phrases for addition, concession and contradiction.**
You may use each word or phrase more than once.

The Piraha people live in a world without numbers. (1) .... they have no words in their language to describe colour (2) .... there is no past tense. (3) .... the language have a simple grammar, it is also simple phonetically. (4) .... to the English language, which has forty-five phonemes, Piraha has only ten speech sounds. The Piraha tribe mainly communicates through humming (5) .... they can whistle their language, too. Dan Everitt argues that the unusual features of the Piraha language are linked to the tribe's way of life. They have no wish to be like other people. (6) .... they do everything they can to avoid being absorbed into the wider world (7) .... one way they do this is by not abstracting anything.

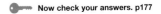 Now check your answers. p177

1 **Read the passage and write TRUE, FALSE or NOT GIVEN.**

> **Writing task 2**
>
> As people in cities are becoming richer, more of them can afford to buy cars. In consequence, city centres are becoming more congested and polluted all over the world. What are the main causes of this problem and what are the solutions?

Traffic congestion is a growing problem in cities throughout the world, so we have to do something about it. Most cities were planned when people used horses and carts, walked or rode bicycles. As a result, the streets are too narrow to take today's traffic. In addition to this, there is not enough off-street parking in the city; therefore drivers leave their cars on the side of the road, making the space even narrower. People may be reluctant to use public transport because it is inconvenient, too expensive or not available for the journey they want to make. Cars are also major status symbols, meaning that more and more people want to own one.

Now that traffic congestion has become such a problem, governments and local councils are desperately seeking solutions. In view of the fact that the number of car drivers has increased, the obvious solution is to build more roads, but this is unpopular owing to its effect on the countryside. Inside cities, one-way systems can be introduced at little cost. Thus, the traffic flow can be eased. Some cities now make drivers pay to enter the city centre, so that they are encouraged to leave their cars at home. Another scheme is 'park and ride', in which people leave their cars outside the city and take a bus to the central district, thereby reducing the number of cars in the city centre.

Overall, it is clear that urgent action needs to be taken, since traffic congestion leads to pollution and frustration. Reliable, cheap and convenient public transport must be the answer.

1 In the old days, most people rode bicycles. ....
2 City streets now need to be wider. ....
3 Most people prefer cars to public transport. ....
4 Everybody agrees that we need more roads. ....
5 'Park and ride' schemes mean that drivers leave their cars at home. ....

Reason and result

Introducing the reason

- *Now that* traffic congestion has become such a problem, governments and local councils are desperately seeking solutions.
- *In view of the fact that* the number of car drivers has increased, the obvious solution is to build more roads.
- *Overall, it is clear that urgent action needs to be taken, **since** traffic congestion leads to pollution and frustration.*

Introducing the result

- *Traffic congestion is a growing problem in cities throughout the world, **so** we have to do something about it.*
- *As a result, the streets are too narrow to take today's traffic.*
- *…there is not enough off-street parking in the city; **therefore** drivers leave their cars on the side of the road…*
- ***Thus**, the traffic flow can be eased.*

Linking words followed by clause or noun phrase

Most linking words are followed by clauses (subject + verb + object), but if the linking word is followed by a preposition, it can be followed by a noun or a noun phrase.

- *People may be reluctant to use public transport, **because** it is inconvenient, too expensive or not available.*

- *People may be reluctant to use public transport **because of** its inconvenience, expense and lack of availability.*

Other linking words which are followed by a noun phrase are:

- *owing to*
- *leading to*
- *due to.*

2 **Read the passage again and say if these expressions introduce (a) a reason or (b) a result.**

| 1 so that | 2 thereby | 3 therefore | 4 meaning that | 5 owing to |

1 ....
2 ....
3 ....
4 ....
5 ....

3 **Match the beginnings 1–6 with six of the endings A–L.**

1 Some of the students were cheating in the test. As a result,
2 Owing to the freezing weather conditions,
3 Travelling by air has become much cheaper recently, meaning that
4 In view of the fact that crime figures have risen sharply,
5 As the room was becoming very hot and stuffy,
6 Pollution is a much bigger problem, now that

A there was a cold wind from the north.
B there were more accidents on the roads than usual.
C I asked him to open a window.
D the window was open.
E children are getting more chest infections.
F more people use cars than public transport.
G planes are faster than trains.
H they hadn't done any revision.
I more people can afford to go abroad for their holidays.
J they were asked to leave the room.
K the government plans to build more jails.
L the police have arrested more criminals.

4 **Complete the sentences using a clause or noun phrase and the correct form of the word in brackets.**

1 We didn't play tennis yesterday because .... (rain)
2 We didn't play tennis yesterday because of .... (rain)
3 As .... (rain), we didn't play tennis yesterday.
4 Yesterday it was raining, so .... (not play tennis)
5 We didn't play tennis yesterday, due to .... (rain)
6 Owing to .... (rain), we didn't play tennis yesterday.

Now check your answers. p177

1 **Read the passage and write TRUE, FALSE or NOT GIVEN.**

Exploring Mars

Since ancient times humans have been fascinated by
Mars and in 2014 NASA's *Maven* spacecraft will
arrive at the red planet to study its atmosphere. In order
to sample the upper layers of Martian 'air', the satellite
will fly low over the planet. It will be followed by the
European Space Agency's *ExoMars* rover, which will
arrive at about the same time and land on the surface
with the aim of studying it. If the European vehicle needs
to relay communications through an orbiting spacecraft, then *Maven* will be equipped to do this. But the
real purpose of sending the satellite is to find out how Mars lost its atmosphere.

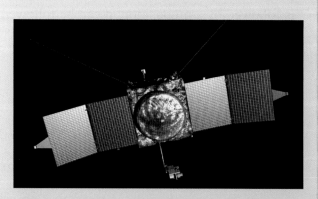

1   The satellite will study all levels of the air on Mars.   ....
2   The *ExoMars* rover is a vehicle from Germany.   ....
3   The *Maven* will be able to send signals from the *ExoMars* rover to Earth.   ....

Phrases of purpose

We use phrases of purpose to answer the question *Why?*
In order to *sample the upper layers of Martian 'air'...*
The *real* **purpose of** *sending the satellite is to find out how Mars lost its atmosphere.*

We introduce clauses of purpose with these words:

in order so as	to + verb
so (that) in order that	subject + could / have to / would
for	+ noun

We can express purpose with these expressions:

for the purpose of with the intention / aim of	+ verb + ing
with a view to	

Note: *so that* is often followed by a modal verb.

We can also use a clause beginning with *to* + infinitive.
NASA's Maven *spacecraft will arrive at the red planet* **to study** *its atmosphere.*
We usually put this clause at the end of the sentence, but can also put it at the beginning of the sentence
for emphasis.

2 **Read the passage in Activity 1 again and answer the questions.**

1   Why will *Maven* fly low over Mars?   ....
2   What will *Maven* be equipped to do?   ....
3   What is the aim of the *ExoMars*?   ....
4   What is the real purpose of *Maven*?   ....

3 Complete the sentences with these words.

so   to   order   to   with

1 .... get to the car park, you go straight through that door.
2 We'll start the project next week .... a view to finishing the following month.
3 We fired three guns at the target .... as to find out their range.
4 Cities in the UK are going wireless .... provide Internet access wherever you want it.
5 James went to bed early in .... not to feel tired the next morning.

4 Join the sentences using the words in brackets.

1 The college put more lights around the campus. The students are safer. (so that)

....

2 They made sandwiches. They were going on a trip. (for)

....

3 There are plans to build a new school of medicine. The government wants to train more doctors.
(in order to)

....

4 A report said an extra 1,000 teachers should be employed. The size of classes can be reduced. (so as)

....

5 The company fitted satellite navigation to their lorries. Their drivers can find their destination easily.
(in order that)

....

5 🔊 Play Track 19. Listen and complete the notes.

Student societies
Societies are for people who like to do (1) .... things.
Three kinds of society:
1 (2) .... e.g., Baseball Society.
2 National society, e.g., (3) ....
3 (4) .... e.g., Drama Society.
Baseball Society meets (5) ....
Saudi Society meets to (6) .... of Arab culture.
Drama Society produces (7) .... every semester.

6 🔊 Play Track 19. Listen again and complete the passage with adverbs and expressions of purpose.

So what is a student society? Well, basically they are clubs (1) .... people who like doing the
same things...the Baseball Society – this society meets every Wednesday (2) .... baseball and
(3) .... the latest American Baseball games...the president of the society says (4) ....
is to have some fun. ...What is (5) .... this society? Well, the Saudi Society meets
(6) .... promote understanding of Arab life and culture through organising events
(7) .... introduce people to the country ...the Drama Society. This society is (8) ....
people who are interested in the theatre and who would like to do acting, too. (9) .... to happen,
the Drama Society produces one play every semester...

🔑 Now check your answers. p177

1 Read the passage and write TRUE, FALSE or NOT GIVEN.

Social responsibility for big business

Corporate social responsibility (CSR) seems to be simple: companies doing or apparently doing good things. Obviously, customers tend not to like companies with bad reputations, and CSR covers everything from looking after employees, to helping the poor, to saving the planet. CSR is clearly in fashion – big companies want to tell the world about their good citizenship. Why the boom? Undoubtedly, companies are working harder to protect their reputations, and if big business thinks it can hide bad behaviour, actually it is mistaken – it is being watched by the media. Unfortunately for companies, bad behaviour, anywhere in the world, can be photographed and published quickly, thanks to the Internet. CSR tends to be made up of three broad layers. The most basic layer is traditional corporate giving – typically companies give about 1% of their profit to good causes. But many companies now feel that, frankly, this is not enough. Hence the second layer of CSR, which is making sure your company does not pollute the environment or use child labour, for example. More surprisingly, the third layer seems to be the idea that CSR can help to create market value and become part of a company's competitive advantage. As a matter of fact, many companies now have mottos like Google's 'Don't be evil.'

1   CSR is when companies always do good actions.   ....
2   Companies do their best to protect their reputations.   ....
3   Google gives 1% of its profits to good causes.   ....

Sentence adverbs

Sentence adverbs show a writer's attitude.
Sentence adverbs

- usually come at the beginning of the sentence
- can cover a wide range of attitudes
- are usually followed by a comma.

Undoubtedly, *companies are working harder to protect their reputation.*

When we believe something is definitely true, we can use words and phrases like:
clearly, in fact, as a matter of fact, obviously, surely, undoubtedly / without doubt.

When we are less sure that something is definitely true (or someone may have told us that it is true), we can use *supposedly* or *apparently.*
To give new and surprising information we may use *actually.*

Note:

- *apparently* = it may or may not be true
- *actually* = it is true, even though we thought it may not be true.

Apparently*, many people thought that the jeans company had stopped producing clothes in developing countries.* ***Actually****, it was trading under a different brand name.*

When we are being honest or truthful, we can use these words and phrases:
frankly, honestly, truthfully, to tell (you) the truth.
Linking verbs like *appear*, *seem* and *look* also show someone is not completely sure of something.

It	appears / seems / looks	as if
It	appears / tends	to be / have

> **Look for...** **IELTS**
> sentence adverbs in the Reading paper with questions asking you about a writer's view or attitude. Using them in your writing will make your answer more natural.

2 **Read the passage again and find words with meanings 1–4.**

1 surprising .... 2 not lucky .... 3 truthfully .... 4 happens often ....

3 **Complete the conversation with** *as if*, *to be* **or** *to have*.

Phil: Is Jane OK, she seems (1) .... a bit dizzy.

Miklos: Did she hit her head?

Phil: No, I don't think so. She tends (2) .... low blood pressure and I think that she stood up too quickly.

Miklos: Well, she seems (3) .... a bit better now, but it looks (4) .... you'll need to sit with her for a while.

4 **Complete the sentences using the words given. There may be more than one answer for some sentences.**

| Actually   Apparently   obviously   To tell you the truth |

1 My parents would like me to work in finance. ...., I think I might travel for a year.

2 According to a survey, the construction industry is seen as an unsafe trade. ...., people believe that the industry has many dangerous jobs.

3 Money can't buy happiness, but .... it helps.

4 I told the tutor I hadn't done my essay because I was ill. ...., I haven't finished it yet!

5 🔘 **Play Track 20. Listen to the candidate and tick his main point.**

1 People are too materialistic. ☐

2 Many people are materialistic, but some are not. ☐

3 Consumerism is bad. ☐

6 🔘 **Play Track 20. Listen again and complete the passage.**

(1) ...., many people are interested in buying the latest products and gadgets – (2) ...., I am too! ... Not everyone likes the latest fashions or technology. (3) ...., one of my classmates even prefers dictionaries to translating machines ...(4) ...., though, while it is true that many people are very consumerist, (5) .... many more are actually turning against this ...(6) ...., some people are choosing not to fly to save the environment, to recycle and repair old things rather than by new products – and things like that... Me? (7) ...., I never repair anything if I can buy a new one!

7 **Rewrite the sentences.**

1 There are more planets like Earth in other solar systems. (You think this is a suprising fact.)
Surprisingly, there are more planets like Earth. ....

2 The banking system needs reforming. (You think everyone knows this.)
....

3 The university is giving all students a free bicycle. (Your friend told you this.)
....

4 The death penalty should be given to all murderers. (You honestly believe this.)
....

Now check your answers. p178

1 **Read the passage and label the diagram.**

Life in a day

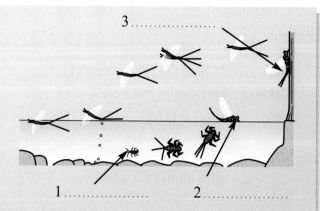

3 ....

Mayflies live for one day only, or even just a few hours as adults. The mayfly life cycle has four stages. To begin with, mayflies start life as eggs in rivers before hatching into a *nymph*. In this stage, the nymph feeds at the bottom of the river for up to two years, before emerging from the surface of the water as an adult. Mayflies are unique among insects in having two adult stages. After emerging from the water they shed their skin to become a *dun* and float until their

1 ....   2 ....

wings are dry. In the third stage of its life, the mayfly flies to the river bank to rest under leaves. The next step of their adult life is to shed their skin again, to become a shiny *spinner*. Following this, they fly back to the water to form mating swarms dancing above the surface of the water. The male and female mayflies mate during this stage. Eventually, the mayflies drop into the water exhausted, to die, but prior to this the female has laid her eggs back into the river for the cycle to begin again.

Staging and sequencing

Words and phrases for staging and sequencing help the reader or listener by ordering the events logically and clearly.

We often help the reader or listener by saying how many stages there are at the beginning of the process.

*The mayfly life cycle **has four stages**.*

***There are four stages to** the mayfly's life cycle.*

*The life cycle of the mayfly **is made up of / is comprised of four stages**.*

> **Use it for IELTS!**
> Staging and sequencing words and phrases are very important when you are describing a process or a natural cycle like the mayfly's life cycle.

First event	Event after event	Two events together	One event before another	Last event
***To begin with,** mayflies start life as eggs.*	***Following this,** they fly back to the water.*	*The male and female mayflies mate **during** this stage.*	***Prior to this** the female has laid her eggs.*	***Eventually,** the mayflies drop into the water.*
initially, the first stage is the first step is to begin with to start with at the outset ... begins with ... commences with	after this, next, then, subsequently, following this, the next step is in the next stage, in the following stage,	at the same time, simultaneously, as / when / while this happens during this step,	before this, previously, prior to this, earlier,	finally, lastly, eventually, ... finishes with ... concludes with in the last stage, the last step is... in the end...

We can use *before / after* + verb + *ing* to show the order of events.

***After emerging** from the water...*

2 Read the passage from Activity 1 again and count the number of words and phrases used for staging and sequencing.

3 Put the sentences in order to make a paragraph.

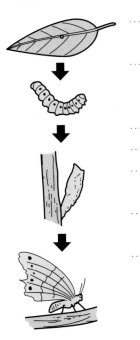

.... A From the chrysalis, the butterfly finally emerges and this is when it moves to new habitats.

.... B There are four separate stages to the life cycle of butterflies and moths, each of which looks completely different and serves a different purpose in the life of the insect.

.... C First, the female attaches the egg to leaves, usually on or near food.

.... D Initially, butterflies and moths start out as eggs.

.... E Then the egg develops into the next stage: the caterpillar (or larva), which is the worm-like stage.

.... F This is the butterfly's feeding and growth stage. While the caterpillar grows, it sheds its skin four times.

.... G Following this, is the transformation stage – the chrysalis – when the caterpillar tissues are broken down and the adult insect's structures are formed.

4 Look at the diagram and complete the passage using the words in the box.

has	The next step	In	Following	at the same time	firstly
stages	finally	At first	concludes	secondly	

THE PRODUCT LIFE CYCLE

A product's life cycle (1) .... several (2) .... : introduction, growth, maturity, decline and withdrawal. Its duration may be as short as a few months or a century or more for products such as the petrol-powered car. (3) ...., when the product is introduced, sales will be low until customers become aware of the product and its benefits. (4) .... the introductory stage, advertising costs are high in order to increase customer awareness of the product. The introduction stage is a period of low profits for two reasons; (5) .... there are low sales and (6) ...., a lot has to be spent on advertising. (7) .... this, at the growth stage, profits grow rapidly – sales increase as customers become aware of the product. (8) .... is the most profitable. However, (9) .... as sales continue to increase, they do so at a slower pace. The product life cycle (10) .... with the decline stage. As sales begin to go down because the market has become saturated, the product becomes technologically out of date, or customer tastes change. The product is (11) .... withdrawn from sale.

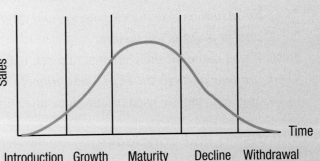

The Product Life Cycle (PLC)

Sales / Time

Introduction   Growth   Maturity   Decline   Withdrawal

Now check your answers. p178

1 **Read the task and the student's response, and write TRUE, FALSE or NOT GIVEN.**

> **Writing task 2**
> In the modern world, more and more people are moving to cities to find a better life. However, many city-dwellers feel that they would have a better lifestyle in the countryside.
> Discuss both these views and give your own opinion. Give reasons for your answer and include any relevant examples from your own experience.

> It is true that there are many advantages to living in the city. For example, facilities such as sports centres, swimming pools and libraries are more readily available in urban areas. It is also easier to find a job. A good illustration of this is my cousin, who found work in a restaurant on his first day in London. There are many places where you can meet new friends too, for instance, evening classes, special interest groups or book clubs. In addition, there is a much wider range of entertainment in the city. A case in point is the theatre. In many cities, you can see a new play or musical every week, if you can afford the tickets.

1   Four advantages of living in the city are mentioned.   ....

2   There are no libraries in the countryside.   ....

3   The writer's cousin is a waiter.   ....

4   People who read a lot will find it hard to meet new friends.   ....

5   Theatre tickets are not cheap.   ....

Exemplification

There are many ways of introducing examples in your writing:

- **For example,** facilities **such as** sports centres, swimming pools and libraries are more readily available.
- **A good illustration of this is** my cousin, who found work in a restaurant.
- **...for instance**, evening classes, special interest groups or book clubs.
- **A case in point is** the theatre.

Note: if you name *all* the elements of a set, use **namely**:

*There are four parts to the IELTS test, **namely** reading, writing, listening and speaking.*

In writing, *e.g.,* can be used to introduce an example.

Summarising and concluding

The final section of your essay should be a summary of your arguments and a statement of the conclusion they lead to.

> **Use it for IELTS!**
> Writing task 2 will always ask you to give examples. It is important to know how to do this.

Summary

- **In short / In a word / In brief**, there are advantages to living in both the town and the countryside.

Conclusion

- **In conclusion / All in all / On the whole**, the countryside may be more suitable for families with young children, whereas young, single people might prefer city life.

2 Read the passage from Activity 1 again and count the phrases that are used to give examples.

3 Complete the passage with the words and phrases in the box. There is one extra phrase.

| for instance   for example   illustration   case in point   such as |

On the other hand, there are also many advantages to country life, (1) .... the peace and quiet of being away from traffic noise and police sirens. Living in the country is safer, too. An (2) .... of this is the low crime figures compared to those in the city. The countryside is an area of natural beauty. We are surrounded by open fields, lakes and mountains, (3) .... , instead of concrete buildings and ugly road signs. Finally, it is much healthier to live outside the city. A (4) .... is the lack of air pollution. There is also more space to exercise and take healthy walks.

4 🔊 Play Track 21. Listen to a talk on vegetarianism, and complete the notes with words or phrases from the box.

| protein   beef   cheese   Hindu   vegan   nuts   children   health   Buddhist animal lovers   butter   beans |

Reasons to be vegetarian
1 ....
religious, e.g., 2 .... , 3 ....
4 ....

Types of vegetarian
5 ....
Lacto-vegetarian – will eat 6 ....
                                     7 ....
No red meat, e.g., 8 ....

Problem
strict vegetarians may not get enough 9 ....

Solution
eat plenty of 10 .... and 11 ....

Conclusion
vegan diet may not be suitable for 12 ....

🔑➡ Now check your answers. p178

1 Read the passage and complete the sentences using NO MORE THAN THREE words.

CLIMATE WATCH

During Spring, people all over Europe are in gardens and parks watching wildlife and taking notes. They record the first time they see a bird, when trees blossom or the first time (1) **they** see a bee. They are taking part in a huge scientific experiment which takes place every year through Spring and Summer. At the end of the season (2) **their** findings are collected and sent to scientists, (3) **who** use these to see if Spring is coming earlier than before. Recording the arrival of the seasons is not new and people have done (4) **so** from ancient times. However, now scientists think that by watching wildlife we can see the immediate effects of climate change. Many types of wildlife become active when the temperature rises; for instance, butterflies do so when the weather is warm, as (5) **do** bees when the temperature reaches 14°C. Phenology is the science of recording (6) **these events** and **changes**.

1 In Spring, some Europeans .... in parks and gardens.
2 Every year in Spring and Summer, a .... happens.
3 When the weather gets warmer, butterflies ....

Cohesion

Cohesion helps the reader or listener follow the subject of a passage by referring them back to the original topic. There are five main ways to do this: reference, substitution, ellipsis, conjunction and repetition.

- **Reference**

Words which refer back to a noun are pronouns. Many kinds of words can be pronouns; common ones are personal pronouns, demonstratives and relative pronouns. (see Activity 3)

Personal pronouns

*They record the first time **they** see a bird.*

subject	*I*	*you*	*he*	*she*	*it*	*we*	*they*
object	*me*	*you*	*him*	*her*	*it*	*us*	*them*
possessive	*mine*	*yours*	*his*	*hers*	*its*	*ours*	*theirs*

> **Look for...**   **IELTS**
> the pronoun *they* – in academic passages, we try to be impersonal in academic English and very often use *they* instead of *he* or *she*.

Demonstratives

*Scientists... use **these** to see if Spring is coming.*

singular	*this / that*	plural	*these / those*

Relative pronouns (see Units A33 and A34)

*A huge scientific experiment **which** takes place every year...*

- **Substitution**

Substitution is replacing an action, idea or event with words and phrases like *do so, if so, not so, one(s)* or words like *the latter / former*. (see Activity 4)

*Butterflies **do so** when the weather is warm. (**do so** = become active)*

- **Ellipsis**

Ellipsis is leaving out part of the sentence because we do not need to repeat it.

*Their findings are collected and **(their findings are)** sent to scientists.*

- **Conjunction**

Conjunction is the use of linking words like *and* and *however.*

***However**, now scientists think...*

- **Repetition, synonyms** (similar words) and **hyponyms** (words which cover a number of other words, e.g., wildlife = birds, animals, insects, etc.) (see Activity 5)

*Phenology is the science of recording **these events** and **changes**.*

2 **Read the passage in Activity 1 again and write who or what the words in bold type refer to.**

1 ....

2 ....

3 ....

4 ....

5 ....

6 ....

3 **Complete the sentences with personal pronouns or demonstratives.**

> her   his (×2)   these   them   he   their

The first phenologist

The first phenologist was Robert Marsham. (1) .... started recording (2) .... findings in 1736. Records of the same events or phenophases were kept by (3) .... family until the twentieth century, when records were kept by Mary Marsham. Unfortunately, this ended with (4) .... death in 1958. Due to the long time period of (5) .... records, we can see (6) .... natural trends over centuries and compare (7) .... with today's findings.

4 **Match the beginnings 1–4 with the endings A–D.**

1 Are you interested in helping to collect data on climate change?

2 Europe is trying to cut its carbon emissions by 20% by 2020.

3 Two measurements were taken to find out the temperature of the sea water – one at 100 metres, the other at 300 metres.

4 Don't you accept that climate change is happening?

A In the <u>former</u> the water temperature was 3°C and in the <u>latter</u> it was –1°C.

B If <u>so</u>, please contact the BBC's weather centre.

C and it has the determination to do <u>so</u>.

D If <u>not</u>, what's your explanation for Spring coming early?

5 **Write what the underlined words in Activity 4 refer to.**

1 ....

2 ....

3 ....

4 ....

5 ....

6 **Cross out the parts of the sentence we do not need to repeat.**

1 The bar chart shows how people travelled to work. We can see that 20 people travelled to work by car, 15 travelled to work by train, and 5 people travelled to work by bicycle.

2 Anne: What did you think to the lecture?
  Sven: I understood it, but Janice didn't understand it.

3 James Lovelock believed in his ideas and fought for his ideas.

4 I thought you were busy writing your essay, but I can see you're not busy writing your essay.

5 Jacques and Joseph Montgolfier were brothers – Jacques, the older brother, was an inventor and Joseph, the younger brother, was a businessman.

7 **Complete the sentences using words from the box.**

| this criticism   the term   this situation   the problem   the theory |

1 'Global warming' was a phrase used by a few scientists for the effects of decades of pollution on weather patterns. Today, ... 'global warming' is well-known.

2 Increasing world temperatures are caused by the amount of CO_2 in the atmosphere, and our growing dependence on fossil fuels is making .... worse.

3 The Gaia hypothesis sees the living and non-living parts of the Earth as a complex system that can be thought of as a single organism. While .... is accepted by many environmentalists, it has not been fully accepted within the scientific community.

4 Developing nations say developed nations are not doing enough to control their CO_2 emissions. .... is accepted by some politicians in developed countries.

5 In some places there will be very little water and in .... the government will need to act quickly.

Now check your answers. p178

1 **Read the passage and classify descriptions 1–4 as referring to Scott (RS) or Amundsen (RA).**

THE DEADLIEST RACE

The race to the South Pole was extremely dangerous and, in the end, deadly, costing five people their lives. In 1911 Norwegian Roald Amundsen was the first explorer to reach the South Pole, beating his British rival, Robert Falcon Scott. In October, both explorers set off, but it was Amundsen who set up camp 60 miles closer to the Pole than Scott. Amundsen decided to use dogs to help him to the Pole: what Scott employed were motor sleds, ponies and dogs. Amundsen's expedition won the race on 14th December, 1911, returning safely to base camp in late January 1912.

Scott's expedition was less fortunate and could not make good time. What happened was that the motor sleds broke down, the ponies had to be shot and the dog teams were sent back. From his team, Scott picked four men and continued on foot. All they wanted was to reach the South Pole first, but what they found on arriving on 18th January, 1912 was Amundsen's Norwegian flag. On the return journey two members died and then a storm trapped Scott and the other two men in their tent, where they froze to death.

The things that helped Amundsen's expedition were good equipment, appropriate clothing, an understanding of dogs and effective use of skis. In contrast to Scott, Amundsen took his team to the South Pole without major problems.

1 His camp was furthest from the Pole.   ....
2 This expedition had lots of bad luck.   ....
3 He planted his flag at the South Pole first.   ....
4 This expedition was well-prepared.   ....

Emphasis

When we want to emphasise part of a sentence we can do this in two ways:
1 By beginning the sentence with *It* or *What...*
- *It + to be* + emphasised point + *that / which / who / when*

It was Amundsen who set up camp 60 miles closer to the Pole.
- *What* + emphasised point + *to be*

What happened was that the motor sleds broke down.

We can choose which thing we would like to emphasise.
Amundsen took his team to the South Pole without major problems.
It was his team *that Amundsen took to the South Pole without major problems.*
It was without major problems *that Amundsen took his team to the South Pole.*
It was to the South Pole *that Amundsen took his team.*
What Amundsen took *to the South Pole **was** his team.*

Note: we use *It is / was...* for people and objects and *What...* for actions or qualities.

2 By beginning the sentence with the phrases below:

The thing The worry The concern The problem The reason why	is / was	that
The question	is / was	which / how / when whether

The things that helped Amundsen's expedition **were** good equipment...

Note: We sometimes see *All...*
All they wanted was to reach the South Pole first...

2 **Read the passage again. Find sentences with *It...* (x1), *What...* (x3), *All...* (x1), *The thing...* (x1), and decide what they emphasise.**

1 ....
2 ....
3 ....
4 ....
5 ....
6 ....

3 **Read the sentences and tick the ones which use emphasis.**

1 It was Amundsen who reached the South Pole first. ☐
2 On the way to the Pole, Scott was taking measurements. ☐
3 The temperature on the way back was –43°C. ☐
4 What Amundsen had done previously was to find a route through the Arctic sea called the North West Passage. ☐
5 One reason why Amundsen succeeded was that he had a lot of experience of polar conditions. ☐

4 **Rewrite the sentence below to emphasise the words in brackets.**

Tony took Noriko to the end-of-term party last Saturday.

1 It was Tony who took Noriko to the end-of-term party last Saturday. .... (Tony)
2 It .... (Noriko)
3 It .... (end-of-term party)
4 It .... (last Saturday)
5 What .... (Tony took)

5 **Read the passage and complete the sentences below.**

Who invented TV?

Who really invented television? This question cost $50 million in the 1930s, as two inventors working on the same invention at the same time claimed television as their own. Vladimir Kosma Zworykin, working for the large company Westinghouse, applied for a patent in 1923 but the idea was on paper only. Philo Taylor Farnsworth, a farm boy, however, successfully demonstrated the transmission of television signals in 1927. Zworykin was not able to do this until 1934 – Zworykin could only manage a poor picture before then. So, although Zworykin had the patent, Farnsworth had the picture.

1 It was Westinghouse who .... Zworykin was working for. (Westinghouse)
2 One reason people consider Zworykin to be the inventor of TV ....
   (patent)
3 What .... was a working signal. (demonstrate)
4 All .... was a poor picture. (had)
5 It .... while Zworykin had the patent. (picture)

6 **Look at the chart and complete the paragraph using the words and phrases in brackets.**

Report on new beetroot juice drink

Strengths (+)	Weaknesses (–)
good market for healthy drinks	not many people like beetroot juice
cheap to produce in Winter	expensive to produce in Summer
young people may buy it	will it sell in cafés or be bought only for home?

While there is a good market for healthy drinks, (1) .... (our concern).
In addition, while it is cheap to produce in Winter, (2) .... (problem).
So the big (3) .... (question / whether) or both.

Now check your answers. pp178–179

1 🔊 **Play Track 22. Listen to the words in *Vocabulary reference*.**

Vocabulary reference

Physical
age – baby   toddler   school age   school-aged   teen   teenager   middle age   middle-aged
adult   pensioner   old age   old-aged
body shape – figure / shape   pear-shaped   hourglass (figure)   slim   overweight   skinny   curvy
face – round   oval   heart-shaped   square
hair – straight   curly   wavy   blond(e)   brunette   bald

Character
amusing   arrogant   brainy   creepy   easy-going   enthusiastic   funny   fussy   generous
gifted   grumpy   hard-working   idle   mean   nervous   punctual   (self-)confident   strange
strict   sulky   thoughtful   unenthusiastic

2 **Match the ages with the words from *Vocabulary reference: Physical – age*.**

   0–1   baby ....

1 1–3   ....   4 18+   ....

2 5–12   ....   5 40+   ....

3 13–19 ....   6 65+   ....

3 **Complete the passage using words from *Vocabulary reference: Physical – age*.**

Age and nutrition

How much and what we should eat changes over the years. By the time babies become (1) ....,
they'll have formed their own likes and dislikes about food. But like (2) ...., they need to eat a
balanced diet. When children reach (3)..................., they're growing fast, so they need foods that satisfy
their high-energy needs. During your teens, your body is still growing and, combined with the active lifestyle
of a (4) ...., this means we need to take in enough food to meet our energy needs. But at the
end of the teenage years, on average, energy requirements are likely to be less and start to decline as we
reach (5) .... and reduce further in (6) ....

4 **Read the passage and complete it using words from *Vocabulary reference: Physical – body shape*.**

What body shape are you?

Every woman has a different (1) ...., and it seems this can affect your life in a number of
different ways. Here are the four main body shapes and what they mean, both in terms of your health and
how to look your very best.

(2) ....: women with this shape have a narrow upper body, but a wider lower body. The good
news is that scientists believe that people with this body shape will live longer, on average, than others.
According to the Institute of Preventative Medicine in Copenhagen, people with wider hips have some level of
protection against heart conditions that is absent in (3) .... people.

Apple: women with this figure will tend to hold weight around their stomach rather than around their hips.
Being this shape makes you more likely to be (4) .... or obese and it puts you at a higher risk of a
number of illnesses.

Ruler: some women are naturally (5) .... – not too thin or fat. While this body type is less common, women with a ruler-shaped figure will have an upper and lower body all of similar width. Those with ruler-shaped bodies often wish they could put on some weight and have a fuller figure.

(6) .... : women with this figure have upper and lower body of a similar width and a smaller waist, giving them classic female curves without looking too thin or (7) .... Researchers at Harvard University found that (8) .... women have better fertility levels than other women.

5 **Match words from *Vocabulary reference: Physical – face* with the pictures.**

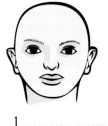 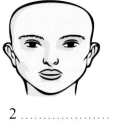 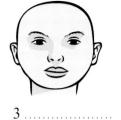 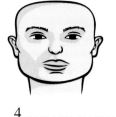

1 ....   2 ....   3 ....   4 ....

6 **Match words from *Vocabulary reference: Character* with their meanings 1–5.**

1 intelligent ....
2 talented ....
3 lazy ....
4 on time ....
5 funny ....

7 **Match the other words from *Vocabulary reference: Character* with the definitions.**

A person who...

1 .... concentrates on unimportant details and is difficult to please.
2 .... becomes upset or excited quickly and can't relax easily.
3 .... does a lot of work.
4 .... does not get worried or angry about things easily.
5 .... is sure about his or her abilities.
6 .... is often unhappy and complains a lot.
7 .... does not like to spend money, especially on other people.
8 .... feels angry and unhappy and refuses to speak to people.
9 .... gives other people a lot of their time or money.
10 .... expects people to obey rules.
11 .... considers other people when they do something.
12 .... is full of energy and excited by things.

8 🔊 **Play Track 23. Listen to a candidate's Speaking task 2 response and tick the adjectives below that you hear.**

1 amusing ☐
2 brainy ☐
3 confident ☐
4 easy-going ☐
5 fussy ☐
6 generous ☐
7 gifted ☐
8 grumpy ☐
9 hard-working ☐
10 idle ☐
11 mean ☐
12 nervous ☐
13 punctual ☐
14 strict ☐
15 sulky ☐
16 thoughtful ☐
17 unenthusiastic ☐

🔑 **Now check your answers. p179**

1 🔊 **Play track 24. Listen to the words in *Vocabulary reference*.**

Vocabulary reference

Dimensions	Shapes
breadth depth height length weight width	circle oval rectangle square triangle pyramid

Size	Patterns
bulky compact enormous huge tiny narrow	plain checked stripy flowery

Age
modern antique used six months old second-hand

2 **Label the diagram using words from *Vocabulary reference: Dimensions*.**

1 ....

2 ....

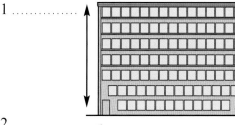

3 ....

4 ....

5 ....

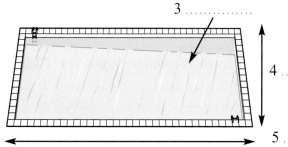

3 **Read the passage and complete the table.**

THE LAST WONDER OF THE WORLD

The Great Pyramid is the last remaining wonder of the ancient world. Built as the tomb of the Pharaoh Khufu, between 2589 and 2566 BC, the Great Pyramid is composed of four triangular sides and a square base. Its dimensions are staggering even today: each side of the square base is over 230 metres long. How heavy is the structure? The total weight would have been 6 million tons and the structure was over 146 metres high before weather eroded it, even now it is still 138.8 metres high. Several passages lead to burial chambers inside the pyramid and one passage goes 105 metres deep into the earth under the pyramid – this passageway is only 1 metre wide and 1.2 metres high. If the scale of the pyramid is astonishing, so is the method of construction, with some surveyors believing that the ancient Egyptians understood the relations of area and circular ratio many years before Pythagoras' Theorem.

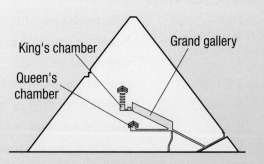

Dimensions						
noun	breadth	width	depth	length	height	weight
adjective	*broad*	1 _____	2 _____	3 _____	4 _____	5 _____
Shapes						
noun	circle	oval	rectangle	square	triangle	pyramid
adjective	6 _____	*oval*	*rectangular*	7 _____	8 _____	*pyramidal*

4 Put the words from *Vocabulary reference: Size* into groups.

large: 1 .... 2 .... 3 ....
small: 4 .... 5 ....
width: 6 ....

5 Match the words from *Vocabulary reference: Patterns* with the designs.

1 .... 2 .... 3 .... 4 ....

6 Play Track 25. Listen to the candidate's response and choose the correct alternative.

1 skiing jacket
   new / used   plain / stripy   bulky / thin   polyfibre / cotton
2 shopping bag
   square / circular   flowery / checked   Italian / French   old / modern
3 flower vase
   big / small   modern / antique   Chinese / Italian   glass / ceramic

7 Read the candidate's responses and label the adjectives with these words.

colour   size   purpose   origin   material   pattern   shape   age

A *It was a*   *used*   *stripy*   *yellow and white* *polyfibre*   *skiing jacket.*
                  1 *age*   2 ....   3 ....   4 ....   5 ....

B *It's a*   *large*   *square*   *flowery*   *Italian*   *shopping bag.*
                  1 ....   2 ....   3 ....   4 ....   5 ....

C *It's a*   *big*   *old*   *blue-coloured*   *Chinese*   *ceramic*   *flower vase.*
                  1 ....   2 ....   3 ....   4 ....   5 ....   6 ....

8 Complete the table with words from Activity 7.

Order of adjectives

1 *size*	2 _____	3 _____	4 _____	5 _____	6 _____	7 _____	8 _____

Note: this is a limited list of adjectives.

Now check your answers. p179

1 🔊 Play Track 26. Listen to the words in *Vocabulary reference*.

Vocabulary reference

Musical instruments
guitar   piano   violin   cello   flute   saxophone

Musical styles
reggae   classical   jazz   rock   hip-hop   world

Events
performance art   street art   concert / gig   carnival   festival

Places
museum   (art) gallery   theatre   exhibition (hall)   opera house

Art
sculpture   sketch   self-portrait   portrait   ceramic

Describing art
abstract   still-life   contemporary   surreal

2 Match the words from *Vocabulary reference: Musical instruments* with the pictures.

1 ....
2 ....
3 ....
4 ....
5 ....
6 ....

3 🔊 Play Track 27. Listen and write which music you hear, using words from *Vocabulary reference: Musical styles*.

1 ....
2 ....
3 ....
4 ....
5 ....
6 ....

4 Complete the examples and definitions using words from *Vocabulary reference: Events.*

1 When a person or group of people doing something is the work of art, this is called ....

2 .... is art that happens in a public place.

3 A .... or .... is when a musical group performs for an audience.

4 A public event that happens at a certain time every year involving music, dancing, dressing up and a parade is called a ....

5 When there is a series of art events, usually held in one place or a day of celebration, often with a religious background, this is a ....

5 Read the passage and find words in *Vocabulary reference: Places* with the same meaning as the underlined phrases.

Guide to Paris

Paris is a world capital built on a human scale, with an unrivalled concentration of artistic and cultural places. One of the most famous of these is the Louvre, (1) where paintings are kept and displayed and people queue to see the *Mona Lisa*. France's national (2) collection of valuable historical objects is in the Musée National d'Histoire Naturelle with three separate centres (3) showing geology, fossils and the ecosystem to the public. The Palais Garnier is the jewel in the crown of Paris music-making and is one of the (4) places to see opera in the capital, but if you prefer a good laugh, you can go to the Comédie Française, (5) where plays are performed.

1 ....

2 ....

3 ....

4 ....

5 ....

6 Complete the passage using words from *Vocabulary reference: Art* and *Describing art.*

One of the greatest influences on (modern) .... (1) art is Picasso. To get a feeling for Picasso's artistic development from the blue and rose periods to the (shapes and patterns) .... (2) period, when he began to paint shapes and colours rather than objects, you can go to the Musée National Picasso in Paris. From a moving (painting of himself) .... (3) and rough (pencil drawings) .... (4) in preparation for the oil painting *Les Demoiselles d'Avignon*, the collection moves to Picasso's (dreamlike) .... (5) *Nude in an Armchair*. It contains (pictures of objects that do not move) .... (6) paintings, and some of his many (paintings of other people) .... (7). The gallery also has (objects made from clay) .... (8) including bowls, cups and vases. A small garden displays larger (pieces of art made from stone and metal) .... (9) from his studio.

Now check your answers. p179

1 🔊 **Play Track 28. Listen to the words in *Vocabulary reference*.**

Vocabulary reference

Location
west(ern)   east(ern)   north(ern)   south(ern)   inland

Type of city
capital city   provincial city   district / regional / provincial capital   port
administrative / commercial capital

Describing cities
physical – suburb   inner city   sector   harbour   bay   waterfront   zone / area / quarter / district
coastal
character – fascinating   vibrant   ancient   tourist   modern   major   world-famous   cosmopolitan
multicultural   metropolitan   historic   industrial
climate – temperate   humid   changeable   tropical

---

2 **Look at the map and write the names of:**

1   the capital city ....

2   a provincial city ....

3   a suburb ....

4   a port ....

5   an inland city ....

6   a coastal city ....

7   an eastern city ....

**There may be more than one answer for
some of the questions.**

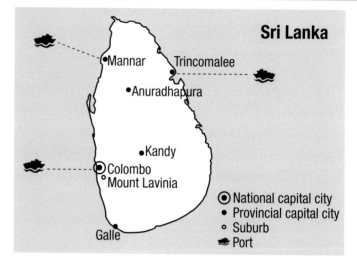

3 🔊 **Play Track 29. Listen and match 1–8 with A–H on the map.**

1   Hargate Hill suburb.........

2   Castle Hill.........

3   harbour.........

4   waterfront.........

5   entertainment district.........

6   inner city residential quarter.........

7   East Bay.........

8   industrial sector.........

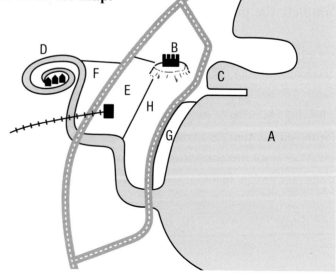

4 **Match some of the words from** *Vocabulary reference: Describing cities – character* **and** *climate* **with their definitions.**

1 full of energy, lively and exciting ....

2 great, important or main ....

3 including people from many different countries ....

4 a very large, industrial and commercial city ....

5 weather which is very hot, wet and uncomfortable ....

6 showing the influence of many different countries and cultures ....

7 very interesting ....

8 weather in or from the warmer parts of the world ....

9 very old ....

10 a mild climate ....

11 new ....

12 something that everyone knows about in many countries ....

5 🔊 **Play Track 30. Listen and complete the passages using words from** *Vocabulary reference.*

Our next city of culture in this lecture is Glasgow. Glasgow became the European City of Culture in 1990. It's a modern, (1) .... city with people from many ethnic backgrounds, in the western part of Scotland, built on both sides of the river Clyde. It is the country's second city and was an (2) .... centre with shipbuilding as its (3) .... industry. Today the shipbuilding industry is less important and the city has reinvented itself as a (4) .... Centre with many visitors to the city.

Examiner: So, Kashif, where do you come from?

Candidate: I come from the capital city of Pakistan, Islamabad, which is one of the most (5) .... cities in the south Asian region.

Examiner: Is that a nice place to live?

Candidate: Yes, it has a (6) .... climate because it's surrounded by mountains. The city is divided into (7) ....: administrative and residential areas, industrial (8) .... and green areas. It's a very young and (9) .... city – it's exciting, with lots to do. With lots of commerce and industry, it's Pakistan's largest (10) .... city.

Yokohama is a (11) .... city on Honshu island on the bay of Tokyo. It's a major (12) .... and also a regional capital. I have lived there all my life and I like it very much. It's very crowded – the second most populous city in Japan, but it has a (13) .... feel to the city because of the Western-style buildings, Chinese temples and international restaurants, especially in the (14) .... of Yamate, just outside the city centre with its churches and teashops – a bit like England, really!

Now check your answers. p179

1 🎵 **Play Track 31. Listen to the phrases in** *Vocabulary reference.*

Vocabulary reference

Collocations connected with success and failure

to give a dismal presentation   to give a winning performance   to make a good impression
to be doomed to failure   to go badly wrong   to be a total flop   to be a recipe for disaster
to be an outstanding success

Collocations connected with change

to make things easier for yourself   to make a real difference   to increase your chances
to make a slight adjustment

Collocations connected with remembering

to keep something in mind   to make a point of doing something   to make sure
to make a note of something

Collocations with *make*

to make a list   to make an effort   to make a mistake   to make notes

---

2 **Match some of the** *Collocations connected with success and failure* **and** *change* **with the definitions.**

   1   cause someone to notice and admire you   ....

   2   a complete failure   ....

   3   to result in a very positive change   ....

   4   to make a small change   ....

   5   lead to major problems   ....

   6   to be certain to fail   ....

   7   to do something very well   ....

   8   to improve the possibility of something happening   ....

3 **Classify the** *Collocations connected with success and failure* **as referring to:**

A success	B failure
....	....
....	....
....	....
....	....

4 🔊 **Play Track 32. Listen to the talk and complete the passage using appropriate *Collocations* from the *Vocabulary reference* on page 128.**

PRESENTATION SKILLS

Preparation is the key to giving a good presentation. It can be the difference between a great success and a
(1) .... So, keep these key points in mind during your preparations in order to
(2) .... on your audience.

Make sure the audience can see both you and any visual aids you plan to use. Your presentation will
(3) .... if you obstruct screens by standing in front of them. You can
(4) .... by checking where you plan to stand in the room in advance and
(5) .... if necessary.

State at the beginning what you are going to talk about and make a list of the main points. Make an effort to ensure that your presentation has a logical order. Emphasising your key points by using visual aids or by alerting your audience to key points coming up can (6) .... Make eye contact with your audience, but don't just focus on one person – look around at different people.

Don't (7) .... of simply reading from a script. It will be a
(8) .... and you will be (9) ....! Not only will it affect the flow of your delivery, you will bore your audience, too. Making notes and using them as prompts will help you sound more natural and increase your chances of (10) ....

5 **Choose the correct alternative.**

1 Make an effort / Make eye contact with your audience while giving your presentation.
2 Make a point of / Make sure you check the audience can see both you and any visual aids you use.
3 Speaking too quietly when you give a presentation is a recipe for success / failure.
4 Always keep in mind / make a note of your audience when planning your presentation.
5 Practise using the equipment you will have so that you can make adjustments / make a difference if necessary.
6 Make a note / Make notes in advance and refer to them during your presentation.

6 **Complete the sentences using *Collocations connected with remembering* and *make*. Use NO MORE THAN FOUR words for each answer.**

1 Why .... you locked the door behind you when you went out last night?
2 She always .... keeping all her shopping receipts so that she knows how much she spends.
3 You can't expect to have friends if you .... to be friendly.
4 .... of the things we need to do before we go on holiday. Is there anything you want to add?
5 I'm not blaming you for the accident – we all ....
6 I .... on the calendar that he was arriving on Tuesday but he didn't come.
7 I still can't decide what to buy him for his birthday, but I .... your suggestion.

👉 Now check your answers. pp179–180

1   (⊙) **Play Track 33. Listen to the words in *Vocabulary reference*.**

Vocabulary reference

Places of study
primary school   secondary school   comprehensive school   grammar school   specialist school
boarding school   independent school   secondary modern school   further education college
university

Qualifications
degree   diploma   A level   GCSE   doctorate   masters

Collocations connected with education
to develop practical skills in   to complete a degree   to learn from experience
to get hands-on experience of   to cover a wide range of subjects
to get a practical grounding in   to acquire theoretical knowledge   to take an exam

---

Jobs / positions in education
administrator   admissions officer   graduate   lecturer   postgraduate   professor   pupil
researcher   tutor   undergraduate

Collocations with *get*	**Collocations with *do***
a place an offer an education a qualification a degree	a degree a course research

2   **Match the descriptions with words from *Vocabulary reference: Places of study.***

1   It takes children of all abilities and provides a wide range of secondary
education for children between the ages of 11–18.   ....

2   It offers a mainly academic education for the 11–18-year-old age group.
Children enter the school on the basis of their abilities and have to sit
an entrance examination first.   ....

3   It specialises in helping students improve their qualifications, especially
for admission to a career-based or degree course.   ....

4   The first one was founded around 800 years ago. Students study for
qualifications such as degrees, diplomas and postgraduate qualifications.   ....

5   It provides education up to the age of 18. Students live at the college and
have to pay fees to attend.   ....

6   It gives pupils a broad secondary education with a strong emphasis on
languages, technology, arts or sport. Pupils do not have to pay fees in
order to attend.   ....

7   Pupils have to pay fees for their education in this type of school.   ....

8   Children attend this school from around the age of 4 or 5 until the
age of 10 or 11.   ....

9   These schools, sometimes called junior high schools, are for pupils aged 11–16.   ....

3 ◉ **Play Track 34. Listen to the speakers and match them with words from *Vocabulary reference: Qualifications*.**

A ....

B ....

C ....

4 **Complete the definitions with words from *Vocabulary reference: Jobs / positions in education*.**

1 a boy or girl attending school – usually in primary or middle school   ....

2 a university or college teacher responsible for teaching students   ....

3 an academic who investigates or studies something in order to find out new facts or make new discoveries   ....

4 a person who works at university or college and teaches large numbers of students in a lecture theatre   ....

5 someone who has completed a course of study or training, especially a person who has got their first degree   ....

6 the person responsible for running an office in an organisation   ....

7 a student at a college or university who has not taken their first degree   ....

8 someone who is taking a higher degree such as a masters or doctorate   ....

9 the most senior teacher in a university or college department   ....

10 this person decides who can be offered a place on a course at college or university   ....

5 **Tick the words that go with *get* or *do*. One word can go with both.**

	a place	a degree	a course	research	a qualification	an offer	an education
get							
do							

6 **Complete the passage using the correct form of words from *Vocabulary reference: Collocations connected with education*.**

Andrew Mitchell tells how he trained to be a pilot.

I always wanted to be a pilot. In fact, I can remember telling my teacher at boarding school about my dream when I was about 12 years old! I was in the air cadets for four years while I was doing GCSEs and A levels. After leaving school I went on to (1) .... in Aeronautics and Astronautics Engineering at (2) .... After graduating I applied to do an Airline Transport Pilot Licence course. The course enables you to acquire (3) .... at the flight deck. During the first part of the course you (4) ...., including meteorology and navigation. For the rest of the course you get (5) .... of flying!

As a pilot you have to get used to (6) .... In fact, I have to take a test in a simulator every six months.

▷ Now check your answers. p180

1 🔊 **Play Track 35. Listen to the words in *Vocabulary reference*.**

Vocabulary reference

Types of power
(hydro-)electric   solar   nuclear   coal- / gas- / oil-fired   wave   wind   geothermal

---

Types of fuel
(non-)renewable source   fossil fuel   radioactive   uranium

Places
(nuclear) power station   wind farm   dam

Working parts
(wind) turbine   solar panel   reactor   generator   transformer

---

Verbs
generate   produce   collect   store   burn   transmit   distribute

---

2 **Match words from *Vocabulary reference: Types of power* with the pictures.**

1 ....   2 ....   3 ....   4 ....

3 **Write *R* if these types of energy are renewable or *N-R* if they are non-renewable.**

1 hydroelectric	....	6 solar	....
2 nuclear	....	7 oil-fired	....
3 geothermal	....	8 wave power	....
4 wind power	....	9 gas-fired	....
5 coal-fired	....	10 oil-fired	....

4 **Match words from *Vocabulary reference* with their definitions.**

1 a solid form of fossil fuel ....

2 the place where energy is generated in a nuclear power station ....

3 something which collects energy from the sun ....

4 a wall which holds back water ....

5 the movement of water in the sea ....

6 set fire to ....

7 supply energy to individual households ....

8 energy which comes from directly under the ground ....

9 a type of fuel which can never be used up ....

10 fuel for nuclear energy ....

5 **Complete the sentences using words from *Vocabulary reference* and enter the words in the grid below.**

1 Solar panels .... energy from the sun.

2 Oil is an example of a ....

3 A .... turns energy into electricity.

4 Traditional power stations .... oil, coal or gas to make electricity.

5 Uranium is a .... substance used in generating nuclear power.

6 Power lines .... electricity from power stations across the country.

7 A solar panel can .... energy until it is needed.

8 Complete this sentence with the word in the blue column:

   A wind .... collects energy from moving air.

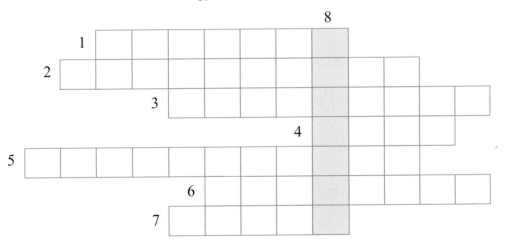

6 **Complete the table using the noun or verb form of the words given. In some cases there is more than one possible answer.**

VERB	NOUN
1	generator
2	reactor
3	transformer
produce	4
store	5
collect	6
transmit	7
distribute	8

🔊 **Play Track 36. Listen and check your answers.**

Now check your answers. p180

1 🔊 Play Track 37. Listen to the words in *Vocabulary reference*.

Vocabulary reference

Geography
north   south   east   west   northern / southern hemisphere   latitude   longitude
North / South Pole   equator

Sea
ocean   gulf   maritime   current   flow   salinity

Land
continent   coast   landmass   mountain range

Climate
atmosphere   high / low pressure   humid   mild   (sub-)tropical   monsoon   trade winds
moisture   precipitation   flood   drought

---

2 Label the compass and parts of the globe using words from *Vocabulary reference: Geography*.

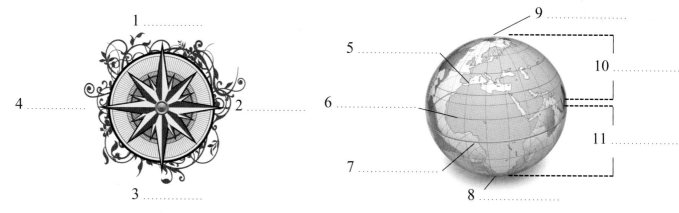

1 ....   9 ....

5 ....

4 ....   2 ....   6 ....   10 ....

7 ....   11 ....

3 ....   8 ....

3 Match words from *Vocabulary reference: Sea* with their definitions.

1   a verb describing the movement of water   ....
2   a large expanse of water   ....
3   a noun meaning the movement of water   ....
4   an adjective relating to navigation, shipping or the sea   ....
5   a deep place where there are strong ocean currents   ....
6   the amount of salt that water contains   ....

4 🔊 Play Track 38. Listen to the talk and complete the summary using words from *Vocabulary reference*.

The Gulf Stream is a warm (1) .... (2) .... It (3) .... in a north-easterly direction across the Atlantic (4) .... from the Gulf of Mexico. The air above the Gulf Stream is (5) .... and (6) .... , and its water has high (7) .... If it were not for the Gulf Stream, places in the UK and Europe at the same (8) .... would be as cold as Canada.

5 Complete the sentences using words from the box.

---

range   hemisphere   flood   continent   pressure   atmosphere   precipitation
trade winds   monsoon   maritime   coast   drought   tropical   moisture

---

1 When the .... arrives, there is plenty of rain to .... the fields, so the farmers can grow rice there.
2 The returning space capsule entered the Earth's .... at a speed of nearly 30,000 km per hour.
3 Asia is the world's largest ....
4 An area of low .... brought unsettled weather to the whole area.
5 Antarctica is in the southern ....
6 If you are interested in ships and the sea, you should visit the .... museum.
7 Fast sailing boats called 'clippers' used to cross the ocean using the .... to bring tea from the East.
8 There are many beautiful beaches along the .... of Australia.
9 .... countries are near the equator, so they are hot and humid all year round.
10 The Andes is a mountain .... in South America.
11 As there is not much .... in the desert, there is very little .... in the ground.
12 There has not been any rain for months in parts of Africa, and the people there are suffering terribly from the ....

6 **Read the article and complete the notes using NO MORE THAN THREE WORDS from the passage for each answer.**

World climates are shaped by the circulation of the atmosphere, which is affected by the positions of mountain ranges, continents and oceans. Landmasses absorb heat and cool more rapidly than the oceans, and the air above them creates the atmospheric pressure systems which control our weather.

Land and sea

Areas of high pressure develop over cold areas where the air is falling, and low-pressure areas, known as depressions, form over warm areas such as the north Atlantic and north Pacific oceans, where the air is rising. In Summer, low pressure builds up over Asia, resulting in the monsoon over the Indian Ocean, because the usual trade winds are replaced by south-westerlies. These carry a lot of moisture, causing heavy precipitation. Because the oceans' temperatures remain steadier than those of the land, maritime climates are milder, or more temperate. In the UK, for example, the temperature range between Summer and Winter is only 10–15°C, whereas in a large landmass such as Canada or Siberia, it can be more than 40°C. However, although the temperatures in maritime climates are more pleasant, they are often wetter.

(1) .... (2) .... (3) ....
↓
Movement of air in (4) ....
↓
World climates

Temperatures of (5) .... change less than temperatures of (6) .... ; hot or cold air change (7) ...., controlling weather systems. (8) .... forms when air is falling, (9) .... when it is rising. Monsoons form when (10) .... builds up and moist winds result in (11) .... Temperatures in (12) .... are less changeable than in areas with (13) ...., so they are more pleasant but also (14) ....

Now check your answers. p180

1 🔊 **Play Track 39. Listen to the words in *Vocabulary reference*.**

Vocabulary reference

Places to eat
café fast food outlet buffet refectory restaurant

Types of food
junk food fast food homemade vegetarian vegan (French / Italian / Chinese, etc.) cuisine

Food and drink
snack starter main course dessert side dish
beverage

Ways of cooking
fry grill roast boil bake steam

Describing food
nutrition – calorie carbohydrate fat protein vitamin mineral fibre
taste and texture – raw fresh oily tough sour sweet savoury bitter spicy tender sugary
adjectives – delicious gorgeous heavenly moreish light heavy bland unhealthy

2 🔊 **Play Track 40. Listen to a talk about where to eat on campus and complete the notes using words from *Vocabulary reference*.**

Types of cooking: Italian, Chinese and (1) ....
Places to eat
1 Uni buffet = a small (2) .... for (3) .... like biscuits and tea, coffee and other hot
   (4) ....
2 Fair and fast – a fast food (5) .... for light meals and burgers, which are (6) .... and
   are not (7) .... food.
3 The refectory, that is the university (8) .... You can get a (9) .... – small dishes or
   (10) .... with chips or garlic bread as a (11) ...., then something sweet for
   (12) ....
   Also (13) .... meals for people who don't eat meat, but there isn't (14) .... food for
   people who don't eat milk or cheese.

3 **Label the pictures using words from *Vocabulary reference: Ways of cooking*.**

1 ....   2 ....   3 ....   4 ....   5 ....   6 ....

4 **Match the words from *Vocabulary reference: Describing food – taste and texture* with the definitions.**

1 fruit or vegetables which have recently been picked   ....
2 food with too much fat   ....
3 food which is difficult to eat or takes a long time to eat   ....
4 having a sharp taste   ....

5	easy to cut and chew	....
6	having a salty taste, not sugary	....
7	having a hot taste	....
8	having an acid taste like lemon or vinegar	....
9	not cooked	....

5 **Match the adjectives with the types of food.**

	bitter	fresh	oily	raw	savoury	sour	spicy	tender	tough
meat		✓							
fruit									
vegetables									
food / a meal					✓				

6 **Read the passage and match the words 1–6 with their functions A–F.**

FOOD GROUPS

Everything we eat is part of one of five food groups. The grain group contains food like bread, rice and pasta. The ingredients in these foods give your body the carbohydrates which it needs for energy, as well as minerals like iron, which helps carry oxygen around the body, and fibre – the part of the grain that helps food to pass through our bodies. The protein group includes: meat, beans, eggs and nuts. We need at least two servings a day from this food, which helps our body to repair itself. The dairy group includes milk and cheese and contains calcium, which makes bones strong. The vegetable group contains different nutrients, especially vegetables that are dark green or orange. Finally, there is the fruit group, which is packed with vitamins like vitamin C, helping protect us from diseases.

1	.... carbohydrates	A	helps our body repair itself
2	.... minerals	B	makes our bones strong
3	.... fibre	C	give us energy
4	.... protein	D	helps food pass through our bodies
5	.... calcium	E	protect us from diseases
6	.... vitamins	F	carry oxygen around the body

7 **Put the words from *Vocabulary reference: Describing food – adjectives* into groups.**

A Good: (1) .... (2) .... (3) .... (4) .... (5) ....

B Bad: (6) .... (7) .... (8) ....

8 🔘 **Play Track 41. Listen to the examiner and the candidate and choose the answers.**

1   The candidate says his country's food is not good for
    A vegans   B vegetarians   C people with allergies.

2   Which food does he call 'fantastic'?   A sour cream   B pork   C pickles

3   What makes his country's food spicy?   A chilli pepper   B paprika   C black pepper

4   Which course does the candidate say is 'heavy'?   A starter   B main course   C dessert

5   What does he say about the cakes? They are   A heavy   B heavenly   C boring.

🔑 **Now check your answers. p180**

1 🔊 **Play Track 42. Listen to the words in *Vocabulary reference*.**

Vocabulary reference

Internal organs
liver   kidneys   lungs   heart   intestines   brain   diaphragm   bladder   spleen   muscle

Bones
skull   spine   vertebrae   ribs

Joints
hip   ankle   knee   wrist

Diseases
arthritis   malaria   infectious diseases   cancer   stroke   heart disease   Alzheimer's disease
HIV / AIDS (Human Immunodeficiency Virus / Acquired Immune Deficiency Syndrome)

Cures
vitamins   holistic medicine   conventional medicine   pills   diet   exercise   injection
operation   radiotherapy   chemotherapy   herbs

People
surgeon   osteopath   psychiatrist   chiropodist   physiotherapist   cardiologist
paediatrician   consultant   optician   GP (General Practitioner)

Places
A&E (Accidents and Emergencies)   clinic   hospice   outpatients   surgery   theatre   ward   waiting room

2 **Label the diagrams using words from *Vocabulary reference: Internal organs, Bones* and *Joints*.**

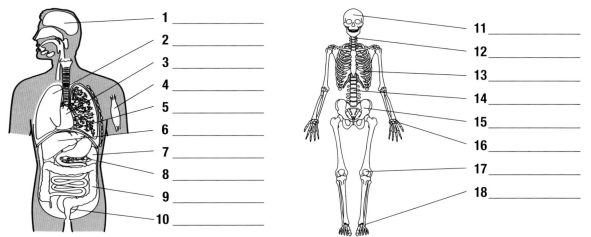

1 _____
2 _____
3 _____
4 _____
5 _____
6 _____
7 _____
8 _____
9 _____
10 _____

11 _____
12 _____
13 _____
14 _____
15 _____
16 _____
17 _____
18 _____

3 **Match the words from *Vocabulary reference: Diseases* with their definitions.**

1   You can catch these from other people by breathing the same air.   ....
2   This is spread by blood or sexual contact.   ....
3   This happens when cells in the body grow uncontrollably.   ....
4   This disease is common in tropical countries where there are a lot of mosquitoes.   ....
5   A sudden attack of the brain which can kill or paralyse.   ....
6   A painful disease of the joints.   ....
7   This is usually a disease of older people.   ....
8   This can often be avoided by having a healthy lifestyle.   ....

4 **Match the medical problems with the medical people who treat them, using words from** *Vocabulary reference: People.*

1 Your own doctor is not sure what is wrong with you.   ....
2 You are very depressed and can't sleep at night.   ....
3 You have painful feet.   ....
4 You have a sick child.   ....
5 You are having an operation.   ....
6 You have back pain.   ....
7 You think you might need glasses.   ....
8 You need to start walking again after a long illness.   ....
9 You are worried about your heart.   ....

5 Play Track 43. **Listen to a talk about Chinese medicine and complete the passage using words from** *Vocabulary reference: Cures.*

Chinese medicine

In Chinese medicine, a more (1) .... view of the patient is taken. Whereas (2) .... in the West primarily treats the symptoms, or signs, of a disease, the Chinese approach is to consider the whole person. In the treatment of cancer, for example, Fu Zhen therapy uses special (3) .... and (4) .... alongside modern (5) .... to strengthen the body's ability to fight the disease. These herbs can help to counter the negative effects of chemicals used in (6) .... and can also help them to work more efficiently. The Chinese believe that good (7) .... and (8) .... are of greater benefit to health than (9) .... or (10) ...., and many westerners are now using Chinese medicine in conjunction with modern techniques.

6 **Complete the sentences using words from** *Vocabulary reference: Places.*

1 When I need advice about my children's health, I go to the .... in the high street.
2 Maria cut her hand very badly, so we had to take her to .... at the big hospital in the city.
3 After the operation, they put him in a bed in the recovery ....
4 There is no need for you to stay in hospital any longer. Just come to the .... department in two weeks' time, and we'll give you a check-up.
5 A lot of people have colds at the moment, so the doctor's .... is very full.
6 I'm afraid he's really very ill, and they don't think he's going to get better, so they've found him a peaceful room in the ....
7 The doctor's .... is open from 8.30 until 3.00 in the afternoon.
8 The operation will take place in the .... on the second floor.

Play Track 44. **Listen and check your answers.**

Now check your answers. pp180–181

1 🔊 **Play Track 45. Listen to the words in *Vocabulary reference*.**

Vocabulary reference

Research methods

case study   experiment   fieldwork   questionnaire   survey   trial

---

Outcomes of research

information – data   findings   figures / statistics (stats)   results   report   recommendation
products – discovery   invention   innovation   design

Verbs connected with research

analyse   investigate   explore   produce   examine   conduct   carry out

---

2 **Complete the definitions using words from *Vocabulary reference: Research methods*.**

1 A(n) .... is a scientific test done in order to discover what happens to something under certain conditions.

2 Detailed information about a person, group or thing and their development over a period of time is a ....

3 When you collect information in the real world, rather than in a laboratory, this is ....

4 If you .... a number of people, you try to find out information about their opinions, usually by asking them questions.

5 A .... is an experiment to test something to see how well it works.

6 A .... is a list of questions answered by a lot of people in order to provide information.

3 **Match the definitions with words from *Vocabulary reference: Outcomes of research – information*.**

1 information in the form of facts or numbers that you can study ....

2 information from research or experiments ....

3 facts which come from studying information shown in numbers ....

4 what you get at the end of a calculation or experiment ....

5 an official document after studying an event or situation ....

6 advice to take specific action ....

4 **Match the examples from *Vocabulary reference: Outcomes of research – products*.**

1 Galileo looked through a telescope and found Jupiter's moons. ....

2 Both Gottlieb Daimler and Karl Benz made a new kind of engine – the internal combustion engine. ....

3 Jony Ive drew the plans for the iPod. ....

4 Momofuku Ando took traditional noodles and used them in a new way to make instant noodles. ....

5 **Complete the sentences using words from** *Vocabulary reference: Verbs connected with research.*

1   to consider something carefully or look at it using scientific methods in order to understand it
    The researchers .... the causes of the disease.

2   if you do this, you think about an idea in detail and comment on it
    On Wednesdays, special workshops .... a particular theme through the work of modern artists.

3   to make or create something
    The new medicine will be .... for the market after testing has shown how effective it is.

4   to look at something very carefully
    The doctor .... his patient very carefully to find out what was wrong with her.

5   to organise and complete an activity or task
    The centre will .... a survey to look at the engineering industry in the area.

6   to do something according to instructions, to complete something
    All government departments have to .... staff reductions.

7   to examine something thoroughly to find the truth
    The scientists at CERN are .... why the Large Hadron Collider broke down.

6 **Complete the table.**

verb:	investigate	analyse	explore	produce	examine
noun:	*investigation*	1 _____	2 _____	3 _____	4 _____

7 **Tick the verbs that go with these nouns.**

	analyse	examine	explore	conduct	carry out
an idea			✔		
an experiment					
statistics					

8 **Choose the correct alternatives to complete the passage.**

This year's (1) data / numbers / recommendations from a (2) report / survey / questionnaire of over 40,000 businessmen and -women suggests that the UK's executives are willing to risk their job security. The number of executives who resign from their job is currently at 6.5%. The survey, done by (3) findings / questionnaires / statistics on the Internet and followed up by interviews, asked companies why their employees left. (4) Production / Analysis / Completion of the (5) findings / innovation / recommendations showed that three-quarters (75%) of organisations blamed competition from other businesses. The (6) recommendation / statistics / innovation showed that almost half (48%) of businesses recognise that they do not provide adequate career opportunities or development programmes. Further (7) survey / examination / discovery of the results shows that one in ten admit that employees left because of frustrations with the working environment (9%). The (8) report / numbers / examination also showed similar proportions leaving due to 'bureaucratic leadership styles' (8%) and (9) recommended / examined / explored that, to keep the best talent, businesses needed to provide good working environments and good long-term career opportunities.

Now check your answers. p181

1 🔊 **Play Track 46. Listen to the words in *Vocabulary reference*.**

Vocabulary reference

> **Hardware**
>
> smartphone   laptop   hard drive   flash drive   keyboard   speakers   scanner
> mouse   monitor   printer   cable   modem

> **Software**
>
> application / program   database   spreadsheet   word processing

> **Computing verbs**
>
> navigate   click   browse   drag   scroll up / down   highlight   download / upload
> back up   freeze   crash   delete   access   hack

> **IT dangers**
>
> hacker   virus   spyware   bug   cybercrime

> **Jobs**
>
> software engineer   applications programmer   technical support
> web / systems designer   network manager

2 **Match the words from *Vocabulary reference: Hardware* with the pictures.**

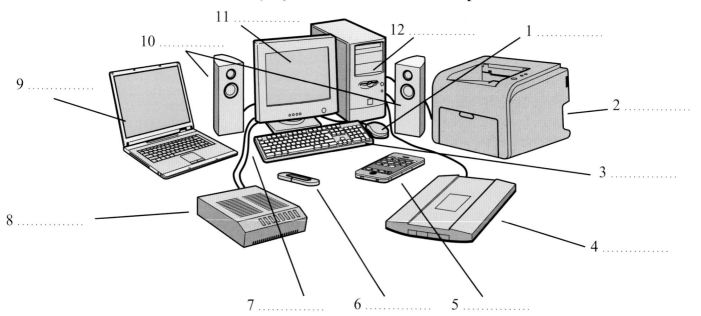

3 **Complete the definitions with words from *Vocabulary reference: Software*.**

1 An .... or a .... is a piece of software designed for a particular purpose – to play music (media software), for example.

2 A collection of information stored in an organised way is called a ....

3 A .... is a computer program used for accounting, in which figures are arranged in rows and columns in a table.

4 We write essays, messages, letters, and so on with a .... program.

4 Complete the passage using words from *Vocabulary reference: Computing verbs.*

IT WORKSHOPS FOR STUDENTS

OK – we **know** you know how to use a computer! But how well do you know how to use it? In our first workshop, we show you how to (1) .... or find your way around the Internet, or go directly to the information you need – how to (2) .... to what you want to know. Do you want to manage your documents better? Our second workshop shows you how to (3) ...., or choose, the files you want and then move or (4) .... them to another place. Our third workshop makes sure you don't lose any work. Learn how to put your work in a safe place by (5) .... your data. Find out how to (6) ...., or transfer, data to another computer to save it, then (7) .... it again to your computer when you need it. Make sure that you're protected if your computer (8) .... or stops working for a few minutes or, worse still, stops completely and (9) .... To reserve a place on the course, (10) .... down to the bottom of the page by moving the scroll bar with your mouse and (11) .... on the link.

5 Complete the newspaper articles using words from *Vocabulary reference: Computing verbs* and *IT dangers.*

Gary McKinnon, also known as *Solo*, illegally entered or (1) .... into 97 US military computers, causing over $700,000 of damage by (2) .... or removing files. McKinnon has never denied entering or (3) .... the US Army, Navy, Air Force and NASA computers, but says he did not damage them.

A mysterious computer (4) ...., or illegal program, has contaminated six million machines in the past three days. The virus, known as *Upandown* or *Confict*, puts a (5) .... computer error onto machines. The virus is a (6) .... program that allows criminals engaged in (7) .... to watch which keys the user is pressing on their keyboard.

6 Read the passages and match the job descriptions with words from *Vocabulary reference: Jobs.*

1 My job is to research, design and develop computer programs for customers. Once the system has been designed, I test and maintain the systems. ....

2 People who monitor and maintain the computers in an organisation. They install computer systems, diagnose hardware / software faults and solve technical problems, either over the phone or face-to-face. ....

3 I have management responsibility for the operation and administration of the company's internal networks, email and network security systems. ....

4 I am responsible for the visual appearance and functioning of a website. ....

5 My role involves planning and designing information systems that integrate hardware, software and communication technologies. ....

Now check your answers. p181

1 🔊 **Play Track 47. Listen to the words in *Vocabulary reference*.**

Vocabulary reference

Features of language

accent   collocation   context   dialect   expression   fluency   intonation   style
syntax   idiom   accuracy   phonetic   slang   saying

Types of talk

argument   chat   debate   discussion   gossip   small talk

Types of language

sign language   body language   mother tongue   common language   bilingual   multilingual

---

Verbs connected with language

interpret   recite   transcribe   translate   pronounce

---

2 **Read the clues and complete the crossword using words from *Vocabulary reference: Features of language*.**

Across

1 An expression whose meaning is different from the meaning of the individual words.

3 A form of a language that is spoken in a particular part of a country and contains some different words, grammar and vocabulary.

6 Two or more words that create a different meaning when used together.

9 The grammatical arrangement of words in a sentence.

10 The way in which people in a particular area, country, or social class pronounce words.

11 Using language in a particular way, e.g., in a formal or informal way.

12 Informal language which is used by particular groups of people who know each other, and is usually spoken rather than written.

Down

1 The sound changes produced by the rise and fall of the voice when speaking.

2 The ability to speak a language easily, well and quickly without many pauses.

4 The relationship of sounds in a language to the writing.

5 The situation in which a text occurs.

7 The ability to speak a language without mistakes.

8 A word or phrase used to give an idea.

9 A well-known statement about life.

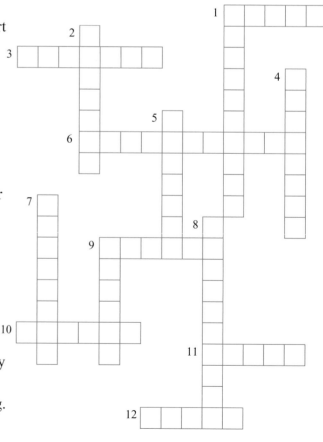

3 Complete the definitions using words from *Vocabulary reference: Types of talk.*

1 Polite conversation about very unimportant things is known as ....
2 To talk in an informal and friendly way usually with someone you know well is to ....
3 To talk about other people, often about things that may or may not be true, is to ....
4 A .... is a formal discussion on a topic in public.
5 To talk about something in a formal way, in order to reach a decision, is a ....
6 To list all the reasons for or against something is to present an ....

4 Match the definitions with words from *Vocabulary reference: Types of language.*

1 a system of communication often used by people who cannot hear ....
2 communicating how we feel using how we move, how we look and how we behave ....
3 this is used to describe a person who can speak more than two languages equally well ....
4 a language two people share ....
5 this is used to describe a person who can speak two languages equally well ....
6 the language we speak from birth ....

5 Read the passage and find words in *Vocabulary reference: Verbs connected with language* for the underlined phrases.

The secret of ancient Egyptian

In 1799, French soldiers found the Rosetta stone. It was covered in ancient Egyptian writing, or *hieroglyph*, and it was thought that the Rosetta stone held the secret of (1) how the ancient Egyptians spoke their language, but no one knew (2) how their spoken language was written down. Jean-François Champollion was told that nobody could (3) change this ancient writing into another language, but he was determined to discover its secret. He had learnt Coptic – the ancient language of Christian Egyptians – and was so fluent that he could (4) read it aloud. He used Coptic to (5) explain the meaning of the writing on the Rosetta stone and discovered that hieroglyphs were phonetic – an alphabet based on sound.

1 .... 2 .... 3 .... 4 .... 5 ....

Now check your answers. p181

1   Play track 48. Listen to the words in *Vocabulary reference.*

Vocabulary reference

Types of material
natural – wood   rubber   metal   aluminium   gold
fabric – wool   silk   cotton
artificial / man-made – plastic   nylon   glass   steel   leather

Qualities
waterproof   reflective   absorbent   flexible   transparent

Processes with materials
melt   heat   evaporate   condense   destroy   mix   combine   merge   split   cool

2   Read the definitions and complete the crossword using words from *Vocabulary reference: Types of material.*

Across

2   A cloth made from the hair that grows on sheep and some other animals.

4   This material is a valuable yellow-coloured metal.

7   A light, strong material produced by a chemical process, often used to make bags.

10   A very strong metal made from iron.

11   A substance made from the liquid inside a tropical tree.

12   A strong artificial fibre often used to make clothes.

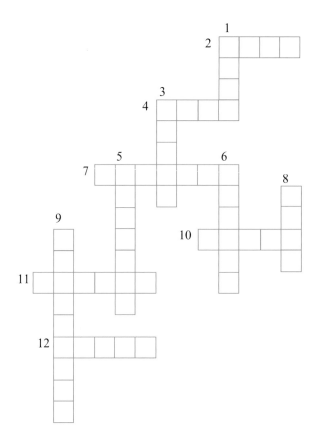

Down

1   Trees are formed from this material.

3   This is a hard, transparent substance used to make windows and bottles.

5   A material made from animal skin.

6   A cloth that is made from the fibres of a plant.

8   A cloth made from a substance produced by a type of worm.

9   A light metal used for making aircraft and computers.

3 Complete the articles using words from *Vocabulary reference: Qualities of materials.*

Scientists have long tried to find an ideal black material that absorbs all the colours of light and is not (1) ...., or does not give off any light back from its surface. Now researchers have created the darkest material ever made by man, which is 99.9% (2) ....of light.

In Japan, scientists have shown their prototype of a glass-like material that they say to be 100% clear, or (3) .... The material also bends and, because it is (4) ...., it can be used to make cables and wires.

Swiss chemists have developed a new material with polyester which they claim is the most (5) ....cloth ever created. Drops of water stay as tiny balls on top of the fabric and roll off it without being absorbed.

4 Complete the descriptions using words from *Vocabulary reference: Processes with materials.* There may be more than one possible answer for some questions.

condense   split   evaporate

Nuclear power divides public opinion: is it an old, dangerous technology or will it save us from global warming? Here's how it works. Water is circulated through the reactor core to absorb the heat that it generates. The heat is generated when the nucleus of a large atom is (1) ...., releasing energy and radiation. The heat from the reaction (2) ....the water and the water vapour is carried to the turbine to create electricity. The steam is then (3) .... by passing it over cool water and is used again.

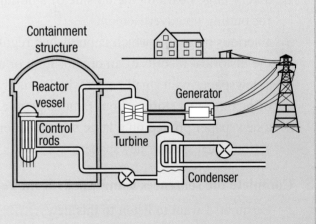

mix   heat   melt   combine   cool   merge   destroy

One of the most important metals is iron. To refine iron, iron ore, charcoal and limestone are (4) .... in a blast furnace. Then the blast furnace is (5) .... to 1,300°C. As the heat (6) .... the raw materials, the calcium in the limestone (7) .... with the iron ore and charcoal to form *slag* – a waste by-product. At the bottom of the blast furnace, liquid iron collects and is taken out periodically and (8) .... Steel can be made by (9) .... or taking out any impurities in the iron. Metal alloys like chrome-moly steel are produced by (10) .... other metals with the steel.

Now check your answers. pp181–182

1 Play Track 49. Listen to the words in *Vocabulary reference.*

Vocabulary reference

Printed media
tabloid   flyer   broadsheet   billboard   archive   journal

Film and television media
trailer   bulletin   broadcast   screening   episode   commercial   channel

People
broadcaster   reporter   viewer   editor   producer   web designer
Disc Jockey (DJ)   camera crew   critic

Verb collocations connected with media
to cover a story   to do an interview   to make the headlines
to launch an advertising campaign   to go on air

2 Match the words in *Vocabulary reference: Printed media* with the definitions.

1 a single sheet of paper which advertises a product or special event and is given
   to a large number of people   ....

2 a very large board on the outside of a building or at the side of a road used
   for putting up advertisements   ....

3 a serious magazine which is published regularly, usually about a specialist subject ....

4 the historical records of an organisation or a place   ....

5 a newspaper with small pages which usually has short articles and contains a lot
   of pictures and stories about famous people   ....

6 a newspaper printed on a large size of paper which is generally considered more
   serious than smaller newspapers   ....

3 Complete the sentences using words from *Vocabulary reference: Film and television media.*

1 Be quiet! I want to listen to this news ....

2 Have you seen the .... advertising the latest Spielberg film? I think it looks really exciting!

3 There are far too many .... on television these days. I hate it when there is a long break for
   advertisements during each programme.

4 There are .... of the film at 3, 5 and 7 pm.

5 Did you see the first .... of that new drama on TV last night? I can't wait to find out what
   happens next.

6 This programme is boring. Let's switch over to a different ....

7 The concert will be .... live tomorrow evening.

4 **Complete the definitions using words from *Vocabulary reference: People*.**

1   A .... presents news and conducts live interviews on television.
2   A .... is a person who watches television.
3   A .... writes reports of events for a television programme or newspaper.
4   An .... corrects and makes changes to texts before they are printed in a newspaper or broadcast on TV.
5   A .... organises the practical and financial matters connected with the production of a film, play or TV programme.
6   A .... creates the look of the pages of an Internet site using programming techniques and Internet tools.
7   A .... is a group of people who operate camera equipment for filming.
8   A .... is someone who plays records and talks on the radio or at an event like a disco, where people dance to music.
9   A .... is someone who judges the quality of something, especially a work of art, literature or music.

5 **Play Track 50. Listen to the extracts and match them with some of the words from *Vocabulary reference: People*.**

1   Extract A   *broadcaster* ....
2   Extract B   ....
3   Extract C   ....
4   Extract D   ....
5   Extract E   ....
6   Extract F   ....

6 **Complete the sentences with the correct form of *Vocabulary reference: Verb collocations connected with media*.**

1   I work on a live radio show so there is always a buzz before I ....
2   As a reporter I can be sent out at a moment's notice to .... It can be anything from a football match to a murder.
3   The scandal .... in newspapers all over the world.
4   My first job as a reporter involved .... with the proud parents of newborn triplets.
5   The government has .... to promote healthy eating among schoolchildren.

Now check your answers. p182

1 🔊 **Play Track 51. Listen to the words in *Vocabulary reference*.**

Vocabulary reference

Money terms
tuition fees   maintenance grant   current account   interest   debit card   overdraft   transactions
direct debit   balance   budget

Verbs connected with money
to set up an account   to check your balance   to pay in cash   to earn an income
to transfer money   to draw up a budget   to take out a loan   to pay back money
to overspend your account   to withdraw money   to be in / go into debt

---

2 **Match the words from *Vocabulary reference: Money terms* with the definitions.**

1 the amount of money that students have to pay in order to attend college
    or university   ....
2 the amount of money you have in your account at any particular time   ....
3 a plastic card which allows you to take money from your account at any time
    of day, including outside banking hours, by using cash machines   ....
4 extra money paid to you on money you have deposited in an account   ....
5 a bank account, with a cheque book, for putting in and taking out money   ....
6 a sum of money that the bank has decided you are allowed to take out of
    your account even when you haven't got any money in there   ....
7 an arrangement for making payments, (e.g. to a gas or electricity company)
    in which your bank moves money from your account into the company's
    account at regular times   ....
8 a sum of money provided to students to help them pay for accommodation
    and living costs   ....
9 a plan to show how much money a person will earn and how much they
    will need or be able to spend   ....
10 amounts of money that are spent regularly   ....

3 **Complete the passage using words from *Vocabulary reference: Money terms*.**

Get answers to these questions before you choose your bank:

- How much (1) .... does the money in your current account earn?
- What is your maximum (2) .... limit? Is it interest-free?
- What are the facilities like, such as the number and location of cash machines? For example, can you use your (3) .... to take out money on campus?
- How easy is it to arrange to pay bills by monthly (4) ....?
- Do they charge you for everyday (5) .... like using cheques or sending you statements which tell you what's happening in your account?
- Do they offer online or telephone banking services so that you can check your (6) .... whenever you want to?

4 Tick the verbs that go with these nouns.

	account	balance	loan	money	interest
to check					
to earn					
to set up					
to transfer					
to pay back					
to overspend					

5 Choose the correct alternatives to complete the passage.

Managing your student loan

It is important to draw up a (1) budget / balance. Making a list of how much you are spending will ensure that you don't go (2) withdrawn / into debt. Some student money advisers argue that the best way to manage your (3) loan / interest is to set up two bank accounts. You can (4) transfer / withdraw the full amount into one of them and then set up a monthly (5) direct debit / overdraft to put money into your (6) current account / tuition fees. This means you will know as soon as you start to (7) overspend / earn. It's definitely worth doing some research into student bank accounts as they are likely to offer interest-free (8) overdrafts / grants.

6 🔊 **Play Track 52. Listen and complete the passage using the correct form of the words from** *Vocabulary reference.*

I have a student (1) .... which pays for my university (2) .... and I have a (3) .... on top of that. This is the money that I have to manage on, on a day-to-day basis. It pays for my accommodation and food. I also have a part-time job and I use that (4) .... to buy other things such as clothes and CDs.

I've actually been very disciplined and careful with my money so far, and regularly (5) .... I keep a note of my (6) .... so that I can keep on top of things. Obviously if I go and get a pizza or something I don't bother writing that down, but if I (7) .... a lot of money, I do keep a note of it so that I know what I spent it on. I know that one day I'll have to (8) .... the loan, but this shouldn't be too much of a problem once I've graduated and got myself a job.

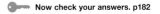 **Now check your answers. p182**

1 🔊 **Play Track 53. Listen to the words in *Vocabulary reference*.**

Vocabulary reference

Decimals

0.75 (zero / nought) point seven five   **2.6** two point six
28.3 twenty-eight point three   **3.657** three point six five seven

---

Percentages

25% twenty-five per cent   **8.56%** eight point five six per cent

---

Fractions

$\frac{1}{2}$ a / one half   **$\frac{1}{4}$** a / one quarter   **$\frac{1}{3}$** a / one third
$\frac{5}{6}$ five-sixths   **$\frac{3}{7}$** three-sevenths   **$\frac{1}{8}$** an / one eighth

---

Mathematical symbols

+ plus / add / and   **–** minus / take away   **x** times / multiplied by   **=** equals / is / is equal to
÷ divided by   **3^2** three squared   **4^3** four cubed   **5^{10}** five to the power of ten
A>B A is greater than B   **A<B** A is less than B

Temperatures

32° C thirty-two degrees Celsius / Centigrade
90° F ninety degrees Fahrenheit
–3° F minus three degrees Fahrenheit

Large numbers

8,567,923 eight million, five hundred and sixty-seven thousand, nine hundred and twenty-three
9,416,892 nine million, four hundred and sixteen thousand, eight hundred and ninety-two
18,576,951 eighteen million, five hundred and seventy-six thousand, nine hundred and fifty-one

---

Metric and imperial weights and measures

length	**liquid measure**
in inch	**fl oz** fluid ounce
cm centimetre	**cm^2** cubic centimetre
ft foot / feet	**gal** gallon
m metre	**lit** litre
yd yard	
km kilometre	
mi mile	

weight	**speed**
oz ounce	**mph** miles per hour
g gram	**kph** kilometres per hour
lb pound	
kg kilogram	
ton	
(metric) tonne	

---

2 Rewrite the percentages as fractions, then write the fractions in words.

1   20% $\frac{1}{5}$ ....   one fifth   4   75%   ....

2   25%   5   80%   ....

3   33.3%   6   90%   ....

3 🔊 Play Track 54. Listen and complete the sentences.

1   One kg is equal to .... lbs.

2   One mile equals .... km.

3   3 cm^3 = ... fl oz.

4   60°F is the same as .... °C.

5   On the Fahrenheit scale, water freezes at ....

6   A gallon of water is equal to .... litres.

4 🔊 Play Track 55. Listen and write the symbols and numbers.

1   6   ....

2   7   ....

3   8   ....

4   9   ....

5   10   ....

5 🔊 Play Track 56. Listen and write how many words it takes to say these numbers. (Count hyphenated words as two numbers, e.g., ninety-eight = two words.)

1   20,482   ....

2   58,926   ....

3   4,000,001   ....

4   10,500,000   ....

5   79,425,672   ....

6 🔊 Play Track 57. Listen to a lecture on uranium production and complete the notes.

World production in (1) .... = (2) .... tonnes

Canada (3) .... tonnes

Australia (4) .... tonnes

Estimated percentage of world resources:

Australia (5) .... (6) nearly ....

Canada (7) ....

China (8) ....

India (9) ....

To produce nuclear warhead:

(10) .... tonnes unprocessed uranium → (11) .... tonnes yellow cake

(12) .... kg weapons-grade uranium (13) ...., or (14) .... kg civil-grade

uranium = (15) .... kwh.

🔑 **Now check your answers. p182**

1 🔘 **Play Track 58. Listen to the words in *Vocabulary reference*.**

Vocabulary reference

Relationships
acquaintance   classmate   girlfriend / boyfriend   friend of a friend   partner   workmate / colleague

Family relationships
immediate family   extended family   brother   sister   father   mother   son   daughter
grandfather   grandmother   uncle   aunt   brother-in-law   cousin   niece   nephew

Describing relationships
take after someone   look like someone   be close to someone   get on (well) with someone
have something in common with someone   get together with someone   see someone

2 **Match the words from *Vocabulary reference: Relationships* with the definitions.**

1   I go to school and college with her. She's my ....
2   We know James very well. In fact, we work in the same building, he's our ....
3   My .... and I have lived together for five years, and we're not married.
4   Lucy's my new ....I only asked her to go out with me last week.
5   I don't know Richard very well. In fact, he's a ....
6   She met Edward only once, very briefly. They see each other sometimes, but they are just ....

3 **Unscramble the letters to complete the family tree.**

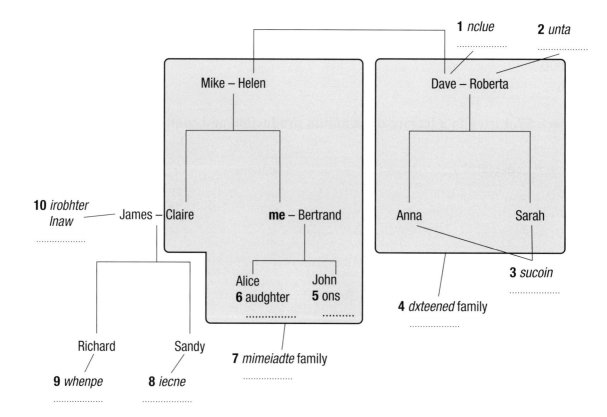

4 Look at the family tree in Activity 3 and complete the passage.

> James is my (1) .... He's married to my (2) .... , Claire – I don't have any brothers. James and Claire have two children – a boy and a girl. Richard is my (3) .... and Sandy is my (4) .... My (5) .... is called Mike and my mother's name is Helen. My mother's brother, my (6) .... , is Dave and my (7) .... is called Roberta. I have two (8) .... , Anna and Sarah, but they live far away and I don't see them often. I've got one (9) .... – his name is John – and my daughter is Alice.

5 Match the phrases from *Vocabulary reference: Describing relationships* with the sentences. There is more than one possible answer for one sentence.

1 What a cute baby, he's got your nose and eyes – he really .... you.
2 Don't you think that Muna .... Julia Roberts? They've got the same hair and she wears similar clothes.
3 Our family is always together – we're very .... to each other.
4 Sara isn't single any more, she's .... Roberto, they .... at a party last week.
5 I think my boss is great, we .... together and I enjoy working for her.
6 We both like rap music and we both support Manchester United – we've got a lot ....

6 (🔊) Play Track 59. Read the Speaking task and the student's notes. Listen and correct the mistakes.

> **Speaking test, part 2 – long turn**
> Describe someone in your family who you like. You should say
> • how this person is related to you
> • what this person looks like
> • what kind of person he / she is
> and explain why you like this person.

Talk about:

~~brother~~-in-law – *father-in-law*

known for 5 years – don't get on with him

my wife looks like her mother – takes after him, serious and sad

unsuccessful business person, never helps people

nothing in common – never get together to play golf and cook

🔑 **Now check your answers. p182**

1 🔊 **Play Track 60. Listen to the words in *Vocabulary reference*.**

Vocabulary reference

> **Activities**
> revise   summarise   paraphrase   plagiarise   note-taking   critical thinking
> references   research   plan   hand / give in

> **University classes**
> seminar   lecture   tutorial   workshop

> **Subjects**
> Agriculture   Biology   Mathematics   Engineering   Pharmacy   Geography
> Archaeology   Management   Psychology   Informatics

2 **Match the words from *Vocabulary reference: Activities* with the definitions.**

1   to give a piece of work to someone to mark   ....
2   to write the main points of a lecture or an article   ....
3   to look for facts to use in a piece of writing or work you are doing   ....
4   to write the title and author of a book you have used in your essay   ....
5   to write something down in words or short sentences   ....
6   to think about both sides of an argument   ....
7   to say someone else's work is your work – to copy   ....
8   to use different words to give the same meaning as the original writer   ....
9   to decide on something and arrange to do it   ....
10 to read your work again to improve your knowledge of a subject, usually to
    prepare for an examination   ....

3 **Complete the paragraph using the correct form of words from *Vocabulary reference: Activities*.**

Our tutor gave us the subject of Operations Management and first of all our group
(1) .... what to do. Then we (2) .... our notes from the tutor's lecture and
(3) .... the references from the lecture in the library and on the Internet. Everyone read
a different article and (4) .... on it. After this we met again and each person
(5) .... their research. A person from another group wanted to copy our work, but
we told him not to (6) .... We (7) .... our work one week early.

4 Match the words from *Vocabulary reference: University classes* with the pictures.

1 .... 2 .... 3 .... 4 ....

5 Cover the words in *Vocabulary reference: Subjects*. Read the definitions and find the words in the word square. (Answers are horizontal → or vertical ↓).

s	i	n	f	o	r	m	a	t	i	c	s
c	c	o	b	m	p	e	o	a	m	i	a
p	g	i	a	a	h	n	h	g	a	e	r
s	e	b	t	n	a	g	r	r	t	p	c
y	o	l	t	a	r	i	r	i	h	a	h
c	g	e	t	g	m	n	r	c	e	i	a
h	r	a	p	e	a	e	i	u	m	r	e
o	a	r	m	m	c	e	h	l	a	s	o
l	p	o	g	e	y	r	n	t	t	a	l
o	h	l	y	n	e	i	e	u	i	a	o
g	y	y	o	t	i	n	b	r	c	m	g
y	b	i	o	l	o	g	y	e	s	m	y

1 the study of cultures of the past, and of periods of history by examining the remains of buildings and objects found in the ground ....
2 the study of how to run and control a business ....
3 the study of electronic equipment, especially computers ....
4 the study of the earth's surface, physical features, divisions, products and population ....
5 the study of how to prepare medicines and drugs ....
6 the activity of applying scientific knowledge to the design, building and control of machines, roads, bridges and electrical equipment ....
7 the science of numbers and shapes ....
8 the scientific study of the life and structure of plants and animals ....
9 the science or practice of farming ....
10 the scientific study of the mind and how it influences behaviour ....

Now check your answers. pp182–183

1 🔊 **Play Track 61. Listen to the words in** *Vocabulary reference.*

Vocabulary reference

Team sports
football / soccer   rugby   baseball   basketball
volleyball   cricket   hockey   cycling   rowing

Other sports
(table) tennis   badminton   golf   gymnastics
swimming   diving   boxing   skiing   ice-skating

Martial arts
judo   karate   kendo   kung fu

Places
football / rugby / baseball / cricket pitch
tennis / badminton / volleyball / basketball court
hockey field   running / cycling track   swimming / diving pool   boxing ring
golf course   ski slope   gym   ice-skating rink

People
football – manager   referee   coach   captain   linesman / lineswoman
tennis – umpire   ball-boy / girl
cricket – team   batsman   bowler   fielder   captain

2 **Match the equipment with the sport.**

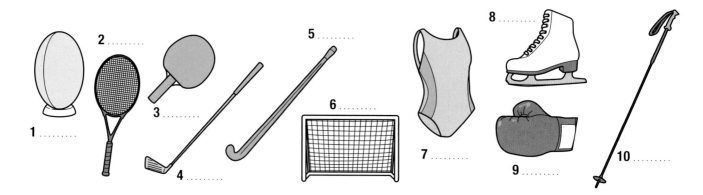

3 **Complete the sentences using words from** *Vocabulary references: Places* **and** *People.*

1 In cricket, the .... on the .... try to catch the ball to get the .... out.

2 In tennis, if the ball goes out of the ...., the .... calls it out and the
   .... announces the score.

3 Football and rugby .... are trained by a .... The .... is on the
   .... with the teams to ensure they are playing by the rules.

4 When a team wins a competition, the .... receives the trophy on behalf of the team.

4 **Use your dictionary to find which word is the odd one out in each group.**

1 Golf: tee, hole, bat, club, links

2 Tennis: court, track, net, umpire, racket

3 Swimming: pool, lane, goggles, saddle, crawl
4 Football: pitch, team, stick, goal, kick
5 Boxing: ring, ropes, corner, round, team
6 Gymnastics: rings, court, beam, horse, balance
7 Cricket: over, under, wicket, bowl, innings
8 Hockey: stick, net, player, team, slope
9 Skiing: snow, piste, pool, pole, slope
10 Martial arts: ju-jitsu, belt, dan, trunks, master

5 Which sports are shown in these photos?

1 ....
2 ....
3 ....
4 ....
5 ....
6 ....

6 Choose the correct verb to complete the sentences.

1 Which team are you going to .... in the World Cup final: Poland or Argentina?
   A have   B like   C play   D support

2 If you want to get fit and lose weight, you should .... running.
   A go off   B take up   C take out   D get on

3 He .... football every Saturday in the park.
   A plays   B does   C makes   D gets

4 If they score one more goal, they're going to .... the championship!
   A lose   B win   C draw   D miss

5 The swimming team .... every evening to prepare for the Olympics.
   A study   B rehearse   C play   D train

6 My aunt is 84, but she still .... swimming in the sea every day.
   A plays   B goes   C does   D makes

7 Manchester United were .... by three goals to two last night.
   A won   B lost   C defeated   D drawn

8 If you don't improve your speed and fitness, you're going to .... the fight.
   A lose   B surrender   C defeat   D mislay

Now check your answers. p183

1 🔊 **Play Track 62. Listen to the words in *Vocabulary reference*.**

Vocabulary reference

Types of holiday camping package self-catering cruise backpacking adventure safari city break beach luxury eco-tourism	**Transport – land** car caravan campervan bus / coach train / rail tram trolleybus funicular bicycle motorbike taxi lorry / truck underground / tube
Transport – sea ship liner / cruise ship hovercraft ferry hydrofoil jet-ski yacht speedboat tanker container ship	**Transport – air** (aero)plane helicopter balloon rocket microlight Zeppelin

Travel – places motorway   airport   railway / coach / bus / tram station   bus / tram stop service station   helicopter pad   docks   port

2 **Match these vocabulary groups with words from *Vocabulary reference: Types of holiday*.**

1 bikini, sunscreen, lounger, tan, sunburn ....

2 market, kitchen, cooking, washing-up, cutlery ....

3 tent, pitch, sleeping bag, open air, groundsheet ....

4 gap year, rucksack, hostel, student, guide book ....

5 five-star, en-suite, comfort, spa, gourmet ....

6 deck, captain, seasick, porthole, gangway ....

7 wildlife, Land Rover, binoculars, tracking, guide ....

8 all-inclusive, economical, unimaginative, wristband, group ....

9 museums, art galleries, weekend, cinemas, crowds ....

10 green, environment, ethical, rainforest, politically correct ....

3 **Think of five things you might do on an adventure holiday.**

1 ....   2 ....   3 ....   4 ....   5 ....

4 🔊 **Play Track 63. Listen to the dialogue again and complete the sentences using words from the box.**

got in   ride   called   adventure   hire   rode   missed   take   got off   catch fare   get on   fell off   go on   caught

1 Jenny and Susie decided to .... an .... holiday.

2 They planned to .... the bus, then .... a train.

3 They wanted to .... bicycles, then .... them to the hostel.

4 The bus was so full that they couldn't .... , so they .... a taxi.

5 When the taxi arrived, they .... but the traffic was bad so they .... the train.

6   The taxi .... was very expensive.

7   They .... the next train and .... at Windermere.

8   They .... their bikes to the hostel, but they .... a few times on the way.

5   **Complete the passage using words from *Vocabulary reference: Travel – places*.**

Holiday delays

If you are going on holiday this Summer, be prepared to spend a large proportion of your break getting there! Results from a recent survey show that delays are an inevitable part of the trip. If you are driving to the (1) .... to catch a plane, there will probably be a traffic jam on the (2) .... And if you stop for petrol, you'll find a queue at the (3) .... too.

It's no better if you take a ferry. Strikes often mean there are hold-ups at the (4) .... Travelling by train is a good way of avoiding the traffic, but you are still likely to spend time waiting at the (5) .... , so take a good book to read.

It seems the only way to be sure of a delay-free holiday is to fly in your private jet or take off from your own (6) .... !

6   **Which types of travel can these words be used for: (A) both sea and air, (B) only sea, (C) only air, or (D) neither?**

1 cabin	....	
2 pilot	....	
3 fuselage	....	
4 spoke	....	
5 bridge	....	
6 crew	....	
7 undercarriage	....	
8 deck	....	
9 helmet	....	
10 galley	....	

7   **Match the words from Activity 6 with their meanings.**

1   staff   ....

2   kitchen   ....

3   part of a bike wheel   ....

4   floor   ....

5   room   ....

6   landing gear   ....

7   outside of a plane   ....

8   control area in a ship   ....

9   hard hat   ....

10 someone who flies a plane ....

Now check your answers. p183

1 🔘 **Play Track 64. Listen to the words in *Vocabulary reference*.**

Vocabulary reference

Positive characteristics, feelings and attitudes
appreciative   cheerful   co-operative   enthusiastic   generous   even-tempered   industrious
kind   optimistic   respectful   sensible   sympathetic

Negative characteristics, feelings and attitudes
rebellious   moody   insensitive   cruel   ungrateful   selfish   pessimistic   idle   miserable
passive   impulsive   stubborn

---

2 **Complete the definitions using words from *Vocabulary reference: Positive characteristics, feelings and attitudes*.**

1   behaving in a way that shows you care about other people   ....
2   a person who does not behave too emotionally   ....
3   being able to understand how others feel   ....
4   being grateful for things others do for you   ....
5   always hoping for the best   ....
6   not doing silly things   ....
7   able to share with others   ....
8   someone who often seems happy or positive   ....
9   being good at working with other people   ....
10 someone who works hard   ....
11 a person who is full of energy and interested in things   ....
12 feeling that someone or something is important   ....

3 **Match the words in Activity 2 with their negatives from *Vocabulary reference: Negative characteristics, feelings and attitudes*.**

1   kind   cruel   7   ....
2   8   ....
3   9   ....
4   ....   10 ....
5   ....   11 ....
6   ....   12 ....

4 **Decide which words from *Vocabulary reference: Positive characteristics, feelings and attitudes* can be made negative using a prefix *un-* or *dis-*.**

1   5   ....
2   6   ....
3   7   ....
4   8   ....

5 Write the nouns for the adjectives.

adjective	noun
ungrateful	(1) ....
idle	(2) ....
moody	(3) ....
cheerful	(4) ....
Group 1: nouns ending with	**(5)** ....
cruel	(6) ....
sympathetic	(7) ....
insensitive	(8) ....
generous	(9) ....
Group 2: nouns ending with	**(10)** .... **or** ....
egotistic	(11) ....
optimistic	(12) ....
pessimistic	(13) ....
Group 3: nouns ending with	**(14)** ....
rebellious	(15) ....
appreciative	(16) ....
co-operative	(17) ....
Group 4: nouns ending with	**(18)** .... **or** ....

6 🔊 **Play Track 65. Listen and complete the passage using words from** *Vocabulary reference.*

ADOLESCENCE

What happened when our loving and (1) .... child turned 13? Where did our (2) .... and (3) .... child go – and who is that (4) .... person in their place? Today I'm going to talk briefly about teenage behaviour. The good news is that it doesn't last long. Studies show that (5) .... behaviour in boys begins at 13, peaks at 17, and by early adulthood most of it has stopped completely. Teenagers are often (6) .... because, although they are physically adult, their brains are not mature enough to think in a (7) .... way. This means that they become frustrated that they are not allowed to do all the things that adults do.

7 🔊 **Play Track 66. Listen and complete the dialogue using words from** *Vocabulary reference.*

Examiner: So, Mina, you've told me about your best friend. Now I'm going to ask you about friends in general. What do you think are the most important qualities for friends to have?

Candidate: For me, the most important things are for friends to be (1) .... and (2) .... They help you if you have problems, so they need to be (3) .... I like people who are (4) .... It's just depressing to be around people who are (5) .... about life. I don't like people who are (6) ...., either.

🔑 **Now check your answers. p183**

1 Play Track 67. Listen to the words in *Vocabulary reference*.

Vocabulary reference

Referring to work	**Work positions**
career vocation occupation profession	trainee labourer consultant director executive

Types of work	**Collocations connected with *work***
service / construction / tourism / heavy industry full- / part-time casual flexitime job share	work with / on / through / for / as

Finding work
application (form) CV (curriculum vitae) job hunt interview
salary vacancy hire contract recruitment (agency)

Stopping work
(to be made) redundant (to be) unemployed
(to be) sacked / fired industrial action / strike (action)
resign / quit (maternity) leave

Use it for IELTS!
In part 1 of the Speaking test, the examiner may ask you about your current work situation.

2 **Match the words from *Vocabulary reference: Referring to work* with the definitions.**

1 a job done for a long period of a person's life   ....
2 a job that involves long training and qualifications   ....
3 a formal word for 'job'   ....
4 a strong feeling of suitability for a particular career or occupation ....

3 **Complete the sentences using words from *Vocabulary reference: Work positions*.**

1 After an accident at the company, they asked an expert for his opinion on safety at the building. The safety .... took two months to complete his report.
2 An .... at Hong Kong Telecom will join the Government's Policy Unit from next month. Lee Yang leaves a senior management position at Hong Kong Telecom.
3 The public relations agency, *Urgency*, asked Abdul Aziz to be account .... with responsibility for the finance department.
4 John does really heavy work during the holidays – he works on a building site as a ....
5 People joining us have a training period of six months to learn about how our company works. So first you join us as a .... employee.

4 **Complete the sentences using words from *Vocabulary reference: Types of work*.**

1 I only work two and a half days a week, I work ....
2 She works in reception in a hotel. She works in the ....
3 People who organise their own working hours work ....
4 A telesales worker calls people and sells products – they work in the ....
5 Someone working five days a week, 9 am – 5 pm, works ....
6 A builder works in the ....
7 I only work during the half-term and Summer holidays. My work is ....

8   James is a steel worker. He works in ....

9   Elaine and Mohammed divide the work of one job, they do a ....

5 **Read the student's Speaking task response and choose the correct alternatives.**

Last year I was working (1) as / for / with / through / at a sales assistant in a supermarket.
The supermarket I worked (2) as / for / with / through / at was Tesco – I did quite a lot of things there
– I worked (3) as / for / with / through / at the checkout and later worked (4) as / for / with / through
the orders for the supermarket. It was a nice job to have for a while. I was working (5) as / for / with /
through some nice people and I worked all (6) as / for / with / through / at the Summer.

6 **Complete the explanations using *as*, *at*, *for*, *with* or *through*.**

1   We work .... someone.
2   We work .... a period of time or a problem.
3   We work .... an organisation.
4   We work .... a place.

7 **Play Track 68. Listen and number the words from *Vocabulary reference: Finding work* in the order you hear them.**

A application (form) ☐   **F** vacancy ☐
B CV (curriculum vitae) ☐   **G** hire ☐
C job hunt ☐   **H** contract ☐
D interview ☐   **I** recruitment (agency) ☐
E salary ☐

8 **Match words from *Vocabulary reference*: *Stopping work* with the definitions.**

1   to take time away from work for a holiday or to have a baby   ....
2   to have no job   ....
3   to lose your job, often because there is not enough work   ....
4   to lose your job because you aren't good at it   ....
5   to stop working, often for better pay or conditions   ....
6   to leave your job   ....

9 **Complete the newspaper stories using words from *Vocabulary reference*: *Stopping work*.**

1 **250 made .... as factory closes**

2 **Number of .... rises to 1.5 million**

3 **Politician .... by Prime Minister after sex scandal**

4 **.................. to be taken by Railway Workers' Union**

5 **Executive of the year .... to join rival firm.**

Now check your answers. p183

Activity 1

1 shows   2 gives   3 represents   4 demonstrates   5 is rising
6 is falling 7 has risen   8 has dropped   9 has remained
10 has stayed

For more help with present tenses, do Units 1 and 2.

Activity 2

1   correct
2   ~~I've listened~~ → I've been listening / ~~have you listened~~ → have you been listening
3   ~~have got~~ → have been getting
4   correct
5   ~~are pushing~~ → have been pushing

For more help with present perfect and present perfect continuous, do Units 4 and 5.

Activity 3

1 is shipped   2 is performed   3 tests   4 is tested
5 has been implemented   6 are integrated   7 is working
8 checks   9 is often done   10 are released

For more help with passives, do Units 6, 7 and 15.

Activity 4

1 was studying / was having   2 was leaving / had left / remembered   3 was orbiting / landed   4 didn't / see / crashed / wasn't watching   5 realised / was waiting

For more help with past simple and past continuous, do Units 10 and 11.

Activity 5

1 dropped   2 had taught   3 thought   4 were not
5 had... thought   6 had proposed   7 had discovered
8 expressed

For more help with past perfect, do Unit 12.

Activity 6

1 'm going to do   2 'm going to see   3 will it take   4 are due to be   5 'm not about to miss 6 'll join   7 're going to take   8 'll try

For more help with *will* and *going to / due to / about to,* do Units 16 and 17.

Activity 7

1 will have visited / will visit   2 will have prescribed
3 will be practising   4 will be working   5 will have increased / risen   6 will have risen / increased

For more help with future continuous and future perfect, do Units 18 and 19.

Activity 8

2   You have to fill in an application form.
3   You shouldn't sleep so much.
4   Ann could speak four languages.
5   Marc should apply for a part-time job.
6   Sarah couldn't get home early.
7   Paul couldn't believe it when he saw the results of his test.
8   To get a driving licence, you have to take a written test.

For more help with modal verbs, do Units 20–24.

Activity 9

1 can   2 May / Can   3 might / may   4 can't   5 can   6 can
7 might / may   8 might / may   9 can't   10 may / might

For more help with modal verbs, do Units 20–24.

Activity 10

1 expensivest → most expensive   2 cheap → cheapest
3 most priciest → priciest   4 live in is → live in as
5 more cheap → cheaper   6 Furtherer → Further
7 least expensive → less expensive   8 costlier → costly
9 most least expensive → least expensive   10 lesser → less

For more help with comparatives and superlatives, do Units 25 and 26.

Activity 11

1 too much   2 too much   3 too much   4 enough   5 too many

For more help with comparatives and superlatives, do Units 25 and 26.

Activity 12

1 doesn't leave / will miss   2 works / will pass   3 are / take
4 are / avoid   5 doesn't practise / will not (won't) improve
6 will be / arrive   7 see / will give

For more help with zero and first conditionals, do Units 27 and 28.

Activity 13

1 ~~would meet~~ → met   2 ~~have~~ → had   3 ~~will~~ go → would go
4 ~~am you~~ → were you   5 ~~Would you still gone~~ → Would you have still gone   6 ~~you sorry~~ → you be sorry   7 ~~wouldn't break~~ → wouldn't have broken   8 ~~missed~~ → miss

For more help with second and third conditionals, do Units 29 and 30.

Activity 14

1 denied   2 told me   3 persuaded me   4 advised me
5 warned me   6 announced

For more help with reported speech, do Units 31 and 32.

Activity 15

2   Steve, whose car was stolen, went to the police.
3   A friend, who met me at the station, carried my bags.
4   The food that Rachel cooked was delicious.
5   A friend who comes from Paris is staying with Peter.
6   The man whose wallet I found gave me £10.

For more help with relative clauses, do Units 33 and 34.

Activity 16

1 brush up   2 looking up   3 look back   4 pick out   5 come across
6 pick up   7 work out   8 looking for

For more help with multi-word verbs, do Unit 40.

Unit A1

Activity 1
1 Diagram B   2 Diagram A   3 Diagram C

Activity 2
14

Activity 3
1 is changing   2 is warming   3 agree   4 is causing   5 are dying
6 are diminishing   7 are (governments) doing   8 are discussing
9 are not co-operating

Activity 4
1 believe (stative verb)   2 is (this) happening   3 are causing
4 are hunting   5 are selling   6 is increasing   7 are disappearing
8 are not adapting   9 are poisoning   10 is resulting
11 are developing

Activity 5
1 is studying   2 (is) working   3 is hoping   4 is joining
5 is enjoying   6 is having

Unit A2

Activity 1
1 work   2 sleep   3 sport and leisure   4 other activities
5 meals/eating   6 care for others

Activity 2
shows   spends   is divided   are   work   sleep   take part   do
do not take   eat   drink   do   care

Activity 3
1 spend   2 shows / gives   3 gives / shows   4 watch   5 don't read
6 listen   7 don't write   8 use

Activity 4
1 covers   2 crosses   3 contains   4 has   5 support   6 represents
7 are cutting   8 are growing

Activity 5
1 Engineering   2 10 am   3 lectures   4 tutorial   5 supervises
6 attends

Unit A3

Activity 1
1 B   2 C   3 C

Activity 2
1 C   2 D   3 A   4 B

Activity 3
1 E   2 D   3 A   4 F   5 B   6 C

Activity 4
1 try to   2 Always   3 never   4 Put   5 make sure   6 close
7 notify   8 Have   9 Remember   10 Don't forget

Activity 5
1 book   2 keep   3 ask for   4 give   5 check   6 don't get in   7 sit
8 ask

Unit A4

Activity 1
1 southeast Asia   2 Oceania   3 North America

Activity 2
The bar chart shows how numbers of people moving to Australia from nine different regions <u>have changed</u> in the past ten years. Overall, there <u>has been</u> a decrease in immigration. Numbers from Europe, southeast and northeast Asia <u>have fallen</u> sharply. Additionally, immigration from India, the Middle East and North America <u>has gone down</u> slightly. <u>Have any regions shown</u> an increase? Numbers from Oceania and Africa <u>have not fallen</u>; in fact, numbers from Africa <u>have more than doubled</u> over the past ten years.

Activity 3
1 have risen, since   2 has fallen, more   3 have moved   4 has not changed   5 Fewer, have left

Activity 4

	Candidate A (female)	Candidate B (male)
Send application form	✓	✓
Receive confirmation		✓
Find passport		✓
Watch speaking test video	✓	
Do practice test	✓	✓
Buy alarm clock		✓

Activity 5
1 questions, negative   2 positive / affirmative

Activity 6
1 Have (you) booked   2 yet   3 have bought   4 have applied
5 hasn't arrived / come   6 haven't packed   7 yet   8 haven't done
9 have checked   10 haven't called   11 yet

Activity 7
1 Have you tried   2 have measured   3 have done   4 has grown
5 have followed   6 has risen   7 have heated

Activity 8
1 have taken / was   2 have finished   3 didn't eat / have had
4 has filled in   5 Have you done   6 rained / has been
7 must have drunk   8 has gone   9 I've written   10 has dropped

Activity 9
2   Police have arrested a bank robber who has stolen £30 million.
3   A damaged aircraft has landed safely. 200 people have survived unhurt.
4   The Prime Minister has been caught in a love triangle. He has offered to resign immediately.

Unit A5
1 B   2 C   3 C

Activity 2
6

Activity 3
1 have been recycling   2 have been paying   3 has been buying
4 has been bringing   5 have been commuting

Activity 4
1 A i, B ii   2 A ii, B i   3 A i, B ii   4 A i, B ii   5 A ii, B i

Activity 5
1 haven't been feeling   2 have been hurting   3 hasn't been working   4 have been avoiding   5 haven't been going   6 haven't been eating

Activity 6

1 she been crying   2 he been working   3 she been sunbathing
4 have you been doing   5 has been tidying up

Unit A6

Activity 1

1 C   2 C   3 B

Activity 2

Coffee is the second largest export in the world after oil and around two billion cups <u>are consumed</u> every day, making it the world's favourite drink. Where <u>is coffee grown</u>? Two-thirds of the world's coffee supply <u>is produced</u> in Central and South America and one third <u>is grown</u> in Brazil. Large amounts of coffee <u>are also grown</u> in Indonesia, Colombia and Vietnam. Worldwide six million metric tonnes of coffee <u>are produced</u> in countries within 1,600 kilometres of the equator – it <u>isn't produced</u> in colder countries. It takes 4,000 coffee beans to make half a kilo of coffee and 60–70 beans <u>are used</u> to make an espresso.

Activity 3

1 are picked   2 are dried   3 (are) separated   4 are sorted
5 are bagged

Activity 4

1 When are coffee beans picked?   2 How are coffee cherries harvested?   3 How are the beans sorted?   4 How are the beans transported?

Activity 5

1 They are picked when they are bright red.   2 They are harvested by hand.   3 They are sorted according to size and weight.
4 They are transported in large containers.

Activity 6

1 are harvested / have been harvested   2 are roasted   3 are heated
4 turn   5 is turned down   6 occurs   7 is produced

Unit A7

Activity 1

1 cleaned   2 washed   3 soaked   4 preserved   5 sealed
6 labelled   7 boxed   8 stored

Activity 2

(a) present passive: fish are tinned   they are cleaned   they are washed and soaked   they must be preserved   the tins are sealed   labels are put on   ready to be put in a box ... and stored.
(b) present perfect passive: they have been caught   they have been cleaned   they have not been cooked   they have been put in tins   the labels have been put on   Why have the fish been tinned?

Activity 3

1 is collected   2 has been taken   3 is put   4 have been cancelled
5 be sorted   6 has been done   7 are delivered   8 has been addressed

Activity 4

1 Alien life **has** been discovered on the planet Europa.
2 46 species of butterfly **have disappeared** because of global warming.   3 Correct   4 This book **was written** by our Professor of Chemistry in 2001.   5 Correct   6 The classrooms have not **been** cleaned properly this term.   7 30 kilos of potatoes **are eaten** in the canteen every day.   8 Correct

Activity 5

1 B, E   2 A, D   3 C, F

Unit A8

Activity 1

1 FALSE   2 TRUE   3 NOT GIVEN   4 TRUE

Activity 2

1 are having (active)   2 looks (stative)   3 am looking (active)
4 has (stative)

Activity 3

1 I   2 C   3 C   4 I   5 C   6 C   7 I   8 C

Activity 4

1 I see what you mean.   4 This curry tastes delicious.
7 This material feels very soft.

Activity 5

1 B   2 C   3 A

Activity 6

dies – intransitive   loses – transitive   replaced – transitive   hunting – transitive   killing – transitive   lived – intransitive   visited – transitive   found – transitive   had – transitive   walked – intransitive   hunted – transitive   ate – transitive   changed – transitive

Activity 7

1 intransitive   2 transitive   3 intransitive   4 transitive

Unit A9

Activity 1

1 C   2 C   3 D (duck)

Activity 2

I like my food. I particularly like duck and eat it <u>regularly</u>, <u>usually</u> with a green salad. I <u>hardly ever</u> eat pasta and I <u>never</u> go near fried potatoes. I've <u>always</u> been a big fan of Asian cooking. I've loved spicy food for as long as I can remember! I <u>normally</u> have fruit for breakfast. It's just become part of my diet over the past few years. I <u>generally</u> mix cereal into that and eat it with milk but <u>occasionally</u> I'll add some yoghurt and honey. I like to relax with a glass of champagne on a Saturday evening. Well, we all need a treat <u>sometimes</u> and it is only <u>once a week!</u> I love barbecues but they <u>generally</u> only work well in warm weather. Climate-wise, Australia is good for barbecues. When the weather gets warm, it's <u>usually</u> one of the first things we do here. People <u>frequently</u> assume that it's all about throwing a prawn on the barbecue at the beach. I don't know if you have <u>ever</u> tried to fry food on a beach but the sand gets everywhere. The reality <u>rarely</u> lives up to the exotic image!

Activity 3

1 often, normally   2 rarely   3 ever   4 generally   5 once a week
6 frequently   7 never   8 don't often

Activity 4

1 never, always   2 sometimes / occasionally, often   3 often
4 never   5 usually / generally / normally, sometimes / occasionally
6 once a week / often, regularly   7 always

Unit A10

Activity 1

1 FALSE   2 NOT GIVEN   3 FALSE

Activity 2

In 2008, the largest users of oil were the US and Canada. They used almost three gallons of oil per day per person, which was double that of other industrial countries and six times that of the rest of the world.

So how did the north American countries use this oil? Figure 2 shows US oil consumption by sector. The biggest demand for oil came from transport; in 2008 this was almost two thirds of the total. The next largest user was the industrial sector, which accounted for 24% of the total. Surprisingly, the US did not consume as much oil to produce electricity as they did for industry.

Activity 3

1 attended   2 passed   3 travelled   4 planned   5 decided
6 studied   7 graduated

Activity 4

1 grew   2 went up   3 had   4 was   5 saw   6 rose

Activity 5

1 did / have – caught   2 did / travel – took   3 Were / born – was
4 did / go – graduated   5 did / take – studied / didn't like / changed

Unit A11

Activity 1

1 four / 4   2 four / 4   3 twenty-two / 22   4 fourteen / 14

Activity 2

I remember that day so clearly. I was skiing in Switzerland. I was living there at the time. It was a bright, clear day. It was about four o'clock in the afternoon. There was no warning. It was instant. Suddenly I was curled up in a ball doing somersaults. Then it was over and I was buried in snow. It was totally dark. My mouth was packed with snow. The pressure was so intense that it was hard to breathe. I didn't know which direction was up. I believed I was going to die. Luckily I was covering my face when it happened. I cleared the snow out of my mouth with my fingers. And then I panicked. I didn't think I was going to survive. I was screaming. I was crying. The tears were flowing. And then I noticed that all the tears were running across my face. I realised that I was lying in an upside down and backwards position. That was a real moment of truth. I knew that I had to get out. I moved my hands around which gave me a bit more room. Then I got my upper body loose and I started digging. I made a little game out of it. I counted to four and then reached out to grab a handful of snow. And then I pushed it all down to my feet and stamped on it. I was digging for twenty-two hours before I finally got out. It was another fourteen hours before I heard the sound of the rescue team coming towards me.

Activity 3

Picture D

Activity 4

1 was skiing, happened   2 remembered   3 didn't think
4 didn't know   5 realised, were running   6 was digging, arrived

Activity 5

1 Was he skiing, struck   2 was he living   3 didn't understand / was lying in   4 He felt frightened   5 He didn't see   6 It took / came
7 Did he hear / approached

Unit A12

Activity 1

1 FALSE   2 TRUE   3 TRUE   4 NOT GIVEN   5 TRUE

Activity 2

1 B   2 C   3 A

Activity 3

I graduated in 2002 with 1st class honours. My friend Anna decided to have a surprise party to celebrate, but she didn't tell me. She invited all my friends, then she booked a large room at the Grand Hotel. She even ordered a stretch limousine to take me there. Imagine my surprise when it turned up at my door! I got dressed up very quickly - but I still didn't know where I was going. When we arrived at the hotel, my friends came out to meet me. We laughed and danced all night long.

Activity 4

1 graduated   2 decided   3 didn't tell   4 invited   5 booked
6 ordered   7 turned up   8 got dressed up   9 didn't know
10 arrived   11 came out   12 laughed   13 danced

Activity 5

1 turned up   2 had ordered   3 got dressed up   4 didn't know
5 arrived   6 came   7 had invited   8 had graduated
9 had decided   10 hadn't told   11 had booked   12 laughed
13 danced

Activity 6

1 talked / hadn't seen   2 rang / realised / had forgotten
3 did the police arrest / had he done   4 had prepared / served

Unit A13

Activity 1

1 2000   2 4%   3 12%   4 8%   5 2005   6 2008   7 10%

Activity 2

1 exports from China   2 exports from America   3 as many goods as America

Activity 3

1 'd been working   2 changed   3 'd been thinking   4 found
5 'd been doing

Activity 4

2 It hadn't been investing in new products.   3 She hadn't been working hard enough.   4 She hadn't been listening to the instructions.   5 He hadn't been watching it.

Activity 5

1 has been increasing   2 had been fluctuating   3 had been rising
4 had been decreasing   5 have been rising / increasing   6 rose / increased   7 has / produced

Unit A14

Activity 1

C, E

Activity 2

Reading a book or an article used to be so easy for me. I would get fully involved in the narrative. In fact, I used to love reading long texts but I don't now. After reading two or three pages my concentration starts to drift. I never used to think like this. I didn't use to have a problem with deep reading, but recently I've been spending a lot of time online, surfing the Internet. Research that in the past would require days searching through books can now be done in minutes. But when I'm reading online, I'm 'power browsing' instead of deep reading in the way I used to.

A recent study of online habits suggests that new ways of reading are emerging. Researchers found that users would hop from one source to another and that they wouldn't necessarily go on to read texts that they had saved. The style of reading promoted by the Internet may be weakening our capacity to think; to interpret text and to make the mental connections that form when we read books and other printed material.

Activity 3
1 C   2 A   3 B   4 A   5 A   6 B   7 B

Activity 4
1 I   2 C   3 C   4 I   5 I   6 I

Activity 5
1 *I used to* read much more as a child than I do now.   4 Even as a child she *wouldn't* put down a book until she had finished it.
5 It *used to* take ages for him to find all the information he needed but now it takes only a few seconds.   6 Do you think people generally read less nowadays than they *used to?*

Activity 6
1 didn't use to buy   2 used to take / would take
3 used to be   4 used to make / would make
5 Didn't we use to study   6 didn't use to be

Unit A15

Activity 1
1 cereal   2 magnet   3 crushed cereal   4 specks of iron

Activity 2
The diagram shows the stages of an experiment for removing iron from flakes of breakfast cereal. Firstly, a beaker was filled with water and some cornflakes were put on top. After that, a magnet was put in the water and the cereal moved towards it, showing that there was iron in it. At the next stage, some cereal was crushed into a powder with a mortar and pestle. The powder was spread on a piece of paper, and the paper was moved over a magnet. Specks of iron in the powder were attracted to the magnet, which could then be removed from the cereal.

Activity 3
1 was used   2 were mixed   3 was placed   4 was poured
5 remained   6 passed   7 was put   8 was placed   9 was heated
10 evaporated   11 left   12 was allowed

Activity 4
1 Care was taken when the chemicals were mixed.   2 The class was shown how to use a Bunsen burner.   3 Science was chosen by all the boys as their favourite subject.   4 An experiment must / has to be described in the Chemistry exam.

Activity 5
1 was made   2 was mixed   3 was heated / was stirred
4 was stirred / was heated   5 separated   6 was filtered
7 were dried   8 was added   9 were stirred   10 was tested

Unit A16

Activity 1
1 young people   2 sense of responsibility   3 expect

Activity 2
will happen   will not be   will become   will be   Will... become
will... become

Activity 3
1 will be   2 will work   3 will be   4 will have / do
5 won't / will not work   6 will be   7 will have   8 will need
9 won't / will not use   10 will be   11 won't / will not be

Activity 4
1 d   2 a   3 c   4 e   5 b

Activity 5
1 I'll go   2 she'll bring   3 I'll have   4 it won't / will not   5 I'll lift

Activity 6
1 offer   2 promise   3 quick decision   4 promise   5 offer

Unit A17

Activity 1
C, E

Activity 2
Clocks around the world are about to change. The world's official timekeepers are going to add a single second or leap second to atomic clocks on Wednesday, the last day of the year. This will be the 24th leap second since 1972, when the practice began. It is going to be the first leap second since 2005.

The move will help match clocks to the Earth's slowing spin on its axis. Because of tidal friction and other natural phenomena, that rotation is slowing down by about two-thousandths of a second a day. The extra second is due to be added in coordination with the world's atomic clocks on New Year's Eve at 23 hours 59 minutes and 59 seconds Co-ordinated Universal Time or UTC. This is the timescale kept by the highly precise atomic clocks around the world.

In today's digital world, the smooth operation of everything from cash machines to the Internet depends on the exactly timed transmission of electronic data. Leap seconds can crash mobile phones and computer networks. However, the passing of the leap second on the 31st December won't make much of a difference to most people. We're not going to notice it.

Activity 3
1 about to be changed   2 going to do   3 going to notice
4 about to change   5 isn't going to crash   6 going to be

Activity 4
1 C   2 I   3 I   4 C   5 I   6 I   7 I

Activity 5
1 Are you **going to go / going** to the shops later? Can you get some bread?
2 The train **is due to leave** in five minutes.
3 When are you **due to take** your driving test?
4 I'm just **about to** sneeze!
5 When is the meeting **due to** finish?

Unit A18

Activity 1
1 a student   2 in a restaurant   3 waiting on tables   4 working / mixing the drinks   5 as a barman   6 as a waiter   7 from tips

Activity 2
1 will (still) be playing   2 will be doing   3 won't be playing   4 will be flying   5 will be taking part   6 will be moving   7 will be developing   8 will be breaking

Activity 3
1 D   2 B   3 E   4 A   5 F   6 C

Unit A19

Activity 1
1 TRUE   2 NOT GIVEN   3 FALSE

Activity 2
4: work, population growth, multinational companies, news

Activity 3
1 I will have been in Australia for one year before I see you next Summer.
2 Tahiye will have completed her Masters when / by the time she is 28 years old.
3 Hsio Wen will have lost 5 kilos by the time / when Summer arrives.
4 A lot of things will have happened before we meet again.
5 They will have repaired your computer when / by the time you return to the shop.
6 We will have been in business for two years before we start making a profit.

Activity 4
1 Where will you have been for one year?
2 When will she have completed her Masters?
3 How many kilos will she have lost?
4 What will have happened (before we meet again)?
5 When will they have repaired your computer?
6 How long will we have been in business before we start making a profit?

Activity 5
1 will have become   2 will have grown   3 will have reached   4 will not have increased   5 will have increased   6 will have become

Unit A20

Activity 1
A i   B ii   C v

Activity 2
1 rule   2 rule   3 permission   4 permission   5 rule

Activity 3
1 have to   2 must / has to   3 don't have to   4 must   5 mustn't

Activity 4
1 prove   2 passport   3 bags and coats   4 anything valuable   5 a dictionary   6 switch off   7 candidates   8 questions   9 transfer   10 any part of

Activity 5
1 are required   2 have to   3 can   4 are not allowed   5 must   6 can't   7 must not   8 may not   9 may not   10 have to   11 are not to   12 have to

Unit A21

Activity 1
1 more attractive, cheaper land   2 more convenient, children from school could use it, might attract people from Waston   3 more expensive land

Activity 2
12:
could be built   may be more attractive   is probably cheaper   could be bigger   might even have   is certainly more convenient   could use it   it might attract   will definitely not be   must be an important consideration   might not be able to   can't be easy

Activity 3
1 can't be   2 must be   3 must be   4 can't be   5 can't be   6 must be   7 must be   8 can't be   9 must be   10 can't be

Activity 4
1 could make   2 probably go   3 might wait   4 definitely   5 might / might not   6 probably not   7 might have   8 may be

Activity 5
1 may / might   2 certainly not   3 may / might   4 must be   5 certainly   6 probably   7 may not be   8 definitely

Unit A22

Activity 1
1 F   2 A   3 E

Activity 2
Ambidexterity is the ability to use both hands or feet with equal ease. However, ambidextrous people still tend to have a 'dominant' hand. Ambidexterity is encouraged in activities requiring skill in both hands or feet, such as juggling and swimming. In pool and snooker, a player can reach further across a table if they are able to play with either hand. In skateboarding, a person is considered to be exceptionally talented if they are able to skate with either foot forward, hence the term 'switch skating'. In surfing, those who can ride in either stance are said to be surfing 'switch foot'. In soccer, being skilled at kicking with both feet provides more options for passing and scoring. Therefore, players who can use their weaker foot with proficiency are more valuable in a team than those who can't.
To be able to use either hand equally well, practice is the key. Wherever you normally use one hand, try to use the other instead. Consciously switch when you are about to do everyday actions such as pouring a glass of water. When you next put on your clothes you could put your other hand or foot into the garment first. You may have difficulty in doing these things at first or be unable to do them at all but with regular practice you'll gradually become good at using your less dominant hand.

Activity 3
1 can / could   2 will be able to   3 could   4 can   5 can   6 could

Activity 4

1 good at   2 are able to   3 is skilled   4 could   5 won't be able to
6 good at

Activity 5

B, C

Activity 6

1 good at swimming   2 not so good at   3 not at all bad at
4 got pretty good   5 won't be able to play   6 not very skilled
7 can't run fast   8 not very adept at   9 pretty bad at

Unit A23

Activity 1

1 NOT GIVEN   2 TRUE   3 FALSE   4 TRUE   5 TRUE

Activity 2

the government ought to provide...
Families shouldn't have to spend...
why not use it to fund...?
Governments should stop complaining / start helping...
How about training...?
what about giving them...?

Activity 3

1 How about going to the library if you want a quiet place to study?
2 If you're feeling sleepy, you should have a cup of coffee.
3 They should stop building new roads and start improving public transport.
4 What about trying acupuncture if you want to give up smoking?
5 If you have a problem with your accommodation, why not go to a local estate agent?
6 If you want to lose weight, you shouldn't eat so many biscuits and you should do more exercise.
7 You ought to take the bus to London. It's cheaper than the train.

Activity 4

1 You shouldn't   2 You should   3 You shouldn't   4 You should
5 You should   6 You should   7 You should   8 You should
9 You shouldn't   10 You should

Activity 5

1 stop relying   2 start working   3 shouldn't use   4 should use
5 ought to practise   6 should do   7 what about working
8 how about asking   9 you shouldn't   10 should see

Unit A24

Activity 1

1 FALSE   2 NOT GIVEN   3 TRUE

Activity 2

could see   could replace   could he figure out   couldn't make
he managed to find   was finally able to use

Activity 3

1 I   2 I   3 C   4 I   5 I

Activity 4

1 he ~~could get~~ was able to / managed to get the third prize
2 I ~~managed to~~ I could / was able to run
4 I ~~could get~~ was able to / managed to book
5 we ~~could~~ were able to / managed to repair it

Activity 5

1 were able to / managed to   2 could   3 managed to / was able to
4 could not / were not able to / did not manage to   5 managed to / were able to

Activity 6

1 How were you able to   2 how long was it before you were able
3 Were you able to   4 Couldn't he understand   5 Didn't you manage to catch

Unit A25

Activity 1

1 S   2 D   3 D   4 S   5 S

Activity 2

(a) 6: warmer than   hotter than   more widely than   less rainy than
much drier than   a little drier than
(b) 8: the hottest   the coldest   the warmest   the least   the most
extreme   the hottest   the rainiest   the most variable

Activity 3

1 cheaper   2 the most expensive   3 much more costly / much
costlier   4 the most inexpensive   5 highest   6 more cheaply
7 the dearest   8 the least expensive   9 lower   10 better

Activity 4

1 I   2 C   3 I   4 I

Unit A26

Activity 1

1 TRUE   2 TRUE   3 NOT GIVEN   4 FALSE   5 NOT GIVEN
6 FALSE

Activity 2

Polygraphs (or lie detectors) measure changes in the body that often occur when people tell lies, such as breathing rhythms and body temperature. They can even monitor the response of the eye during questioning. If the iris contracts <u>too suddenly,</u> this may indicate that a person is lying. The questions used fit into three categories. The first are a set of control questions such as 'Have you ever borrowed anything and not returned it?' These are questions which almost everyone should answer 'yes' to, but which may be <u>too uncomfortable</u> for some people to give honest answers to. These are followed by irrelevant questions such as 'Do you think you drink <u>too much coffee</u>?' 'Do you take <u>enough exercise</u>?' They can help distract the respondent from the relevant questions that follow. These are specific questions such as 'Did you drive <u>too fast</u> last night and exceed the speed limit?' that should determine whether you are telling the truth or not. The problem is that polygraphs only really work with those who become stressed when they lie. Those able to remain <u>calm enough</u> can easily beat the test. Recent scientific research also suggests that the tests themselves may not be <u>reliable enough</u>. One study has found their level of accuracy to be <u>as low as</u> 65%.

Activity 3

1 A   2 A   3 B   4 B   5 C

Activity 4

1 He is <u>strong enough</u> to carry the machine.
2 You are <u>too young</u> to take the test.
3 She was <u>too nervous</u> to answer the questions.

4   You weren't <u>calm enough</u> to pass the test.
5   She is <u>too honest</u> to tell lies.
6   I'm <u>not clever enough</u> to understand how the machine works.

Activity 5

1 as... as   2 too much   3 too many   4 not enough
5 too little / not enough

Unit A27

Activity 1

A iii   B i   C iv

Activity 2

<u>If you want help with your visa</u>   <u>if you are having problems</u>   <u>If you want to see us</u>   <u>When you want to call us</u>   <u>If we are not here</u>   <u>When we pick up messages</u>   <u>if you want to book an appointment</u>   <u>if you don't need help</u>

Activity 3

1 D   2 E   3 A   4 C   5 B

Activity 4

1 forms   2 gains   3 is created   4 rises   5 are blowing   6 reaches

Activity 5

1 want   2 take   3 stick   4 find   5 is cut   6 is cut   7 separates

Activity 6

1 D   2 B   3 C   4 A

Activity 7

1 pour / separates   2 disturb / am trying   3 is feeling / can see
4 can't <i>or</i> don't find / don't worry,   5 isn't hardening / isn't high enough

Unit A28

Activity 1

1 C   2 B   3 E

Activity 2

1   If carbon dioxide emissions continue to grow at current rates, then the level of this gas in the atmosphere will double.
2   If there is a slight increase in the global temperature, this will lead to climate change.
3   If this happens, increasing temperatures will raise sea levels.
4   When the environment changes, many endangered species are not going to survive.
5   If climate change is happening, we must work together against its worst effects.

Activity 3

if people ~~will~~ dislike work   ~~when~~ then the result   if managers ~~will~~ explain   they simply ~~are telling~~ tell their employees

Activity 4

1   If the equipment is too old, the experiment will not / may not / might not work.
2   If your computer crashes, you could lose your work.
3   If Agata doesn't use her dictionary more, her vocabulary won't improve.
4   If he plays computer games all night, his eyesight will / may / might get damaged.
5   If the value of the dollar falls, American products will be cheaper to buy.

Activity 5

1   If you have already had dinner, we can go straight to the cinema.
2   Don't worry about finding a bed for me. I will stay with Helen if Mike is visiting you.
3   You will have to pay a lot of money to the library if you don't return that book soon.
4   If you come back late at night again, I will lock you out of the flat.
5   If you still haven't finished the project, I will help you at the weekend.
6   If you go to Budapest, you must / should visit the Fisherman's Bastion.
7   Alex will fix your car if he hasn't done it already.
8   If you plan / are planning to live off-campus, you will need to make arrangements well in advance.

Activity 6

1 If you see / will you tell   2 will you do / if they offer
3 If Joe says (he is) / will you forgive   4 If we miss / will we fail / will we have failed   5 will happen / if I write

Unit A29

Activity 1

1 overpopulation   2 education   3 poor(er)   4 problems   5 birth control   6 work   7 (more) money   8 children

Activity 2

<u>if people were better educated, I believe this could solve the problem.</u>   <u>They might not do this if they understood the problems it causes. If they had proper education in schools, they would know how to control their lives. If the women used birth control and didn't have so many children, they would be able to go back to work... if the government punished people for having children, people who are already poor would become even poorer. If that happened, who would suffer? If only governments would spend more money on education, we could avoid the problem altogether.</u>

Activity 3

1 spent / would be   2 would have   3 ruled / would build
4 would be / were   5 would you help / won   6 wouldn't touch / were   7 earned / would have   8 valued / would starve

Activity 4

(answers can be in either order)
1   I could go to England. / I could get a visa.
2   I didn't have to work. / I could study psychology.
3   I could have a big piece of chocolate cake. / I wasn't / weren't on a diet.
4   I could understand what he is saying / this lecture wasn't so difficult.

Activity 5

1 would be more space   2 everybody lived like   3 would have six children   4 would be left

Unit A30

Activity 1

1 NOT GIVEN   2 FALSE   3 TRUE

Activity 2

<u>If they had ended their meeting without further action, America would have been very different.</u>

Women might not have won the vote in 1920 if Elizabeth Cady Stanton and her friends had not met.

If they hadn't campaigned for financial independence, women may not have had control over their own money.

Would the 1972 Equal Rights Amendment have been passed if it had not been for the Movement?

Activity 3

1 Greece   2 teamwork   3 teambuilding   4 sharing responsibilities
5 contribute / work hard   6 had started   7 of time   8 planned

Activity 4

2 If he had bought a ticket, he could / would have won the lottery. *or* He would / could have won the lottery if he had bought a ticket.
3 If he had learnt to play the guitar, he would / could have been a rock star. *or* He would / could have been a rock star if he had learnt to play the guitar.
4 If she had passed the exam(s), she would have gone to university. *or* She would have gone to university if she had passed the exam(s).
5 If they had not fought for women's rights, women would not have been able to vote today. *or* Women would not have been able to vote today if they had not fought for women's rights.

Activity 5

1 be waiting   2 write   3 had got   4 had taken   5 'd go

Unit A31

Activity 1

1 ambitious   2 compassionate   3 equal

Activity 2

40% said that decisiveness was the most important quality. → '*Decisiveness is the most important quality.*'
Americans told the Pew Research Center that compassion was the most important thing. → '*Compassion is the most important thing.*'
They said compassion was not important at all for men. → '*Compassion is not important at all for men.*'
They told the Pew Research Center that the next most important characteristic for women leaders was to be creative. → '*The next most important characteristic for women leaders is to be creative.*'
People said that that men and women were equal. → '*Men and women are equal.*'

Activity 3

1 became overweight because they needed   2 showed that obese people had   3 were eating more   4 obese people experienced
5 the results could help

Activity 4

1 if they had any money   2 if they spent more money on food or fuel   3 if they spent money on luxury goods   4 what else they spent money on   5 how they paid for things

Activity 5

1 missed   2 've been reading   3 'm not going   4 spoke
5 haven't read   6 will   7 must   8 will be

Activity 6

Andreas said that he **wasn't** ill. He told Lili that he **had been reading** a lot about accounting lately and he wasn't really

interested in it. He said he **was not going to** take the option in it. Lili said that Dr Kesevan **had covered** more than just accounting. She said that he **had spoken** about the marketing mix too. Andreas told her that he **hadn't read** about that and Lili said that it **had been** only a short introduction and that he **was going to** / **would** talk about it in more detail **the following week**. She said he **had to** make sure he was there. Andreas said he **would be there** for sure.

Unit A32

Activity 1

1 rebellious types   2 independent-minded (people) / independent thinkers   3 forward-thinking (people) / forward thinkers
4 risk takers   5 strong communicators

Activity 2

It has been suggested in a recent study that there are definite patterns in people's behaviour depending on where they sit on a double-decker bus. Researchers from Salford University discovered that forward-thinking people sat at the front of the bus and noticed that the independent-minded chose the middle. It was also noted that those with a rebellious character usually opted for the rear. The findings revealed seven distinct groups of passengers. Passengers at front on the top deck are said to be forward thinkers, while those at the back are believed to be rebellious types who tend to guard their own personal space. Passengers sitting in the middle are thought to be independent thinkers because they read a newspaper or listen to music during their journey. It is claimed that people who sit on the bottom deck at the front are out going and sociable, while those in the middle are strong communicators. Passengers who head for the rear of the downstairs deck are said to be risk takers. The researchers defined one final group as chameleons and explained that these are travellers who do not care where they sit because they feel that they can fit in anywhere.

Activity 3

1 C   2 A   3 B   4 C   5 A   6 B   7 C

Activity 4

1 E   2 A   3 G   4 D   5 C   6 F   7 B

Activity 5

1 He admitted that he didn't always obey the rules.
2 She explained that she always thought ahead and didn't only focus on the present.
3 She insisted that she could take responsibility for herself.
4 She agreed that she also liked keeping her distance from other passengers.
5 She confirmed that she preferred being around other people.
6 He reckoned he found it quite easy to express his ideas clearly.
7 He claimed that he always wanted to try something new even when there was a chance he wouldn't succeed.

Activity 6

1 130,000   2 umbrellas / glasses   3 25%   4 3 months
5 £10,000

Activity 7

1 It is thought that   2 It is understood   3 were handed in
4 explained   5 remained   6 It is believed   7 found

Unit A33

Activity 1
1 British Council / IDP Australia / University of Cambridge
2 interlocutor   3 test centre   4 Saturday   5 entrance to university
6 No, the NHS requires doctors to have band 7.0 IELTS
7 multiple choice / short answer / chart, table, note or sentence completion / labelling / labelling   8 invigilator   9 listening
10 20 minutes

Activity 2
1 Do you know <u>the name of one of the three organisations which administer</u> the IELTS test?
2 What is the correct word for <u>the examiner who asks</u> the questions in the IELTS speaking test?
3 What do we call <u>the place where</u> the test is taken?
4 What is <u>the day of the week when</u> the test is usually taken?
5 What is <u>the reason why</u> most people take the IELTS test?
6 Can <u>a doctor whose</u> IELTS score is 6.5 work for the National Health Service in Great Britain?
7 Name <u>a type of question which</u> might be in the listening test.
8 What is the word for <u>a person who</u> sits in the room while people are taking an examination?
9 Can you name <u>the part of the IELTS test that</u> takes about 35 minutes?
10 What is <u>the maximum length of time that</u> you should spend on Writing task 1?

Activity 3
1 F Those are the people whose test papers have been lost.
2 H I'd like to buy a book which will help me to pass the test.
3 C He isn't the same man who was in the canteen yesterday.
4 E That reminds me of the day when I saw real snow for the first time.
5 G Do you know the reason why the sky is blue?
6 A That lady over there is the one whose dog bit the Vice Chancellor.
7 D The police are looking for the girl who / that set fire to the school.
8 J There are some subjects that / which are harder to learn than others.
9 B Is this the room where I will be teaching this afternoon?
10 I The end of Autumn is the time when all the clocks go back in Europe.

Activity 4
1 The book he wrote was *On the Origin of Species*.
2 It was a subject he hated.
3 He thought Religious Studies was a topic he might be more interested in.
4 These were papers he did not publish until 1859.
5 This was the same year he published his book.
6 He could not ignore the evidence he had found.
7 He married a woman he loved very deeply, Emma Wedgewood.

Unit A34

Activity 1
1 drunk   2 situated   3 abroad   4 rain / rainfall   5 to bear

Activity 2
which include Phoenix and Riyadh;   which is the capital city of Saudi Arabia;   many of whom are foreigners;   where temperatures can reach 45°C in Summer;   in which government, education and commerce are important elements

Activity 3
1 , which are called silos,   2 , which   3 which / that   4 , where
5 which / that   6 when

Activity 4
1 which shows the number of people being made unemployed
2 which may account for / have accounted for the falling rate
3 which meant that there was

Activity 5
1 The speed of economic growth is influenced by many factors, some of which we can control.
2 The rugby society has many members, three of whom play for Bradford Bulls.
3 The Prime Minister has visited Japan many times, the most recent of which was in May.
4 The Prime Minister had dinner with the Prime Minister of Japan, during which he made a speech.

Activity 6
1 in which my parents still live   2 about which she can't remember much   3 on which they rely for business

Unit A35

Activity 1
1 memory capacity   2 (biometric) fingertip sensor   3 (remote) computer mouse   4 projected images

Activity 2
A manage to, decide to, need to, happen to, choose to, want to, wish to   B imagine   C allow you to, expect you to, enable you to   D let you put   E stops someone doing

Activity 3
1 allows   2 lets   3 to see   4 to develop   5 owning   6 expect you

Activity 4
1 to work   2 to book   3 expect (you) to   4 to ask / to leave
5 to lend   6 to complete   7 to know   8 winning

Unit A36

Activity 1
1 NOT GIVEN   2 TRUE   3 FALSE   4 TRUE   5 NOT GIVEN

Activity 2
C egg, vegetable, cup of tea, century, dish, potato, meal, diet
U simplicity, flour, batter, rice, spaghetti, gravy
B curry, fish, food, haddock, water, sauces, paper, beer, chicken, fat

Activity 3
1 advice   2 shows   3 job   4 experience   5 flour   6 salt
7 stock / some   8 a lot   9 a little

Activity 4
The wide range of British regional food <u>are</u> reflected in the names of our favourite <u>dish</u>. Several <u>region</u> are famous for their local <u>produces</u>. Cheeses <u>is</u> produced in many <u>area</u> and Cheddar is one of the most popular <u>variety</u>. Many dishes are named after <u>place</u>, such as the Bath buns – a very sweet cake containing <u>much</u> sugar, some dried fruit and a little <u>spices</u>.

Answer key **A** Grammar

Unit A37

Activity 1

1 a soldier 2 a few drinks, a lot of friends 3 an officer
4 a soldier, an officer 5 a medal, an officer, a retirement home
6 once a week 7 the medal, the officer, the army, the rice, the
vegetables 8 the Sun, the Second World War 9 the Ganges, the
Himalayas 10 the White Swan Hotel 11 the happiest 12 India,
Rishikesh 13 rice, vegetables 14 lunch 15 school 16 by bus

Activity 2

	the	a / an	no article
Uncountable noun *(water)*	✓	✗	✓
Plural noun *(tables)*	✓	✗	✓
Singular countable noun *(chair)*	✓	✓	✗

Examples
3 Water is essential for life. (*all water, water in general*)
4 We'll have to move the tables out of the classroom. (*we know which tables*)
6 Furniture shops sell chairs, beds and tables. (*any tables, tables in general*)
7 You sit on the sofa, I'll sit on the chair. (*we know which chair*)
8 We need to buy a chair for the living room. (*we don't know which chair*)

Activity 3
TRUE

Activity 4

I agree with **the** statement. When I first started (**no article**) school, I could already read and write a bit because my mother had taught me. She always used to read me **a** bedtime story, and I got to know **the** shapes of the different letters. Some of the other children in **the** class couldn't even count up to ten.
The only problem was, I was very bored at first. Everything **the** teacher taught us, I already knew. **The** book we had was too easy for me, but **the** girl who sat next to me couldn't read it. I asked **the** teacher if I could read **a** book from **the** library, but she said I had to use **the** same one as the other children in our class.
To sum up, I think all (**no article**) parents should help their children learn to read and write before they start (**no article**) school. They should also teach **the** alphabet and numbers up to ten. Unless they do this, their children will learn more slowly and they will never be top of **the** class.

Activity 5
1 I 2 I 3 C 4 I 5 I 6 C 7 I 8 I 9 I 10 C

Activity 6
1 **The** Moon is very bright tonight.
2 I usually have (–) breakfast at 7.30 a.m.
4 Large numbers of (–) Japanese tourists travel abroad every year.
5 China produces **a** lot of (–) rice.
7 I usually like chocolate, but **the** bar I had yesterday was horrible.
8 Once **a** week I go to Manchester by (–) train.
9 She's **an** engineer, I'm **a** student and he's **a** teacher.

Activity 7
1 We saw **a** light in **the** sky which looked like **a** spaceship.

2 Will you have (–) dinner with me tonight at **the** Hilton?
3 **The** Thames is one of **the** most famous rivers in **the** world.
4 (–) Advice from friends can be hard to take, but **the** advice Sharif gave me was a great help.
5 I had **a** sandwich, **a** banana and **an** apple for lunch.
6 Look! There's **a** football in **the** garden.
7 I need to buy **a** new mobile phone – I've lost **the** one Michelle gave me.
8 After leaving (–) school, many young people now take **a** year off before they start (–) university.
9 I don't like (–) snakes, but I'm not afraid of (–) spiders.
10 My uncle was born in (–) Manchester, but now all my cousins live in (–) Spain.

Unit A38

Activity 1
1 NOT GIVEN 2 TRUE 3 TRUE 4 NOT GIVEN

Activity 2

Big Ben is the name of the bell in the famous clock at the Houses of Parliament in London. The bell was named after Sir Benjamin Hall, who commissioned the bell as part of the rebuilding of the Palace of Westminster <u>following a fire</u> there <u>in 1834</u>. The original bell was cast <u>in 1856</u> but <u>during a sounding test in December of that year</u> it cracked and had to be broken up <u>shortly after</u>. A new bell was installed <u>two years later</u> – <u>in 1858</u>. This second bell has been a tourist landmark and symbol of London <u>ever since</u>.
    The clock is wound up by hand <u>on Mondays, Wednesdays and Fridays</u>. The process takes <u>over an hour</u> because it is not possible to wind while it is chiming. And when it is going a bit fast or a bit slow (which is <u>nearly always</u> the case) a mechanic places or removes a penny from the pendulum; adding one speeds up the clock by two-fifths of a second a day. The keeper of the clock checks the clock by ringing up the speaking clock. He does this from a phone in the clock room <u>at five minutes to the hour</u> precisely, <u>before</u> going to the belfry to check that the hammer on Big Ben strikes on the hour. <u>Over the years</u> the clock has been stopped by snow <u>in Winter</u> and mechanical failure but is still going strong. And it looks likely that it will continue to ring out across London <u>during the twenty-first century</u> too.

Activity 3
A in 1834; in 1856; during a sounding test in December of that year; two years later; in 1858; on Mondays, Wednesdays and Fridays; at five minutes to the hour; in Winter; during the twenty-first century
B following a fire; shortly after; ever since; over an hour; nearly always; before; over the years

Activity 4
1 in 2 at 3 during 4 in 5 after 6 by

Activity 5
1 on 2 at 3 at / over 4 during / in 5 in 6 over / during 7 over

Unit A39

Activity 1
3

Activity 2

14 in on to across on under at along through up to
towards from from into

Activity 3

1 SS (Student Services) 2 R (reception) 3 C (café) 4 T (toilets)
5 SSC (self-study centre)

Activity 4

1 in 2 in front of 3 on your left 4 to the right 5 at 6 behind

Activity 5

A Senior common room B Dining room C Kitchens
D Sharwood room E Foundation Studies office

Activity 6

1 past 2 towards 3 along 4 up 5 into 6 through 7 across

Activity 7

1 at 2 over / above 3 above / over 4 up to 5 under

Unit A40

Activity 1

1 FALSE 2 NOT GIVEN 3 FALSE

Activity 2

1 set back 2 let down 3 made up of 4 cater for 5 go back to
6 keep up with

Activity 3

1 B 2 C / D 3 F 4 I 5 A 6 C 7 E 8 J 9 H 10 G

Activity 4

1 looked up to look down on = not respect someone / something;
look around = search
2 thought about think through = think about a problem;
think up = have an idea
3 asked for ask in = invite someone into a room; ask over = ask
someone to visit your house
4 tried out tried on = see if clothes fit you; tried for = attempt
5 brought out bring up = to raise a child; bring forward = to move
a plan earlier

Activity 5

1 separable – *iron their differences out* is also possible 2 separable
3 inseparable – a three-word verb 4 inseparable – intransitive verb
5 inseparable – a three-word verb; inseparable – intransitive verb

Activity 6

1 C 2 I 3 C 4 C 5 I 6 I

Activity 7

2 face up to them (take responsibility) 5 put it off (delay)
6 he still stood out (noticeable)

Activity 8

1 threw him out (make someone leave) 2 watch out for her (take
notice of her) 3 work it out (solve) 4 filled it out (completed)
5 held it up (display) 6 get along with her (have a good relationship)

Activity 9

1 tie up (complete) 2 speak out (say something you want to say)
3 stop off (break a journey) 4 used up (use everything)
5 give out / off (emit) 6 read up on (revise) 7 cut it out (stop)
8 sitting on (delay)

Unit B1

Activity 1

1 B 2 A

Activity 2

1 B 2 E 3 D 4 A 5 C

Activity 3

1 As a matter of fact 2 and 3 Actually
4 Indeed 5 In contrast 6 also

Activity 4

1 In fact / As a matter of fact / Indeed 2 and 3 Not only does
4 In contrast 5 but 6 In fact / As a matter of fact / Indeed 7 and

Unit B2

Activity 1

1 NOT GIVEN 2 TRUE 3 TRUE 4 FALSE 5 FALSE

Activity 2

1 b 2 b 3 b 4 b 5 a

Activity 3

1 J 2 B 3 I 4 K 5 C 6 F

Activity 4

1 it was raining 2 the rain 3 it was raining 4 we didn't play
tennis 5 the rain 6 the rain

Unit B3

Activity 1

1 FALSE 2 NOT GIVEN 3 TRUE

Activity 2

1 to sample the upper atmosphere 2 relay communications
3 to study the surface 4 to find out how Mars lost its atmosphere

Activity 3

1 To 2 with 3 so 4 to 5 order

Activity 4

1 The college put more lights around the campus so that the
   students are safer.
2 They made sandwiches for the trip.
3 The government plans to build a new school of medicine in
   order to train more doctors.
4 An extra 1,000 teachers should be employed so as to reduce the
   size of classes.
5 The company fitted satellite navigation to their lorries in order
   that their drivers can find their destination easily.

Activity 5

1 the same 2 sports society 3 Saudi Society 4 interest society
5 every Wednesday 6 promote understanding 7 one play

Activity 6

1 for 2 to play 3 to watch 4 the real purpose 5 the aim
6 so as to 7 in order to 8 for 9 in order for that

Unit B4

Activity 1

1 FALSE   2 TRUE   3 NOT GIVEN

Activity 2

1 surprisingly   2 unfortunately   3 frankly   4 typically

Activity 3

1 to be   2 to have   3 to be   4 as if

Activity 4

1 Actually / To tell you the truth   2 Apparently   3 obviously
4 Actually / To tell you the truth

Activity 5

2 ✓

Activity 6

1 Obviously   2 as a matter of fact   3 Apparently   4 Seriously
5 it seems   6 In fact   7 Frankly

Activity 7

1   Surprisingly, there are more planets like Earth.
2   Obviously, the banking system needs reforming.
3   Apparently, the university is giving all students a free bicycle.
4   Frankly, the death penalty should be given to all murderers.

Unit B5

Activity 1

1 nymph   2 dun   3 spinner

Activity 2

13: The mayfly life cycle has four stages; To begin with; before
hatching; In this stage; before emerging; two adult stages; After
emerging; In the third stage; The next step; Following this; during
this stage. Eventually; prior to this

Activity 3

1B → 2D → 3C → 4E → 5F → 6G → 7A

Activity 4

1 has   2 stages   3 At first   4 In   5 firstly   6 secondly
7 Following   8 The next step   9 at the same time   10 concludes
11 finally

Unit B6

Activity 1

1 TRUE   2 FALSE   3 NOT GIVEN   4 FALSE   5 TRUE

Activity 2

5: For example; such as; A good illustration of this is; for instance;
A case in point is

Activity 3

1 such as   2 illustration   3 for example / for instance
4 case in point

Activity 4

1 animal lovers   2 Hindu *or* Buddhist   3 Hindu *or* Buddhist
4 health   5 vegan   6 cheese *or* butter   7 cheese *or* butter   8 beef
9 protein   10 nuts *or* beans   11 nuts *or* beans   12 children

Unit B7

Activity 1

1 watch wildlife   2 huge scientific experiment   3 become active

Activity 2

1 people in Europe   2 people taking part in the experiment
3 scientists   4 recording the arrival of the seasons
5 become active   6 butterflies and bees becoming active

Activity 3

1 He   2 his   3 his   4 her   5 their   6 these   7 them

Activity 4

1 B   2 C   3 A   4 D

Activity 5

1 the first measurement 2 the second measurement   3 if you are
interested in collecting data on climate change   4 cut carbon
emissions   5 if you do not accept climate change is happening

Activity 6

1   We can see that 20 people travelled ~~to work~~ by car, 15 ~~travelled
to work~~ by train, and 5 ~~people travelled to work~~ by bicycle.
2   Sven: I understood it, but Janice didn't ~~understand it~~.
3   James Lovelock believed in ~~his ideas~~ and fought for his ideas.
4   I can see you're not ~~busy writing your essay~~.
5   Jacques, the older brother, was an inventor and Joseph, the
younger ~~brother~~, was a businessman.

Activity 7

1 the term   2 the problem   3 the theory   4 This criticism   5 this
situation

Unit B8

Activity 1

1 RS   2 RS   3 RA   4 RA

Activity 2

1   It was Amundsen who set up camp 60 miles closer to the Pole
than Scott – who was closer to the Pole.
2   What Scott employed were motor sleds, ponies and dogs – the
things Scott took to help him.
3   What happened was that the motor sleds broke down – what
happened to Scott.
4   What they found on arriving on 18th January, 1912 was
Amundsen's Norwegian flag – what Scott found.
5   All they wanted was to reach the South Pole first – what they
wanted to do.
6   The things that helped Amundsen's expedition were good
equipment... – the things that helped Amundsen.

Activity 3

1 ✔   4 ✔   5 ✔

Activity 4

1   It was Tony who took Noriko to the end-of-term party last
Saturday.
2   It was Noriko who Tony took to the end-of-term party last
Saturday.
3   It was the end-of-term party that Tony took Noriko to last
Saturday.
4   It was last Saturday when Tony took Noriko to the end-of-term
party.

5 What Tony took Noriko to was the end-of-term party.

Activity 5
1 It was Westinghouse who Zworykin was working for.
2 One reason people consider Zworykin to be the inventor of TV was because he applied for a patent.
3 What Philo Taylor Farnsworth demonstrated was a working signal.
4 All Zworykin had was a poor picture.
5 It was Farnsworth who had the picture, while Zworykin had the patent.

Activity 6
1 our concern is that not many people like beetroot juice.
2 the problem is that it is expensive in Summer.
3 So the big question is whether it will sell in cafés, be bought only for home,

Answer key | C | Vocabulary

Unit C1

Activity 2
1 toddler   2 school age / school-aged   3 teen / teenager   4 adult
5 middle age / middle-aged   6 pensioner / old age / old-aged

Activity 3
1 toddlers   2 adults   3 school age   4 teenager   5 middle age
6 old age

Activity 4
1 figure   2 Pear-shaped   3 slim   4 overweight   5 slim
6 Hourglass   7 skinny   8 curvy

Activity 5
1 oval   2 heart-shaped   3 round   4 square

Activity 6
1 brainy   2 gifted   3 idle   4 punctual   5 amusing

Activity 7
1 fussy   2 nervous   3 hard-working   4 easy-going   5 self-confident   6 grumpy   7 mean   8 sulky   9 generous   10 strict
11 thoughtful   12 enthusiastic

Activity 8
1 amusing   5 generous   6 gifted   7 grumpy   9 hard-working
13 punctual   14 confident   15 strict   16 thoughtful
17 unenthusiastic

Unit C2

Activity 2
1 height   2 breadth   3 depth   4 width   5 length

Activity 3
1 wide   2 deep   3 long   4 high   5 heavy   6 circular   7 square
8 triangular

Activity 4
1 bulky   2 enormous   3 huge   4 tiny   5 compact   6 narrow

Activity 5
1 plain   2 flowery   3 stripy   4 checked

Activity 6
1 used; stripy; bulky; polyfibre   2 square; flowery; Italian; old
3 big; antique; Chinese; ceramic

Activity 7
A 1 age   2 pattern   3 colour   4 material   5 purpose
B 1 size   2 shape   3 pattern   4 origin   5 purpose
C 1 size   2 age   3 colour   4 origin   5 material   6 purpose

Activity 8
1 size   2 age   3 shape   4 pattern   5 colour   6 origin   7 material
8 purpose

Unit C3

Activity 2
1 piano   2 saxophone   3 guitar   4 flute   5 violin   6 cello

Activity 3
1 reggae   2 classical   3 world   4 jazz   5 rock   6 hip-hop

Activity 4
1 performance art   2 Street art   3 concert / gig   4 carnival
5 festival

Activity 5
1 art gallery   2 museum   3 exhibition   4 opera house   5 theatre

Activity 6
1 contemporary   2 abstract   3 self-portrait   4 sketches   5 surreal
6 still-life   7 portraits   8 ceramics   9 sculptures

Unit C4

Activity 2
1 Colombo   2 Trincomalee / Mannar / Anuradhapura / Kandy / Galle   3 Mount Lavinia   4 Trincomalee / Mannar / Colombo
5 Kandy / Anuradhapura   6 Mannar / Trincomalee / Colombo / Galle   7 Mannar / Colombo / Galle.

Activity 3
1 D   2 B   3 C   4 G   5 H   6 E   7 A   8 F

Activity 4
1 vibrant   2 major   3 multicultural   4 metropolitan   5 humid
6 cosmopolitan   7 fascinating   8 tropical   9 ancient / historic
10 temperate   11 modern   12 world-famous

Activity 5
1 multicultural   2 industrial   3 major   4 tourist   5 modern
6 temperate   7 zones   8 sectors   9 vibrant   10 metropolitan
11 coastal   12 port   13 cosmopolitan   14 suburb

Unit C5

Activity 2
1 make a good impression   2 a total flop   3 make a real difference
4 make a slight adjustment   5 a recipe for disaster   6 doomed to failure   7 give a winning performance / be an outstanding success
8 increase your chances

Activity 3
A: to make a good impression; to be an outstanding success; to give a winning performance
B: to give a dismal presentation; to go badly wrong; to be a total flop; to be a recipe for disaster; to be doomed to failure

Activity 4

1 total flop   2 make a good impression   3 go badly wrong
4 make things easier for yourself   5 make slight adjustments
6 make a real difference   7 make the mistake   8 recipe for disaster
9 doomed to failure   10 giving a winning performance

Activity 5

1 Make eye contact   2 Make sure you   3 failure   4 keep in mind
5 make adjustments   6 Make notes

Activity 6

1 didn't you make sure   2 makes a point of   3 don't make an
effort   4 I've made a list   5 make mistakes   6 made a note
7 'll keep in mind

Unit C6

Activity 2

1 comprehensive school   2 grammar school   3 further education
college   4 university   5 boarding school   6 specialist school
7 independent school   8 primary school   9 secondary school

Activity 3

A Masters   B A levels   C GCSEs

Activity 4

1 pupil   2 tutor   3 researcher   4 lecturer   5 graduate
6 administrator   7 undergraduate   8 postgraduate   9 professor
10 admissions officer

Activity 5

get: a place, a degree, a qualification, an offer, an education
do: a degree, a course, research

Activity 6

1 complete a degree   2 university   3 theoretical knowledge
4 develop practical skills   5 hands-on experience   6 taking exams

Unit C7

Activity 2

1 hydroelectric   2 nuclear   3 solar   4 wind

Activity 3

1 R   2 N-R   3 R   4 R   5 N-R   6 R   7 N-R   8 R   9 N-R
10 N-R

Activity 4

1 coal   2 reactor   3 solar panel   4 dam   5 wave   6 burn
7 distribute   8 geothermal   9 renewable   10 uranium

Activity 5

1 collect   2 fossil fuel   3 generator   4 burn   5 radioactive
6 transmit   7 store   8 turbine

Activity 6

1 generate   2 react   3 transform   4 product, production   5 storage
6 collector, collection   7 transmitter, transmission   8 distribution

Unit C8

Activity 2

1 north   2 east   3 south   4 west   5 longitude   6 equator
7 latitude   8 South Pole   9 North Pole   10 northern hemisphere
11 southern hemisphere

Activity 3

1 flow   2 ocean   3 current   4 maritime   5 gulf   6 salinity

Activity 4

1 ocean   2 current   3 flows   4 Ocean   5 humid / mild
6 humid / mild   7 salinity   8 latitude

Activity 5

1 monsoon; flood   2 atmosphere   3 continent   4 pressure
5 hemisphere   6 maritime   7 trade winds   8 coast   9 Tropical
10 range   11 precipitation; moisture   12 drought

Activity 6

1, 2, 3 Mountain ranges; Continents; Oceans   4 atmosphere
5 oceans   6 landmasses   7 (atmospheric) pressure (systems)
8 High pressure   9 low pressure / depressions   10 low pressure
11 (heavy) precipitation   12 maritime climates   13 large
landmasses   14 wetter

Unit C9

Activity 2

1 British   2 café   3 snacks   4 beverages   5 outlet   6 homemade
7 junk   8 restaurant   9 starter   10 a main course   11 side dish
12 dessert   13 vegetarian   14 vegan

Activity 3

1 fry   2 roast   3 boil   4 steam   5 grill   6 bake

Activity 4

1 fresh   2 oily   3 tough   4 bitter   5 tender   6 savoury   7 spicy
8 sour   9 raw

Activity 5

	bitter	fresh	oily	raw	savoury	sour	spicy	tender	tough
meat		✓		✓			✓	✓	✓
fruit	✓	✓		✓		✓			
vegetables		✓		✓					
food / a meal	✓	✓	✓	✓	✓	✓	✓	✓	

Activity 6

1 C   2 F   3 D   4 A   5 B   6 E

Activity 7

A   1 delicious   2 gorgeous   3 heavenly   4 moreish   5 light
B   6 heavy   7 bland   8 unhealthy

Activity 8

1 B   2 C   3 B   4 B   5 B

Unit C10

Activity 2

1 brain   2 lung   3 heart   4 muscle   5 diaphragm   6 liver
7 kidney   8 spleen   9 intestines   10 bladder   11 skull
12 vertebrae   13 ribs   14 spine   15 hip   16 wrist   17 knee
18 ankle

Activity 3

1 infectious diseases   2 HIV / AIDS   3 cancer   4 malaria
5 stroke   6 arthritis   7 Alzheimer's disease   8 heart disease

Activity 4

1 consultant   2 psychiatrist   3 chiropodist   4 paediatrician
5 surgeon   6 osteopath   7 optician   8 physiotherapist
9 cardiologist

Activity 5

1 holistic   2 conventional medicine   3 vitamins   4 herbs
5 radiotherapy   6 chemotherapy   7 diet   8 exercise   9 pills
10 injections

Activity 6

1 clinic   2 A&E   3 ward   4 outpatients   5 waiting room
6 hospice   7 surgery   8 theatre

Unit C11

Activity 2

1 experiment   2 case study   3 fieldwork   4 survey   5 trial
6 questionnaire

Activity 3

1 figures / statistics   2 findings   3 data   4 results   5 report
6 recommendation

Activity 4

1 discovery   2 invention   3 design   4 innovation

Activity 5

1 analysed   2 explore   3 produced   4 examined   5 conduct
6 carry out   7 investigating

Activity 6

1 analysis   2 exploration   3 production / product   4 examination

Activity 7

	analyse	examine	explore	conduct	carry out
an idea	✓	✓	✓		
an experiment	✓			✓	✓
statistics	✓	✓			

Activity 8

1 data   2 survey   3 questionnaires   4 Analysis   5 findings
6 statistics   7 examination   8 report   9 recommended

Unit C12

Activity 2

1 mouse   2 printer   3 keyboard   4 scanner   5 smartphone
6 flash drive   7 cable   8 modem   9 laptop   10 speakers
11 monitor   12 hard drive

Activity 3

1 application / program   2 database   3 spreadsheet
4 word processing

Activity 4

1 browse   2 navigate   3 highlight   4 drag   5 backing up
6 upload   7 download   8 freezes   9 crashes   10 scroll   11 click

Activity 5

1 hacked   2 deleting   3 accessing   4 virus   5 bug   6 spyware
7 cybercrime

Activity 6

1 applications programmer / software engineer   2 technical support
3 network manager   4 web designer   5 systems designer

Unit C13

Activity 2

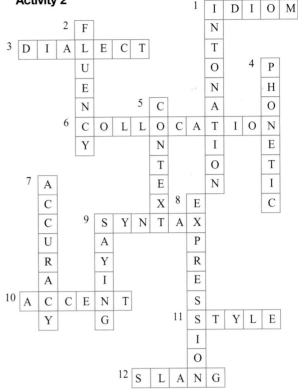

Activity 3

1 small talk   2 chat   3 gossip   4 debate   5 discussion
6 argument

Activity 4

1 sign language   2 body language   3 multilingual   4 common
language   5 bilingual   6 mother tongue

Activity 5

1 pronounce   2 transcribe   3 translate   4 recite   5 interpret

Unit C14

Activity 2

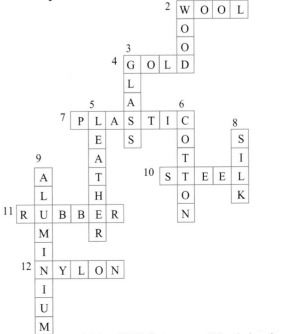

Activity 3

1 reflective 2 absorbent 3 transparent 4 flexible 5 waterproof

Activity 4

1 split 2 evaporates 3 condensed 4 combined / mixed 5 heated
6 melts 7 combines 8 cooled 9 destroying 10 merging /
melting / combining / mixing

Unit C15

Activity 2

1 flyer 2 billboard 3 journal 4 archive 5 tabloid 6 broadsheet

Activity 3

1 bulletin 2 trailer 3 commercials 4 screenings 5 episode
6 channel 7 broadcast

Activity 4

1 broadcaster 2 viewer 3 reporter 4 editor 5 producer
6 web designer 7 camera crew 8 Disc Jockey (DJ)
9 critic

Activity 5

1 broadcaster 2 reporter 3 DJ / Disc Jockey 4 web designer
5 editor 6 critic

Activity 6

1 go on air 2 cover a story 3 made the headlines 4 doing an
interview 5 launched an advertising campaign

Unit C16

Activity 2

1 tuition fees 2 balance 3 debit card 4 interest 5 current
account 6 overdraft 7 direct debit 8 maintenance grant
9 budget 10 transactions

Activity 3

1 interest 2 overdraft 3 debit card 4 direct debit 5 transactions
6 balance

Activity 4

	account	balance	loan	money	interest
to check	✓	✓			
to earn				✓	✓
to set up	✓				
to transfer		✓		✓	
to pay back			✓	✓	✓
to overspend	✓				

Activity 5

1 budget 2 into debt 3 loan 4 transfer 5 direct debit
6 current account 7 overspend 8 overdrafts

Activity 6

1 loan 2 tuition fees 3 maintenance grant 4 income
5 check my balance 6 transactions 7 take out 8 pay back

Unit C17

Activity 2

1 $\frac{1}{5}$ – a / one fifth 2 $\frac{1}{4}$ – a / one quarter 3 $\frac{1}{3}$ – a / one third
4 $\frac{3}{4}$ – three-quarters 5 $\frac{4}{5}$ – four-fifths 6 $\frac{9}{10}$ – nine-tenths

Activity 3

1 2.205 / two point two oh (zero) five 2 1.60934 / one point six
oh (zero) nine three four 3 0.1056 / zero point one / oh (zero) five
six 4 16 / sixteen 5 32° / thirty-two degrees 6 4.54596 / four
point five four five nine six

Activity 4

1 24 + 8 = 32 2 906 – 12 = 894 3 72 ÷ 11= 6.5454545
4 $\sqrt{16}$ = 4 5 1 fl oz = 2.84131 cm^3 6 12 in = 1 ft, 3 ft = 1 yd
7 73 kph 8 64% 9 $520.99 10 6,522,313

Activity 5

1 7 2 8 3 4 4 5 5 14

Activity 6

1 2007 2 41,279 3 9,476 4 8,611 5 23% 6 $\frac{1}{4}$ 7 8% 8 1%
9 1% 10 12,000 11 10 12 20–25 13 235 14 600
15 30,000,000

Unit C18

Activity 2

1 classmate 2 workmate / colleague 3 partner 4 girlfriend
5 friend of a friend 6 acquaintances

Activity 3

1 uncle 2 aunt 3 cousin 4 extended family 5 son 6 daughter
7 immediate family 8 niece 9 nephew 10 brother-in-law

Activity 4

1 brother-in-law 2 sister 3 nephew 4 niece 5 father 6 uncle
7 aunt 8 cousins 9 son

Activity 5

1 takes after / looks like 2 looks like 3 close 4 seeing / got
together 5 get on well 6 in common

Activity 6

Talk about:
~~brother~~-in-law → father-in-law
known for ~~5 years~~ → 10 years
~~don't~~ get on with him
my wife looks like her ~~mother~~ → father
takes after him, ~~serious and sad~~ → funny and full of life
~~un~~successful business person, ~~never~~ → always helps people
~~nothing~~ → lots in common
~~never get together~~ to → both play golf and cook

Unit C19

Activity 2

1 hand in 2 summarise 3 research 4 references 5 note-taking
6 critical knowledge 7 plagiarise 8 paraphrase 9 plan
10 revise

Activity 3

1 planned 2 revised 3 researched 4 took notes 5 summarised
6 plagiarise 7 handed in

Activity 4

1 lecture 2 workshop 3 tutorial 4 seminar

Activity 5

1 archaeology 2 management 3 informatics 4 geography
5 pharmacy 6 engineering 7 mathematics 8 biology
9 agriculture 10 psychology

s	i	n	f	o	r	m	a	t	i	c	s
c	c	o	b	m	p	e	o	a	m	i	a
p	g	i	a	a	h	n	h	g	a	e	r
s	e	b	t	n	a	g	r	r	t	p	c
y	o	l	t	a	r	i	r	i	h	a	h
c	g	e	t	g	m	n	r	c	e	i	a
h	r	a	p	e	a	e	i	u	m	r	e
o	a	r	m	m	c	e	h	l	a	s	o
l	p	o	g	e	y	r	n	t	t	a	l
o	h	l	y	n	e	i	e	u	i	a	o
g	y	y	o	t	i	n	b	r	c	m	g
y	b	i	o	l	o	g	y	e	s	m	y

Unit C20

Activity 2

1 rugby 2 tennis 3 table tennis 4 golf 5 hockey 6 football
7 swimming 8 ice-skating 9 boxing 10 skiing

Activity 3

1 fielders; pitch; batsman
2 court: linesman / lineswoman; umpire
3 players; coach; referee; pitch
4 captain

Activity 4

1 bat 2 track 3 saddle 4 stick 5 team 6 court 7 under
8 slope 9 pool 10 trunks

Activity 5

1 cricket 2 rugby 3 football 4 tennis 5 boxing 6 ice-skating

Activity 6

1 D 2 B 3 A 4 B 5 D 6 B 7 C 8 A

Unit C21

Activity 2

1 beach 2 self-catering 3 camping 4 backpacking 5 luxury
6 cruise 7 safari / eco-tourism 8 package 9 city break
10 eco-tourism

Activity 3

Suggestions: horse-riding, canoeing, sailing, rock-climbing,
abseiling, white-water rafting, bungee-jumping, paintballing,
sky-diving

Activity 4

1 go on; adventure 2 take; catch 3 hire; ride 4 get on; called
5 got in; missed 6 fare 7 caught; got off 8 rode; fell off

Activity 5

1 airport 2 motorway 3 service station 4 port 5 station
6 helicopter pad

Activity 6

1 (A) – both 2 (A) – both (at sea, a pilot guides a larger boat into
the docks with a smaller boat) 3 (C) – only air 4 (A) – neither
5 (B) – only sea 6 (A) – both 7 (C) – only air 8 (A) – both

9 (D) – neither 10 (A) – both

Activity 7

1 crew 2 galley 3 spoke 4 deck 5 cabin 6 undercarriage
7 fuselage 8 bridge 9 helmet 10 pilot

Unit C22

Activity 2

1 kind 2 even-tempered 3 sympathetic 4 appreciative
5 optimistic 6 sensible 7 generous 8 cheerful 9 co-operative
10 industrious 11 enthusiastic 12 respectful

Activity 3

1 cruel 2 moody 3 insensitive 4 ungrateful 5 pessimistic
6 impulsive 7 selfish 8 miserable 9 stubborn 10 idle
11 passive 12 rebellious

Activity 4

1 unkind 2 unsympathetic 3 unappreciative 4 ungenerous
5 uncooperative 6 unenthusiastic 7 disrespectful

Activity 5

1 ungratefulness 2 idleness 3 moodiness 4 cheerfulness 5 -ness
6 cruelty 7 sympathy 8 insensitivity 9 generosity 10 -y or -ty
11 egotism 12 optimism 13 pessimism 14 -ism 15 rebellion
16 appreciation 17 co-operation 18 -ion or -tion

Activity 6

1 cheerful 2 co-operative 3 enthusiastic 4 rebellious
5 unco-operative 6 moody 7 sensible

Activity 7

1 even-tempered 2 kind 3 sympathetic 4 cheerful
5 pessimistic 6 selfish

Unit C23

Activity 2

1 career 2 profession 3 occupation 4 vocation

Activity 3

1 consultant 2 executive 3 director 4 labourer 5 trainee

Activity 4

1 part-time 2 tourism industry 3 flexitime 4 service industry
5 full-time 6 construction industry 7 casual 8 heavy industry
9 jobshare

Activity 5

1 as 2 for 3 at 4 with 5 with 6 through

Activity 6

1 with / for 2 through 3 for 4 at

Activity 7

A 4 B 5 C 1 D 6 E 9 F 2 G 7 H 8 I 3

Activity 8

1 (maternity) leave 2 (to be) unemployed 3 (to be made)
redundant 4 (to be) sacked / fired 5 industrial action / strike
6 resign / quit

Activity 9

1 redundant 2 unemployed 3 sacked / fired 4 Industrial action /
Strike action 5 quits / resigns

Unit A1

Activity 5 Track 1

E: Now, Petros, Let's talk about what you do. Do you work, or are you a student?

C: I'm doing both things at the moment. I'm studying English, but I'm also working as a waiter in a Greek restaurant.

E: I see. Why are you studying English?

C: Well, I'm hoping to get into university here. I'm planning to study economics, and when I get my degree I'm joining my father's business in Athens. He's living in America now, and he's taking his MBA examinations next month.

E: OK, and are you enjoying your studies?

C: Yes, I am, but I'm having a problem paying my fees. That's why I'm working as a waiter.

Unit A2

Activity 5 Track 2

A: Hi, I'm here to pick up the new timetable.

B: OK, which course are you on?

A: It's the Foundation course in Civil and Structural Engineering.

B: So, in semester 1 you take Mathematics, Mechanics, Physics and Information and Communications Technology. Lectures are in the Chesham building and they start at 10 o'clock in the morning.

A: What time do the lectures end?

B: The lectures finish at 12. You have lab work in the afternoon every Wednesday and Thursday; Dr Boot supervises these sessions and a Lab Technician attends the lab work sessions too. On Monday and Tuesday, you go to your tutor for a tutorial session.

A: So what happens on Friday?

B: You don't have any classes on Fridays; that is for research time.

Unit A4

Activity 4 & Activity 5 Track 3

A: Hi Jules. I'm so nervous about the exam. Have you sent your application form yet? I've only just posted mine.

B: Yes, I have. I sent it last week. I've already received confirmation of the test date and time. It's Saturday 18th July at nine in the morning.

A: Have you found your passport? Mine's still missing. I've looked everywhere but I can't find it.

B: Yes, I've found it. It was in the inside pocket of my backpack.

A: Oh! I haven't looked there yet. I'll check when I get home.

B: What about that video of the speaking test? Have you finished with it yet? I'd like to watch it.

A: Yes, I've seen it twice already. It's very helpful. You can have it tomorrow.

B: And have you done any practice tests?

A: I've done the one on the IELTS website, but they don't give you the answers!

B: Well, I've got a book of tests. I've done all of them, so you can have it.

A: Thanks! There's just one more thing I haven't done yet. I need a good alarm clock. Have you got one?

B: Yes, I have. But you can't have that – I'm going to need it myself!

Unit A7

Activity 5 Track 4

Good morning, and welcome to the fresher's week programme at the University of Wickham. I'm here to talk about your timetable. First of all, the police lecture on campus safety has been cancelled, unfortunately, due to illness. All lectures this week are being held in the Sunleigh lecture theatre in the Arts building. The register is taken every day, so make sure you attend. Thirty more students have been enrolled today. They are being taken to their accommodation now, so you can meet them later on. Lunch is served in the canteen from 12.30 every day, and I expect you're all hungry, so that's all from me for now. Are there any questions?

Unit A11

Activity 1 & Activity 3 Track 5

I remember that day so clearly. I was skiing in Switzerland. I was living there at the time. It was a bright, clear day. It was about four o'clock in the afternoon. There was no warning. It was instant. Suddenly I was curled up in a ball doing somersaults. Then it was over and I was buried in snow. It was totally dark. My mouth was packed with snow. The pressure was so intense that it was hard to breathe. I didn't know which direction was up. I believed I was going to die. Luckily, I was covering my face when it happened. I cleared the snow out of my mouth with my fingers. And then I panicked. I didn't think I was going to survive. I was screaming. I was crying. The tears were flowing. And then I noticed that all the tears were running across my face. I realised that I was lying in an upside down and backwards position. That was a real moment of truth. I knew that I had to get out. I moved my hands around, which gave me a bit more room. Then I got my upper body loose and I started digging. I made a little game out of it. I counted to four and then reached out to grab a handful of snow. And then I pushed it all down to my feet and stamped on it. I was digging for twenty-two hours before I finally got out. It was another fourteen hours before I heard the sound of the rescue team coming towards me.

Unit A12

Activity 5 Track 6

The party I enjoyed most of all was my graduation party. I'll never forget the moment when the stretch limousine turned up at my door. My friend Anna had ordered it. I got dressed up very quickly and got in the car, but I really didn't know where I was going. Then we arrived at the Grand Hotel, and all my friends came out to meet me. What a surprise! Anna had invited all my friends from university. I had graduated with 1st class honours, so she had decided to have a party for me, but she hadn't told me about it. She had booked a large room at the hotel, where we laughed and danced all night long.

Unit A15

Activity 5 Track 7

A: Hey, we did a really good experiment in chemistry class this morning.

B: What did you do?

A: We made glue from milk!

B: Wow! How did you do that?

A: Well, first we mixed some vinegar with a cupful of milk in a beaker. Not too much vinegar, just about two spoonfuls. Then we heated it and stirred it until it went lumpy – you know, the milk separated into solid bits and watery stuff. It's called curds and whey.

B: So which part was the glue?

A: It was the solid part – the curds. We filtered off the liquid into a flask through a funnel with special filter paper in it, like they use for making coffee. Then we dried the curds as much as we could with a paper towel, to get rid of the vinegar and the whey. We added some water and stirred it again, and the teacher said, 'Now it's glue!'

B: How did you test it?

A: We used it to stick pictures in our notebooks. It really worked!

Unit A18

Activity 3 Track 8

Question 1: Will you be using the projector this afternoon?
Question 2: Will you be going to the post office when you go to town?
Question 3: Will your party be going on much longer?
Question 4: Will you be needing the car tonight?
Question 5: When will you be finishing in the bathroom?
Question 6: How will you be getting to the conference?

Unit A20

Activity 4 & Activity 5 Track 9

Tutor: OK, now quite a few of you have asked me about what to do on the day of the test, what to take, what you can do and what you mustn't do. So, I'll explain some of the rules and regulations you have been asking about. Now, I'm going to talk about just some of these – you must read all of them for yourself later, and you can find these on the official IELTS website. First of all, before the test – you are required to prove who you are – so take your passport or another form of identity. Remember, you have to leave your bags and coats outside the test room, so don't take anything valuable with you. A lot of people have asked me if they can use a dictionary in the test – I'm afraid not, dictionaries are not allowed, and you must remember to switch off your mobile phone – in fact, it's better not to take it to the test at all because you can't take it into the exam room. You must not talk to any other candidates once the test has started. What happens if you're late? You need to speak to the supervisor – he or she may not let you in. During the test you may not ask about any of the questions. If you need to leave the room for any reason, you must ask the supervisor.
Before the end of the test, remember you have to transfer your answers to the answer sheet – you are not to remove any part of the test from the room or copy any part of the test. After the test, you have to wait for around two weeks for the results, which you can get from the test centre. Now, are there any other questions?

Unit A22

Activity 5 Track 10

E: So, Ahmed, do you do any sports?

A: Yes, I'm good at swimming and I've won a couple of tournaments.

But I'm not so good at getting up in the morning to do two hours of training, though! That's the hardest part for me. I'm not at all bad at football either – I've got pretty good coordination. However, I injured my knee during a game last weekend so won't be able to play for a few weeks. I like playing tennis but I'm not very skilled. I can't run fast enough and have difficulty keeping my eye on the ball. It's the same with basketball. In fact, I think it would be true to say that I'm not very adept at all. I'm pretty bad at badminton too – I've never won a game yet!

Unit A23

Activity 5 Track 11

Now you have reached the second year of your degree, it's time to stop relying on your tutor and start working independently. You shouldn't use a dictionary to look up all the words you don't know – this is time-consuming and unnecessary. Instead of reaching for the dictionary when you don't understand a word, you should use the context to guess the meaning. You do this in your own language, so why not in English? Students ought to practise recognising the type of word it is, for example, is it a noun, verb, adjective or adverb? You can recognise the word type from its position in the sentence. The other thing you should do is to improve your reading speed. I have some suggestions for you regarding this. First of all, what about working with a friend? If you work together, you can time each other. When you have finished reading, how about asking each other questions to test how well you have understood? But when you do this, you shouldn't look back at the text again. Instead, you should see how much you remember. It is no use reading fast if you don't understand!

Unit A29

Activity 5 Track 12

Today I'm going to look at overpopulation and its impact on the world's resources. Overpopulation is seen as one of the world's leading environmental problems. If we had fewer people, there would be more space and food for everyone. To add to the problem, the population of the earth is not evenly distributed, and neither is the wealth. If everybody lived like the average north American, we would need six planets the size of Earth. However, population growth tends to be higher in developing countries, and some have taken action to control it. China, for example, has introduced a one-child policy. Statistics show that the average Chinese woman would have six children, if there was no law against it. India, on the other hand, has a population growth of 1.8% per year. Currently, the population of India is one billion people – that's one sixth of the total number of people in the world. Many of them are poor and live very simply, but if they all had the lifestyle of a citizen of the USA, how much would be left for the rest of us?

Unit A30

Activity 3 Track 13

Tutor: OK Nilgun, so you've brought your final draft of your group project for me to look at.

Nilgun: Yes, it's about new archaeological sites in Greece – I was hoping that you could give me some advice on it before I handed it in.

Tutor:	Of course I can. I read through it last week and made some notes on how you could improve it, if you have the time.
Nilgun:	OK – I hope there's nothing too terrible in there!
Tutor:	No, not really, just a few minor points. But first of all, let me ask you how you thought the project went.
Nilgun:	I'm not sure what you mean.
Tutor:	Well, I mean how did you approach the project, did your group work well together, was there anything you thought worked well and anything you would have changed, if you had the opportunity to do the project again?
Nilgun:	Our group worked very well as a team, but it took a little bit of time before we were able to work really well together. If we had the opportunity to do this again, we would have done some team-building activities first – things like going for a meal together, going away for the weekend. But it was OK in the end.
Tutor:	That's good – and what did you find worked well?
Nilgun:	We were good at sharing our responsibilities. We could divide the work equally and everyone did their share of the project.
Tutor:	So all of the group contributed equally?
Nilgun:	Well, we would have liked one member of the group to have worked harder if he could, but he explained that one of his brothers was ill and he had to spend a lot of time helping him.
Tutor:	And what did you do then?
Nilgun:	We discussed his workload – what he could do and what he couldn't do – and divided it between the other group members.
Tutor:	Anything else?
Nilgun:	Yes, if we had started everything earlier, it would have been better. If we'd been a bit more organised, we would have been able to make a better timetable and we wouldn't have been in such a rush to finish.
Tutor:	Yes, it's always the way. But would you have worked so well as a team if there hadn't been a little bit of time pressure?
Nilgun:	Actually, I hadn't thought about that, but if I had the choice, I still would have planned better and started sooner!

Unit A31

Activity 5 Track 14

Lili:	Were you ill today? You missed a good lecture today about accounting.
Andreas:	No, I'm not ill. I've been reading a lot about accounting lately, and I'm not really interested in it. I'm not going to take the option in it.
Lili:	Dr Kesevan covered more than just accounting though. He spoke about the marketing mix too – the 4Ps: Product, Price, Place and Promotion.
Andreas:	Oh, really? I haven't read about that yet.
Lili:	Well, it was only a short introduction. He'll talk about it in more detail next week, so you must make sure you're there.
Andreas:	Don't worry – I'll be there for sure.

Unit A32

Activity 6 Track 15

Have you ever left anything important on a bus? Or have you handed in something strange to the lost property office? It is thought that Transport for London deals with more than 130,000 items of lost property each year on its buses, trains and taxis. It is understood that last year alone, over ten thousand mobile phones were handed in to its lost property office on Baker Street – ten thousand, six hundred and fourteen of them to be exact! And that's not forgetting the seven thousand umbrellas and around six thousand pairs of glasses that were left behind by passengers in a hurry. However, there is some good news. About twenty-five percent of these items find their way back to their true owners. When we enquired about what happened to the remaining unclaimed lost items, a spokesman for the office explained that after a period of three months they are auctioned off and any money raised goes towards the cost of providing the lost property service. Some of the things that have been handed in to the lost property office over the years are unusual, to say the least. It is believed that someone once handed in a briefcase containing over ten thousand pounds!

Unit A33

Activity 1 Track 16

QM:	Our next contestant is Susan Shaw, from Liverpool University. The subject she has chosen this afternoon is the IELTS test. Good afternoon, Susan.
S:	Good afternoon.
QM:	Here's your first question. Do you know the name of one of the three organisations which administer the IELTS test?
S:	Yes, I think I know all of them. There's the British Council, the University of Cambridge, and um... the Australian one, er... IDP Australia!
QM:	That is the correct answer. My next question is, can you tell me the correct word for the examiner who asks the questions in the IELTS speaking test?
S:	Yes, that would be the interlocutor.
QM:	Yes, that's the right word. Well done. Now, what do we call the place where the test is taken?
S:	Oh, that's an easy one. It's just called a test centre.
QM:	Yes, that's correct. Can you answer this: what is the day of the week when the test is usually taken?
S:	Well, I'm not sure if it's the same everywhere in the world, because Muslim countries have a different weekend, but here in Britain it's normally on a Saturday.
QM:	That's the answer I have here, so it's another point for you, Susan. On to question number five. What do you think is the reason why most people take the IELTS test?
S:	I think around 80% of IELTS candidates take it because they want to get into university in an English-speaking country. Yes, university entrance is the answer.
QM:	That is the correct answer. Your next question is this – can a doctor whose IELTS score is 6.5 work for the National Health Service in Great Britain?
S:	Oh, dear. I don't think I know this one. 6.5 is quite a high score – you can take a Masters degree at most universities with that. I'll say yes.

QM: I'm sorry, Susan. The correct answer is 'no'. Doctors need a band 7.0 before they can practise medicine in the NHS. What a pity. Here's the next question. Can you name a type of question which might be in the reading test?

S: Um... multiple choice?

QM: Yes. The others are labelling, short answer questions and completing a chart, table, note or sentence. Next question: what is the word for a person who sits in the room while people are taking an examination?

S: Er... um... No, I can't remember the word. Pass.

QM: On to question nine, then. Can you name the part of the IELTS test that takes about 35 minutes?

S: Oh, yes. That's the listening test.

QM: That is the correct answer. This is your final question. What is the maximum length of time that you should spend on Writing task 1?

S: You should spend no more than 20 minutes on question 1.

QM: Yes, that's the right answer. You have scored a total of eight points. You passed on one question. A person who sits in the room while people are taking an examination is an invigilator. Well done, Susan!

Unit A39

Activity 3 & Activity 4 Track 17

Andreas: Can you tell me where the self-study centre is, please?

Maria: Yes, it's in C101, just in this building here.

Andreas: Where exactly is it?

Maria: Go into the Richmond Building through the main entrance, just there, and in front of you, you'll see the main stairs into the main part of the building.

Andreas: So I take the stairs to the main building.

Maria: Ah, no. When you go into the building, you'll see the main stairs in front of you, and Student Services on your left.

Andreas: Student Services?

Maria: Yes, you have course enquiries, accommodation services and international student services.

Andreas: OK, that's on the left of the stairs.

Maria: And to the right is the main reception for the university. Go right and walk straight on into the Atrium; it's a large open space. You'll see students at the computer cluster station on the left and then a seating area. In front of the seating area there's a café selling sandwiches, tea, coffee and things.

Andreas: That's good to know. Maybe I'll go there first before I go to the self-study centre.

Maria: Well, you need to go past the café to get to the self-study centre. Just a little bit further and you'll see the exit to Great Horton Road in front of you with the ladies' and gents' toilets on the right.

Andreas: OK.

Maria: Turn left there and with the café behind you you'll see a door with steps leading down. Go down there and the self-study centre is in there.

Activity 5 & Activity 6 Track 18

Xinzhu: Oh, excuse me – I'm looking for Trinity College, it's part of the University of Melbourne. Do you know where it is?

Pete: Well, you're actually very close to where you want to be. From here – we're at the main entrance – go straight on past the College Oak – the oak tree on your left, and the Bulpadock – that's the grassy area on your right.

Xinzhu: So the College Oak is on the left?

Pete: That's right, and go towards Bishops – the building with the tower.

Xinzhu: I see – so is the main reception in there?

Pete: No, but it's not too far away. Next to Bishops is the senior common room, and you need to go in there and out again the other side. Go right along the path, past the senior common room, on your left and you'll see a door – this is the entrance to the senior common room. Go up the stairs, into the senior common room building and straight through the other side.

Xinzhu: OK, into the senior common room building and out again.

Pete: Yes, and you'll see another path – the dining room is on your right and the kitchens are a bit further on the right too, alongside Sharwood Court.

Xinzhu: I see.

Pete: Go across Sharwood Court and turn right at the building in front of you – this is the Sharwood room. Just opposite the Sharwood room, across the lawn from it, is the Foundation Studies office.

Xinzhu: Is it far? It sounds like a long way.

Pete: It's not too far, you'll find it quite easily once you go out of the senior common room building.

Xinzhu: Thanks very much.

Unit B3

Activity 5 & Activity 6 Track 19

Student Union Officer Hi, I'm Sara and I'm the Student's Union Officer responsible for Student Societies in the university, and I'd like to tell you about them today – what they are, what they do and how to join them and get involved. So, what is a student society? Well, basically they are clubs for people who like doing the same things to get together on a regular basis. I'll illustrate what I mean by focusing on three different kinds of society: a sports society – the Baseball Society, a national society – the Saudi Society, and an interest society – the Drama Society. So, the Baseball Society – the society meets every Wednesday to play baseball and to watch the latest American Baseball games. Although it's supposed to be a sports society, the president of the society says the real purpose is to have some fun. The Saudi Society, on the other hand, is very different. Anyone can join the society, but it tends to have a lot of members from Saudi Arabia. What is the aim of this society? Well, the Saudi Society meets so as to promote understanding of Arab life and culture through organising events in order to introduce people to the country. And on to our last society – the Drama Society. This society is for people who are interested in the theatre and who would like to do acting, too. In order for that to happen, the Drama Society produces one play every semester and need people not only for acting but also backstage to do lighting, costume and make-up. Those are just three examples and there are many more of these societies. So, how can you join one of these societies...?

Unit B4

Activity 5 & Activity 6 Track 20

E:　So let's move on now to part 3. Do you think that people are too consumerist today – that is, do you think that people are too interested in consumer goods?

C:　Obviously, many people are interested in buying the latest products and gadgets – as a matter of fact, I am too! I love buying the latest music player or newest telephone. But that doesn't mean that people are too materialistic – interested in consumer products.

E:　Can you expand on that a little?

C:　Not everyone likes the latest fashions or technology. Apparently, one of my classmates even prefers dictionaries to translating machines. Imagine that! Seriously, though, while it is true that many people are very consumerist, it seems many more are actually turning against this.

E:　Uh huh.

C:　In fact, some people are choosing not to fly to save the environment, to recycle and repair old things rather than buy new products – and things like that.

E:　And what about you?

C:　Me? Frankly, I never repair anything if I can buy a new one!

Unit B6

Activity 4 Track 21

Today I'm going to talk about vegetarianism. There are a number of reasons why people may choose to become vegetarian. For example, many young people in the West today are animal lovers, and do not think it is right to eat animals. Others choose not to eat meat for religious reasons; for instance, Hindus and Buddhists. Others feel that it is better for their health not to eat meat, as it is difficult to digest, and takes a long time to pass through the body. A case in point is beef, which takes at least three hours to leave the stomach.

There are three types of vegetarians, namely vegans, lacto-vegetarians and those who eat no red meat, but will eat fish and eggs, for example. Vegans eat no animal products at all, and will not use any animal by-products, such as leather shoes or handbags. Lacto-vegetarians eat dairy products like cheese and butter. A vegan diet may lack protein, which is essential for healthy growth. Some vegetables, such as beans and nuts, contain protein, so vegans must make sure that they eat plenty of these types of food. To sum up, there are many reasons why people choose vegetarianism, and many different types of vegetarian. In conclusion, it is everybody's right to choose their own diet, but care must be taken – and for children in particular – that the body has all the protein it needs to grow.

Unit C1

Activity 8 Track 23

E:　OK, you can begin to tell me about a person you admire now.

C:　I've had many teachers throughout my education, but of the teachers who have taught me through my school life, Bahar-hanim is the one that I most admire. She was my English teacher at high school. In contrast to our other teachers, who were grumpy and unenthusiastic, she was always amusing and thoughtful. Bahar-hanim won everyone over to her as soon as she began teaching us. But, although she was fun and helpful in class, she was also quite strict – she pushed us to do our best – and punctual. Everyone had to be in class on time every time, and this was something that all of us appreciated. Bahar-hanim had a real interest in her job and in her students, so she was always in a good mood when she entered the classroom. Her classes were always interesting and lively – she was a confident and hard-working teacher and nothing was too much trouble for her – if a student needed help, she was very generous with her time. To sum up, I can say she was a gifted and talented teacher and I learned a lot from her – not just English.

Unit C2

Activity 6 Track 25

E:　Have you ever lost anything that was really valuable?

C:　I haven't lost anything that was expensive, but I have lost things that were valuable to me, but only to me. Two years ago I lost a great jacket. It was a used, stripy, yellow and white, polyfibre skiing jacket. It was quite soft and smooth, but a bit bulky to keep out the cold.

E:　What's the most important thing you own and why is it important to you?

C:　One of my most important possessions is my bag – because I keep all my other important things in it. It's a large, square, flowery, Italian shopping bag – quite old and battered now, but I still use it because I can get all my stuff inside it.

E:　Tell me: what's the most embarrassing thing that's happened to you?

C:　Oh, that was when my husband's colleague invited us round for dinner. I had a bit of wine, and we were having a good chat about valuable old objects, when Roberto brought out this big, antique, blue-coloured, Chinese, ceramic, flower vase and asked me to hold it. Well, you can guess what happened – it slipped – crash – into a million pieces all over the floor.

Unit C4

Activity 3 Track 29

Lucy:　So when are you thinking of visiting Hargate?

Kemal:　Next weekend, actually. Have you been there at all?

Lucy:　My parents live there – let me tell you something about it.

Kemal:　Great – here's a pen and paper, draw me a map.

Lucy:　Right, we'll start with the coast – Hargate is on a bay, East Bay, and the river runs through the town and into the bay.

Kemal:　OK.

Lucy:　So the bay area is very popular with people and if you go to the waterfront – that's the road that goes along the bay – in the evening you'll see lots of people walking along, doing exercises, street theatre – all kinds of things.

Kemal:　That sounds nice. What's that to the north of the bay?

Lucy:　North of the bay is the harbour – sailing is very popular, and lots of people have boats there, some rich people even have very large boats. The area behind the harbour is Castle Hill.

Kemal:　Because there's a castle there.

Lucy:	There's a really nice park there and good views over the town. If you look south you'll see the entertainment district – with bars, restaurants, hotels and lots of nightlife.
Kemal:	OK.
Lucy:	And to the west of the entertainment district, where the railway station is, you can find the inner-city residential quarter where a lot of the people who live and work here all year live.
Kemal:	Is there another residential area?
Lucy:	Yes, it's on another hill outside the town – it's a suburb called Hargate Hill. Between Hargate Hill and the main town is the industrial sector, where you can find the factories and small businesses – some supermarkets too.
Kemal:	So really the interesting places for me are the waterfront, Castle Hill, the harbour and the theatre district.
Lucy:	I think so.
Kemal:	So tell me more about the nightlife...

Activity 5 Track 30

Extract 1

Our next city of culture in this lecture is Glasgow. Glasgow became the European city of culture in 1990 – it is a modern, multicultural city with people from many ethnic backgrounds, in the western part of Scotland, built on both sides of the river Clyde. It is the country's second city and was an industrial centre with shipbuilding as its major industry. Today the shipbuilding industry is less important and the city has reinvented itself as a tourist centre with many visitors to the city.

Extract 2

E: So, Kashif, where do you come from?

C: I come from the capital city of Pakistan, Islamabad, which is one of the most modern cities in the south Asian region.

E: Is that a nice place to live?

C: Yes, it has a temperate climate because it's surrounded by mountains. The city is divided into zones: administrative and residential areas, industrial sectors and green areas. It's a very young and vibrant city – it's exciting, with lots to do. With lots of commerce and industry, it's Pakistan's largest metropolitan city.

Extract 3

Yokohama is a coastal city on Honshu island on the bay of Tokyo. It's a major port and also a regional capital. I have lived there all my life and I like it very much. It's very crowded – the second most populous city in Japan, but it has a cosmopolitan feel to the city because of the Western-style buildings, Chinese temples and international restaurants, especially in the suburb of Yamate just outside the city centre with its churches and teashops – a bit like England, really!

Unit C5

Activity 4 Track 32

Preparation is the key to giving a good presentation. It can be the difference between a great success and a total flop. So, keep these key points in mind during your preparations in order to make a good impression on your audience.

Make sure the audience can see both you and any visual aids you plan to use. Your presentation will go badly wrong if you obstruct screens by standing in front of them. You can make things easier for yourself by checking where you plan to stand in the room in advance and make slight adjustments if necessary.

State at the beginning what you are going to talk about and make a list of the main points. Make an effort to ensure that your presentation has a logical order. Emphasising your key points by using visual aids or by alerting your audience to key points coming up can make a real difference. Make eye contact with your audience, but don't just focus on one person – look around at different people.

Don't make the mistake of simply reading from a script. It will be a a recipe for disaster and you will be doomed to failure! Not only will it affect the flow of your delivery, you will bore your audience too. Making notes and using them as prompts will help you sound more natural and increase your chances of giving a winning performance.

Unit C6

Activity 3 Track 34

A: Well, I've finished doing my research so I need to start working on my dissertation. I've never written one before but basically I know what I need to do. I'll be explaining what I set out to learn and why, how I conducted my research and what I discovered. And what conclusions I reached, of course! That's the most important part!

B: We usually take these exams between the ages of 16 and 18. I'm taking three but some people do five of them. They are really important because they are the entrance requirement for university degrees.

C: We start studying for them at the age of 14. I'm taking eight but some of my friends are doing ten! What I like about them is that we are not just assessed on exams – our coursework is taken into consideration too.

Unit C7

Activity 6 Track 36

1 generate   2 react   3 transform   4 product, production
5 storage   6 collector, collection   7 transmitter, transmission
8 distribution

Unit C8

Activity 4 Track 38

Today I'm going to talk about the Gulf Stream. This is a warm ocean current which originates in the Gulf of Mexico, and then flows northeast across the Atlantic Ocean. It influences the climate of the UK and north-western Europe by bringing humid, mild air with it. Within the Gulf of Mexico, the Gulf Stream is very narrow, only 80 kilometres wide, and travels very fast at nearly 5 kilometres per hour, carrying water at 25 degrees Centigrade. When it reaches the North Atlantic it widens considerably to many hundred kilometres and splits into several smaller currents. Because the water in the Gulf Stream has high salinity, it sinks to the bottom of the ocean when it gets there.

The Gulf Stream is one of the strongest currents known anywhere in the world. Without its influence, the UK and other places in Europe would be as cold as Canada at the same latitude.

Unit C9

Activity 2 Track 40

...and as we approach the main atrium you can see some people walking about with sandwiches and coffee. The food court is located here and you can get most things here – from snacks and light meals to a full three-course meal, and there are lots of different cuisines to choose from: Chinese, Italian and of course British. So let me tell you a bit more about what you can get here. Over there is the uni buffet – it's a small café where you can get snacks like a chocolate bar, or biscuits. You can also get tea, coffee and other hot beverages or drinks – it's great when you're running out of one lecture to get to another and you need to eat something quickly. Next to it is the *Fair and fast* food – it's a fair trade fast food outlet and sells sandwiches, salads, light meals, even homemade hamburgers, which are very good by the way and are made by Melissa over there. There's no junk food here, though, even the burgers are healthy. Finally, on D floor we have the university refectory – that is, the university restaurant, you can get a three course meal here, or a starter – something small like a soup before the main meal – or main course where you have a choice of full meals and side dishes like garlic bread or chips to go with the main meal, and of course a sweet or dessert to finish off your meal. People who don't eat meat can get a vegetarian meal, but for people who don't eat meat or dairy products like milk and cheese – vegans, that is – there isn't really a great choice of vegan food.

Activity 8 Track 41

E: So how would you describe the food in your country? What kind of things do people like to eat where you are from?

C: Well, I'm from Hungary, from Szeged, and our town is quite famous in Hungary for its cuisine. How would I describe Hungarian food? Well, it's delicious – that's the first thing to say, but it's not for people who want to lose weight and it's not for vegetarians! We use a lot of meat – mainly pork, and we like to eat sour cream and pickles too – our pickles are fantastic. And of course we use a lot of red pepper or paprika in our cooking, and this makes it slightly spicy. Some people can find Hungarian main courses quite heavy, but our starters – our soups – are quite light and our cakes are just heavenly. The best way to spend an afternoon in Hungary is to go to a coffee shop, buy a cake and chat with a few friends.

E: That sounds like a great way to pass the time.

Unit C10

Activity 5 Track 43

In Chinese medicine, a more holistic view of the patient is taken. Whereas conventional medicine in the West primarily treats the symptoms, or signs, of a disease, the Chinese approach is to consider the whole person. In the treatment of cancer, for example, Fu Zhen therapy uses special vitamins and herbs alongside modern radiotherapy to strengthen the body's ability to fight the disease. These herbs can help to counter the negative effects of chemicals used in chemotherapy and can also help them to work more efficiently. The Chinese believe that good diet and exercise are of greater benefit to health than pills or injections, and many westerners are now using Chinese medicine in conjunction with modern techniques.

Activity 6 Track 44

1   When I need advice about my children's health, I go to the clinic in the high street.

2   Maria cut her hand very badly, so we had to take her to A&E at the big hospital in the city.

3   After the operation, they put him in a bed in the recovery ward.

4   There is no need for you to stay in hospital any longer. Just come to the outpatients department in two weeks' time, and we'll give you a check-up.

5   A lot of people have colds at the moment, so the doctor's waiting room is very full.

6   I'm afraid he's really very ill, and they don't think he's going to get better, so they've found him a peaceful room in the hospice.

7   The doctor's surgery is open from 8.30 until 3.00 in the afternoon.

8   The operation will take place in the theatre on the second floor.

Unit C15

Activity 5 Track 50

A   I present the evening news on live television, which involves doing live interviews on the main news stories of the day. To do my job you've got to be quick-thinking and not panic under pressure.

B   My job combines a mixture of researching interesting stories, writing, going out and filming and talking to people about what they've done. I film with a camera crew and work with an editor. I like working to deadlines. It forces you to write accurately in the time slot you are allocated to deliver the story on TV.

C   I present my own radio show and it's a mixture of Rn'B and hip-hop. Presenting isn't just about talking though! It includes a lot of research. I've got to interview people so a lot of background work goes into that.

D   At the moment I'm working on a website aimed at students. I've got to come up with a new look and feel. It's fun because I can experiment with the design. It's a very creative job and it's great when you see your final work go live.

E   I edit the output for interactive television news – a lot of my time is spent cutting or changing the material. I really enjoy dealing with breaking news and I like the fact that the job keeps changing as new ways of presenting news are developed in response to new technology.

F   I review all the new films and DVDs each week on a radio programme. You have to have patience and an open mind, although watching bad films at 9 am screenings can make this very difficult indeed. But I love watching films pure and simple.

Unit C16

Activity 6 Track 52

I have a student loan which pays for my university tuition fees and I have a maintenance grant on top of that. This is the money that I have to manage on, on a day to day basis. It pays for my accommodation and food. I also have a part-time job and I use that income to buy other things, such as clothes and CDs.

I've actually been very disciplined and careful with my money so far, and regularly check my balance. I keep a note of my transactions so that I can keep on top of things. Obviously if I go and get a pizza or something I don't bother writing that down, but if I take out a lot of money, I do keep a note of it so that I know what I spent it on. I know that one day I'll have to pay back the loan, but this shouldn't be too much of a problem once I've graduated and got myself a job.

Unit C17

Activity 3 Track 54

1 two point two oh five   2 one point six oh nine three four
3 zero point one oh five six   4 sixteen   5 thirty-two degrees
6 four point five four five nine six

Activity 4 Track 55

1 twenty-four plus eight equals thirty-two   2 nine hundred and six minus twelve is eight hundred and ninety-four   3 seventy-two divided by eleven is six point five four five four five four five
4 the square root of sixteen is four   5 one fluid ounce is the same as twenty-eight point four one three one cubic centimetres
6 twelve inches equal one foot, 3 feet equal one yard
7 seventy-three kilometres per hour   8 sixty-four per cent
9 five hundred and twenty dollars, ninety-nine cents
10 six million, five hundred and twenty-two thousand, three hundred and thirteen

Activity 5 Track 56

1 twenty thousand, four hundred and eighty-two   2 fifty-eight thousand, nine hundred and twenty-six   3 four million and one
4 ten million, five hundred thousand   5 seventy-nine million, four hundred and twenty-five thousand, six hundred and seventy-two

Activity 6 Track 57

Uranium concentrate is vital for nuclear power production, but the by-products can also be used to make nuclear weapons. World production of uranium in 2007 was 41,279 tonnes. Nationally, Canada produced the most uranium – 9,476 tonnes, followed by Australia with a total of 8,611 tonnes. Australia has the highest resources of all the nations, with an estimated 23% of all the uranium in the world. That's nearly a quarter. Canada, by comparison, has only 8% of the global uranium resources, about a third of Australia's. Surprisingly, the huge nations of China and India have only 1% of the total uranium resources.
So, how much uranium is needed to make a nuclear warhead? Well, it takes 12,000 tonnes of unprocessed uranium to make 10 tonnes of yellow cake. This yellow cake then has to be further processed to produce weapons-grade uranium. 10 tonnes of yellow cake can produce only 20–25 kg of this weapons-grade uranium-235, which is enough for one nuclear warhead. It could also provide 600 kg of civil-grade uranium, which is equivalent to 30 million kilowatt hours – enough to power Greater London for a day.

Unit C18

Activity 6 Track 59

I've got a very close immediate family and I love them all, of course. But I've also got a large extended family – 32 people altogether – and I'm going to tell you about one of them. I'm going to talk about my father-in-law. I've known him for about ten years now and he's a person I really respect and get on well with. We became related when I married his daughter! My wife looks quite like him and she takes after him in many ways – they are both

funny and full of life. I like him most because, although he's a successful business person, he doesn't show off and he always finds time to help you. Finally, we have lots of things in common – we both like golf and we're both great cooks, so we often do these things together.

Unit C21

Activity 4 Track 63

Jon: Hi, Jenny! What did you do in the holidays?
Jenny: Well, Susie and I decided to go on an adventure holiday in the Lake District, but most of the adventures happened before we even got there. We were going to take the bus to Euston, then catch a train to Windermere. After that we thought we could hire bicycles and then ride them to the hostel. It's about 15 miles, but we're both quite fit.
Jon: So what happened?
Jenny: When the bus finally came, it was full so we couldn't get on. There wasn't enough time to wait for the next one, so we called a taxi. We got in the taxi and asked the driver to go to Euston as quickly as possible, but the traffic was so bad it took nearly half an hour and we missed the train!
Jon: Oh, no! You must have been really worried.
Jenny: I was nearly ready to give up and go home, but Susie was determined to carry on. The taxi fare was nearly £50, as well. But we caught the next train, and when we got off at Windermere, it was so beautiful I was glad we had carried on. We got our bikes and rode them to the hostel, but we fell off a couple of times because our rucksacks were so heavy.
Jon: And what about the rest of the holiday?
Jenny: It was great! We did a lot of walking and all kinds of watersports: canoeing, sailing, white-water rafting, and we went rock-climbing and horse-riding. Susie did a bungee jump, but I didn't want to do that – I went sky-diving instead! It was great!

Unit C22

Activity 6 Track 65

What happened when our loving and cheerful child turned 13? Where did our co-operative and enthusiastic child go – and who is that rebellious person in their place? Today I'm going to talk briefly about teenage behaviour. The good news is that it doesn't last long. Studies show that uncooperative behaviour in boys begins at 13, peaks at 17, and by early adulthood most of it has stopped completely. Teenagers are often moody because, although they are physically adult, their brains are not mature enough to think in a sensible way. This means that they become frustrated that they are not allowed to do all the things that adults do.

Activity 7 Track 66

E: So, Mina, you've told me about your best friend. What do you think are the most important qualities for friends to have?
C: For me, the most important things are for friends to be even-tempered and kind. They help you if you have problems, so they need to be sympathetic. I like people who are cheerful. It's just depressing to be around people who are pessimistic about life. I don't like people who are selfish, either.

Unit C 23

Activity 7 Track 68

E: So is it easy or difficult getting a job in your country nowadays?

C: It's really not easy – it's so difficult. Before I came here I was working in an accounts department as a trainee, but it was so hard to get the job.

E: What did you have to do to get it?

C: Well I was looking for a job – job hunting – for about two months before I found a vacancy – a job with a company.

E: Was that in the newspaper or on the Internet or...?

C: Actually it was through a recruitment agency – a kind of office where they find jobs for people. Then I had to complete an application form – a form where you give details of your qualifications and experience to the company, together with my CV – a list of my work and education experience. Luckily, I was asked to go for an interview – a formal talk with the company and they gave me the job – they hired me – right after the interview.

E: That's quite unusual.

C: I guess they liked me – I got my contract, my agreement to work for them, a week later and started working for my salary – my monthly pay with them – after signing the contract.